# WALKING IN THE BRECON BEACONS

# WALKING IN THE BRECON BEACONS

## 45 CIRCULAR WALKS IN THE NATIONAL PARK

by David Whittaker and Andy Davies

JUNIPER HOUSE, MURLEY MOSS,
OXENHOLME ROAD, KENDAL, CUMBRIA LA9 7RL
www.cicerone.co.uk

© David Whittaker and Andy Davies 2022
Third edition 2022
ISBN: 978 1 78631 089 7
Reprinted 2024 (with updates)
Second edition 2010
First edition 1995

Printed in Czechia on behalf of Latitude Press Ltd on responsibly sourced paper.
A catalogue record for this book is available from the British Library.

© Crown copyright and database rights 2022 OS AC0000810376
All photographs are by the authors unless otherwise stated.

*To our families and friends who have shared this area with us and especially to Tim, David and Jean.*

### Acknowledgements

Special thanks are due to Jean Davies for transcribing many of the cassette tapes made while walking the routes, to David Davies for producing the finished diagrams and to Dorothy Whittaker for patient forbearance during long evening hours of writing.

Thanks are due to Richard Preece, the warden for the Brecon Beacons National Park National Nature Reserves, for his informative comments on the routes that pass through Craig Cerrig-gleisiad and Craig Cwm-du. Help was also received from Suzanna Jones (Interpretation Officer), Eifion Jones (Rights of Way Officer) and Richard Farquhar (Warden) of the Brecon Beacons National Park Authority. Ben Evans, Project Manager, South Wales Coalfield Geo Heritage Network, gave expert assistance with geological information together with Professor Tony Ramsey.

**Since this book was published in 2022, the national park has officially reverted back to its Welsh name and is now known as Bannau Brycheiniog. This will be amended in the next edition.**

*Front cover:* The Sawdde Valley leading up to Bannau Sir Gaer, from the north-west (Walk 31)

# CONTENTS

Map key . . . . . . . . . . . . . . . . . . . . . . . . . . . . . . . . . . . . . . . . . . . . . . . . . . . . . . . . . 8

**INTRODUCTION** . . . . . . . . . . . . . . . . . . . . . . . . . . . . . . . . . . . . . . . . . . . . . . . . 11
Geology of the Brecon Beacons . . . . . . . . . . . . . . . . . . . . . . . . . . . . . . . . . . . 12
Changing woodland . . . . . . . . . . . . . . . . . . . . . . . . . . . . . . . . . . . . . . . . . . . . 14
Human impact . . . . . . . . . . . . . . . . . . . . . . . . . . . . . . . . . . . . . . . . . . . . . . . . 15
Birdlife . . . . . . . . . . . . . . . . . . . . . . . . . . . . . . . . . . . . . . . . . . . . . . . . . . . . . . . 17
Getting to and staying in the national park . . . . . . . . . . . . . . . . . . . . . . . . . . 18
A solitary guided walk? . . . . . . . . . . . . . . . . . . . . . . . . . . . . . . . . . . . . . . . . . 18
Using this guide . . . . . . . . . . . . . . . . . . . . . . . . . . . . . . . . . . . . . . . . . . . . . . . 18

**1 NORTH-EASTERN VALLEYS AND RIDGES** . . . . . . . . . . . . . . . . . . . . . . . . . . 21
Walk 1    Corn Du and Pen y Fan via Cwm Llwch . . . . . . . . . . . . . . . . . . . . . . 22
Walk 2    Pen y Fan via Cwm Sere . . . . . . . . . . . . . . . . . . . . . . . . . . . . . . . . . 30
Walk 3    Cribyn via Cwm Sere . . . . . . . . . . . . . . . . . . . . . . . . . . . . . . . . . . . 35
Walk 4    Cwm Sere ridge ascending Cribyn and Pen y Fan . . . . . . . . . . . . . . 39
Walk 5    Cribyn via Cwm Cynwyn . . . . . . . . . . . . . . . . . . . . . . . . . . . . . . . . . 43
Walk 6    Fan y Bîg via Cwm Cynwyn . . . . . . . . . . . . . . . . . . . . . . . . . . . . . . 48
Walk 7    Cwm Cynwyn ridge ascending Fan y Bîg and Cribyn . . . . . . . . . . . 51
Walk 8    Fan y Bîg via Cwm Oergwm . . . . . . . . . . . . . . . . . . . . . . . . . . . . . . 55
Walk 9    Cwm Oergwm and Gist Wen . . . . . . . . . . . . . . . . . . . . . . . . . . . . . 60
Walk 10   Cwm Oergwm ridge ascending Fan y Bîg . . . . . . . . . . . . . . . . . . . . 64
Walk 11   Cwm Oergwm Valley . . . . . . . . . . . . . . . . . . . . . . . . . . . . . . . . . . . 68

**2 EASTERN VALLEYS AND RIDGES** . . . . . . . . . . . . . . . . . . . . . . . . . . . . . . . . . 71
Walk 12   Bryn . . . . . . . . . . . . . . . . . . . . . . . . . . . . . . . . . . . . . . . . . . . . . . . . 72
Walk 13   Cwm Tarthwynni circuit . . . . . . . . . . . . . . . . . . . . . . . . . . . . . . . . . 75
Walk 14   Blaen-y-glyn and Allt Forgan . . . . . . . . . . . . . . . . . . . . . . . . . . . . . 80
Walk 15   Blaen-y-glyn and Craig y Fan Ddu . . . . . . . . . . . . . . . . . . . . . . . . . 86
Walk 16   Torpantau circuit . . . . . . . . . . . . . . . . . . . . . . . . . . . . . . . . . . . . . . 91

**3 SOUTH-WESTERN VALLEYS AND RIDGES** . . . . . . . . . . . . . . . . . . . . . . . . . 95
Walk 17   Neuadd Horseshoe: Corn Du, Pen y Fan and Cribyn . . . . . . . . . . . 96
Walk 18   Cwm Llysiog and Waun Wen . . . . . . . . . . . . . . . . . . . . . . . . . . . . 101
Walk 19   Corn Du and Pen y Fan via Cwm Crew . . . . . . . . . . . . . . . . . . . . 105
Walk 20   Corn Du and Pen y Fan from Pont ar Daf . . . . . . . . . . . . . . . . . . . 112

**4 FFOREST FAWR** . . . . . . . . . . . . . . . . . . . . . . . . . . . . . . . . . . . . . . . . . . . . . 115
Walk 21   Craig Cerrig-gleisiad . . . . . . . . . . . . . . . . . . . . . . . . . . . . . . . . . . 116
Walk 22   Fan Fawr . . . . . . . . . . . . . . . . . . . . . . . . . . . . . . . . . . . . . . . . . . . 120
Walk 23   Craig Cwm-du and Fan Frynych . . . . . . . . . . . . . . . . . . . . . . . . . . 122

| Walk 24 | Fan Frynych, Fan Dringarth and Fan Llia | 126 |
| Walk 25 | Fan Gyhirych and Fan Nedd | 130 |

## 5 WATERFALL COUNTRY ... 137
| Walk 26 | Elidir Trail: Sgwd Gwladus and Sgwd Ddwli waterfalls | 138 |
| Walk 27 | Waterfall walk | 143 |
| Walk 28 | Sgwd yr Eira | 154 |
| Walk 29 | Ystradfellte Falls | 162 |
| Walk 30 | Afon Nedd and Afon Mellte | 169 |

## 6 THE BLACK MOUNTAIN (MYNYDD DU) ... 177
| Walk 31 | Carmarthen Fans and glacial cwms | 178 |
| Walk 32 | Tair Carn Isaf via Cwm Pedol | 182 |
| Walk 33 | Sinc Giedd and Carmarthen Fans | 184 |
| Walk 34 | Afon Twrch | 191 |
| Walk 35 | Henrhyd Falls and River Tawe | 196 |
| Walk 36 | Garreg Las via Cwm Sawdde | 200 |
| Walk 37 | Cribarth | 203 |
| Walk 38 | Carmarthen Fans via Cwm Giedd | 207 |
| Walk 39 | Carreg Cennen | 211 |

## 7 THE BLACK MOUNTAINS (Y MYNYDDOEDD DUON) ... 215
| Walk 40 | Pen Cerrig-calch and Table Mountain | 216 |
| Walk 41 | Craig y Cilau | 220 |
| Walk 42 | Crug Mawr and Sugar Loaf | 223 |
| Walk 43 | Llanthony Priory, Offa's Dyke and Bal Mawr | 230 |
| Walk 44 | Lord Hereford's Knob | 234 |
| Walk 45 | Castell Dinas and Waun Fach | 237 |

| **Appendix A** | Route summary table | 240 |
| **Appendix B** | Routes by interest | 243 |
| **Appendix C** | Brief Welsh–English glossary | 246 |
| **Appendix D** | Useful contacts | 248 |

*Sgwd Henrhyd, the tallest waterfall in South Wales with a drop of 28m (Walk 35)*

**Route symbols on OS map extracts**
(for OS legend see printed OS maps)

 route

 alternative route

 alternative route

 start/finish point

 alternative start/finish point

 alternative start point

▶ route direction

SCALE: 1:50,000

**Features on the overview map**

 National Park
eg **BRECON BEACONS**

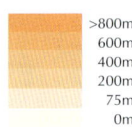
>800m
600m
400m
200m
75m
0m

**GPX files** for all routes can be downloaded free at www.cicerone.co.uk/1089/GPX.

### Updates to this Guide

While every effort is made by our authors to ensure the accuracy of guidebooks as they go to print, changes can occur during the lifetime of an edition. Any updates that we know of for this guide will be on the Cicerone website (www.cicerone.co.uk/1089/updates), so please check before planning your trip. We also advise that you check information about such things as transport, accommodation and shops locally. Even rights of way can be altered over time. We are always grateful for information about any discrepancies between a guidebook and the facts on the ground, sent by email to updates@cicerone.co.uk.

**Register your book:** To sign up to receive free updates, special offers and GPX files where available, create a Cicerone account and register your purchase via the 'My Account' tab at www.cicerone.co.uk.

# Mountain safety

Every mountain walk has its dangers, and those described in this guidebook are no exception. All who walk or climb in the mountains should recognise this and take responsibility for themselves and their companions along the way. The authors and publisher have made every effort to ensure that the information contained in this guide was correct when it went to press, but, except for any liability that cannot be excluded by law, they cannot accept responsibility for any loss, injury or inconvenience sustained by any person using this book.

**International distress signal** *(emergency only)*
Six blasts on a whistle (and flashes with a torch after dark) spaced evenly for one minute, followed by a minute's pause. Repeat until an answer is received. The response is three signals per minute followed by a minute's pause.

**Helicopter rescue**
The following signals are used to communicate with a helicopter:

Help needed: raise both arms above head to form a 'Y'

Help not needed: raise one arm above head, extend other arm downward

**Emergency telephone numbers**
In an emergency, dial 999 and ask for 'police' and then 'mountain rescue'. Be prepared to give your location (with grid ref if possible), the nature of the accident or emergency, the name, age and gender of any casualties, the number of people in your party and your mobile number. Then stay where you are and await help.

**Weather reports**
www.mwis.org.uk
www.metoffice.gov.uk/weather/specialist-forecasts/mountain

**Mountain rescue can be very expensive – be adequately insured.**

*Cribyn from Pen y Fan (Walk 3)*

# INTRODUCTION

*Bannau Brycheiniog from Mynydd y Llan (Walk 31)*

Situated in an unspoilt area of South Wales, just north of the former coal-mining valleys, the Brecon Beacons National Park is a place of beautiful and diverse landscapes. One of three national parks in Wales, more than half of its 519 square miles are over 1000ft above sea level and it boasts a rich mixture of majestic valleys, dramatic waterfalls and high mountain peaks and ridges.

A striking feature of the park is the number of rich and varied walks that can be found in a relatively small area, so you don't have to travel great distances by car to sample the multitude of different landscapes and varied terrain on offer. The routes in this guide mainly take you to wooded gorges and upland valleys that even the locals may be unaware of. All of the 45 routes are circular (with the exception of Walk 26, which is there-and-back) and avoid using stretches of road wherever possible.

The park falls naturally into four geographic areas. These are (from west to east): Mynydd Du (the Black Mountain), Fforest Fawr (the Great Forest), the Brecon Beacons and Y Mynyddoedd Duon (the Black Mountains). These all have different characters, making the park unique in offering such varied walking experiences.

Mynydd Du has some of the remotest upland wilderness in England and Wales. This is the area to choose when you really want to get away from it all. In contrast, Fforest Fawr, a former royal hunting ground, has both upland walks and deeply incised river gorges and waterfalls to rival any in the UK. The

*Pen y Fan from Cribyn (Walk 5)*

Brecon Beacons are the highest summits in the park, with Pen y Fan falling just short of the 3000ft threshold. Although this area lacks the challenges of the narrow rocky ridges of the Lake District and Snowdonia, it does provide opportunities for a real mountain expedition in exciting winter conditions. Finally, the Black Mountains, on the English border, have a softer feel to them, without the coarse and rugged Welshness of Mynydd Du.

There is also a plethora of things to see and activities for visitors of all ages and tastes, making the park a great place for families to visit. Favourite attractions for children include the Dan-yr-Ogof Show Caves in the Swansea Valley, the Brecon Mountain Railway at Penderyn and the Big Pit National Coal Museum near Blaenavon. Picturesque market towns lie on the edges of the park, such as Llandovery, Brecon, Crickhowell and Abergavenny, and are also great places to explore.

### GEOLOGY OF THE BRECON BEACONS

The rocks that shape the park belong to the Old Red Sandstone and were deposited some 395–345 million years ago in the Devonian Period. Old Red Sandstone is a generic term which refers to a group of sedimentary rocks laid down by rivers flowing across coastal plains. Three distinct rock types, conglomerates, sands and muds, were formed from river gravels, sands and muds, respectively.

The area now known as South Wales lay south of the equator in latitudes typically occupied by deserts. Prior to this, much of Britain was affected by strong earth movements which caused uplift and sharp folding, resulting in a tract of upland (St George's Land) that probably extended from the Midlands through central and northern Wales and into Ireland.

Flash floods washed down red muds, sands and grits along ephemeral river channels, building an extensive

## Geological cross-section of the Brecon Beacons

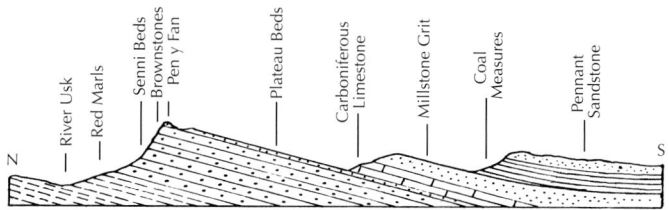

river floodplain. To the south was the Devonian shoreline, approximately where the Bristol Channel is now, and the warm Devonian Sea where the first fish swam. Europe at this time was drifting northward and when it crossed the equator, the semi-arid floodplains were gradually submerged beneath tropical Carboniferous seas.

The Old Red Sandstone in the Brecon Beacons can be split on geological grounds into Lower and Upper; the Middle is missing. The Lower Old Red Sandstone comprises a group of up to 850m of red marls, followed by a group of sandstones divided into two formations: the Senni Beds, some 310m of dark-green chloritic layers interbedded with red, and the Brownstones, 330m of very dark-red and purple sandstones. The steep craggy slopes are formed from these regularly bedded Brownstones.

A secondary escarpment is well developed on the northern ridges of Cefn Cwm Llwch, Bryn Teg and Cefn Cyff where the ridge drops steeply from the main scarp, flattens between 540 and 600m and then drops again, the steeper slopes beneath this being cut in the Senni Beds, which underlie the Brownstones.

The Upper Old Red Sandstone comprises three groups of rocks. The Plateau Beds are red quartzites and conglomerates up to 33m thick, which overlie the Brownstones. The summits of Corn Du and Pen y Fan are capped by an isolated outlier of some 14m of overlying, massively bedded Plateau Beds. The second group, the Grey Grits, are sandstones and conglomerates up to 60m thick and these pass laterally eastwards into the Quartz Conglomerates, which comprise red and brown sandstones, quartzites and coarse conglomerates. Further earth movements during the Middle Devonian Period uplifted South Wales, resulting in renewed erosion, creating a distinct break in the geological record, and forming the distinctive ridges and valleys that walkers enjoy today.

### Earth movements

The mountain-building earth movements that took place at the base of the Old Red Sandstone and at the end of the Upper Palaeozoic have been named the Caledonian and Hercynian Periods, respectively. The Caledonian movements spanned a time interval of more than 100 million years, at least from the latest Cambrian Period to the post-Silurian, and were responsible for the folding and faulting of rocks, resulting in geological structures aligned in a north-east to south-west direction. After these Mid-Devonian movements died away, there was little mountain building until late Carboniferous times. At the end of the Coal Measures, the Brecon Beacons were on the southern flanks of a southward-moving continent that eventually collided with a northward-moving land mass to the south. Enormous compressive forces caused the strong folding and faulting of Upper Palaeozoic rocks. The outstanding feature that resulted from these tectonic movements is the syncline of the South Wales Coalfield, and the regional southward tilt of the rocks of the Brecon Beacons originated as part of its northern limb. A major structure disrupts the northern rim of the coalfield and runs through the lower parts of Waterfall Country. This complex fault system, known as the Neath Disturbance, grew intermittently from Dinantian times, reaching its zenith in late Carboniferous times.

## Glacial origins of U-shaped valleys

The valleys were originally formed by streams cutting down through the Old Red Sandstone rocks, forming a V-shaped cross-section. For some two million years this area was in the grip of the Ice Age which ended about 12,000 years ago. Glacier ice carved out U-shaped valleys and towards the end of the Pleistocene, when climatic conditions were still sufficiently cold for significant quantities of snow to collect, many cwms (valleys) were formed.

### CHANGING WOODLAND

Trees started to recolonise the Brecon Beacons after the last Ice Age around 12,000 years ago. Arctic–alpine vegetation first established itself and was then

*Bluebell woods near Trecastle (Walk 31)*

invaded by a scrubland of dwarf birch with some juniper. Taller birches and, to a lesser extent, Scots pine, followed.

The climate continued becoming warmer and drier and, around 9000 years ago, pine and birch remained on lower hill slopes but the upland was covered in hazel, with valleys full of damp oak woodland with lime and elm. Woodland grew at much higher altitudes than it does today, up to 600m, above which grew alpine grassland.

Climatic conditions became even warmer and more humid, allowing the formation of blanket peats 7000–5000 years ago. Alder, elm and oak thrived in damp valleys. Drier conditions returned, elm disappeared and beech made its first appearance. The climate started to grow colder again but is now growing warmer once more due to global climate change. A forest pasture ecosystem developed during this period with sessile oak, ash and beech woodland interspersed with meadows. The vegetation supported a number of grazing and browsing animals that likely included auroch, European bison, red deer, horse and wild boar. These were preyed on by lynx, brown bear, wolf and wildcat. The river corridors were managed by beaver that was hunted to extinction here 400 years ago. Salmon and sea trout, known as sewin in Wales, spawned in the rivers and streams.

## HUMAN IMPACT

The Brecon Beacons may appear to be a bleak and inhospitable place to live but prehistoric man is known to have settled here since Mesolithic times (Middle Stone Age c.6000BC). The climate in Mesolithic, Neolithic (New Stone Age c.3000–1800BC) and Bronze Age times (c.1800–400BC) was much warmer and drier than today's, and the mountains were covered in oak, birch, alder and lime woodland, with an understorey of hazel and willow.

Woodland glades would have contained grasses, heathers, species of roses and various flowers. Prehistoric man fed, clothed and housed himself by hunting and gathering, and, by about 2500BC, woodland clearance and mixed farming was practised. During the very dry summer of 1976, when the water level was extremely low, many scrapers, arrowheads and knife blades were found in the Upper Neuadd reservoir.

An improvement in Britain's climate from about 4500 years ago heralded the start of the Bronze Age and was associated with the spread of agriculture into the uplands at the expense of the wildwood. This change is suggested by a gradual decline in tree pollen and an increase in plantain pollen and bracken spores in peat cores taken locally. It is also known that cereals were cultivated in the Brecon Beacons area. The climate deteriorated again from about 3000 years ago, resulting in the retreat of farming from the uplands, which led to the recovery of birch and hazel woodland. By the end of the Bronze Age, peat bogs had spread across formerly productive farmland.

The Neolithic tradition of constructing stone circles continued into the Bronze Age, followed by the construction of large drystone cairn burial mounds on the summits of Mynydd Du and Fforest Fawr. Copper tools and other unearthed objects date back to at least 4500 years ago. The use of copper was followed shortly by bronze. However, stone tools continued to be made and used in Wales until about 3400 years ago.

A marked increase in deforestation took place during pre-Roman Iron Age times in order to create new upland heather moorland, as sheep were an important part of the subsistence economy. There is also some evidence of arable cultivation. Many hill forts were built during the Iron Age, with the greatest concentration found in the Usk Valley to the west of Brecon. These were probably used by the Welsh tribe of the region, the Silures, who fought the invading Roman legions for around 25 years, winning many battles and preventing them from building permanent forts until they were defeated in AD79.

During their military occupation the Romans built a number of permanent forts that were linked by well-constructed roads, such as Sarn Helen. No towns were established and only two villas are known of, with one at Llanfrynach. Brown bears roamed the Beacons at this time and their remains have been found at the Roman legionary fortress of Isca on the banks of the Usk at Caerleon. They would have been used as entertainment in the stone amphitheatre and may have been exported to Rome. They had been hunted to extinction by around AD1000.

Roman rule had ended by the fifth and sixth centuries when the princedom of Brycheiniog was established. This dynasty came from Irish ancestry that is thought to have resulted from a movement of people up the Usk Valley utilising the fertile land around Brecon and the upland areas for summer grazing. They made use of the Roman roads and some of their gravestones have been found beside them. One of these is the 3.4m high Maen Madoc on the side of Sarn Helen near Ystradfellte.

Two hundred years of warfare began in 1088 when the Norman baron Bernard Newmarch invaded through the Talgarth Gap. He built motte and bailey castles of earth and wood at Hay, Bronllys and Talgarth, and at Brecon in 1091–93. The occupying force then spread down the Usk Valley, constructing castles at Pencelli, Blaenllynfi, Tretower and Crickhowell. These were later replaced by stone-built castles. The Normans divided up the land in a manorial field arrangement of strips of arable and meadow similar to the existing Welsh system. This settlement pattern continues to the present day.

Some of the rocks of the park have been quarried, with Cribarth mountain being extensively modified by more than 30 large-scale workings for limestone, silica sand and rottenstone. Sought-after rock types include limestone, which was used in the iron and copper smelting industry in South Wales. There are more than 171 disused lime kilns just around the limestone pavements of Blaen Nedd and Ystradfellte, with major works also in Cwm Twrch. Limestone was also used in agriculture and in lime mortar and whitewash.

The Sychryd Valley was once a busy industrial site from which large quantities of silica were mined for the manufacture of refractory bricks for furnace linings. The lower part of the Mellte Valley nearby was once a hive of activity with the manufacture of gunpowder.

The area covered in this guide was designated a national park in 1957. The largest landowner is the National Trust with over 5000 hectares, much of this common land. This includes the Central Beacons massif, which was gifted by the Eagle Star Insurance Company in 1964.

Climate change is the latest threat to some species, with Arctic–alpine plants being at the greatest risk of extinction. These are already at their most southerly limit and are barely surviving, except on the steep cliffs of Craig Cerrig-gleisiad and Pen y Fan, where sheep cannot graze and the high altitude keeps temperatures low.

## BIRDLIFE

Ravens, buzzards and red kites are numerous in the Brecon Beacons and are the great scavengers of the hills, finding sheep carcasses wherever they can. The kites are now a common sight in the park but were once persecuted almost to extinction. A small population survived in Mid Wales and a recovery programme, which began in 1989, has been successful in extending their range over the whole of the UK.

Curlews can be found nesting among the rushes of the higher streams but their camouflage is so good that you will rarely spot a sitting bird. Dunlins nest among eroding peat hags and are at their most southerly breeding limit in the world. Golden plovers are another true wader of mountain moorland and are also close to their southerly limit. You may disturb red and black grouse when walking across open moorland such as Waun Llysiog. Both species spend the winter on the mountains but the loss of bilberry, heather and cotton-grass moorland through conifer planting has resulted in their decline.

Bracken-covered valley slopes support dense populations of whinchat and also provide nesting areas for the mallard, nightjar, stonechat, wren, tree pipit and yellowhammer. Damper patches may hide the dark-capped reed bunting. Skylarks are constant companions in spring and summer on grassy uplands, the air full of song as they fly above you. The white-rumped wheatear resides in drystone walls and bouldery scree. Look out for stonechats, linnets and yellowhammers in the gorse.

Woodland birds include the blue tit, great tit, coal tit, pied flycatcher, nuthatch, redstart, tawny owl, green woodpecker, lesser-spotted woodpecker, great-spotted woodpecker, jay, wood pigeon, blackbird, treecreeper and wren. Warblers migrate in summer from southern climes to nest on the woodland floor.

*The stunning kingfisher can be seen on many of the rivers in the park*

The fields, wooded slopes and rivers of Waterfall Country provide a wide variety of habitats for numerous birds. Lapwings are commonly seen in the valleys, together with redshanks and snipes. Birds associated with woodland and the riverbank include the breeding dipper, grey wagtail, goosander, pied flycatcher, redstart, wood warbler, woodcock, buzzard and sparrowhawk.

## GETTING TO AND STAYING IN THE NATIONAL PARK

The Brecon Beacons National Park is a day trip from Swansea, Cardiff, Bristol and the Midlands and an ideal short-break destination from London, only 200km (120 miles) away. There are excellent rail and motorway links with the rest of the UK and Cardiff International Airport is just over an hour from the park.

In summer, the Beacons Bus offers the opportunity of a car-free day in the mountains on Sundays and Bank Holidays, from May to September, from many places in South Wales and Herefordshire.

The park has accommodation to suit all pockets, from grand country hotels to secluded campsites. Tourist information can be found at Brecon Beacons Our National Park www.breconbeacons.org. The main towns that make good bases for walking holidays are Brecon, Crickhowell and Abergavenny, which all lie in the picturesque Usk Valley.

## A SOLITARY GUIDED WALK?

The inspiration for this guide came from a realisation that many walkers wish to know more about the countryside they have come to enjoy and explore. One solution is to join one of the many guided walks organised by the Brecon Beacons National Park Authority. However, these are so popular that as many as a hundred people may join a single ramble. As well as being a logistical problem for the warden, the sheer numbers destroy the wilderness quality of a walk in the countryside, with little chance of seeing undisturbed wildlife.

Another approach is a 'guided walk' with a difference: a walk guided by a book that gives you all the interesting facts that an expert would provide, but which still lets you retain the magical wilderness feeling of an isolated mountain summit or the tranquillity of a river ramble. This guide aims to provide you with information on all aspects of the landscape, as if you were being accompanied and advised by several experts at the same time.

All the route descriptions are complemented by a commentary that includes geomorphology, hydrology, geology, botany, zoology, ecology, ornithology, archaeology, local history, land-use and environmental issues. Designed to be used by all ages, the guide does not assume any previous mountain walking experience or countryside knowledge.

## USING THIS GUIDE

This book is divided into seven geographic sections: Brecon Beacons – north-eastern valleys and ridges; Brecon Beacons – eastern valleys and ridges; Brecon Beacons – south-western valleys and ridges; Fforest Fawr; Waterfall

## USING THIS GUIDE

*Tree lungwort lichen, a species typical of high rainfall and clean air*

Country; the Black Mountain/Mynydd Du (Western Brecon Beacons National Park) and The Black Mountains/Y Mynyddoedd Duon (Eastern Brecon Beacons National Park).

It is designed to be used in conjunction with the Ordnance Survey's Brecon Beacons National Park Explorer maps (1:25,000): Western area OL12, Central area OL11 and Eastern area OL13. Note that place-name spellings may vary slightly between different maps.

The 45 routes described include low-level and high-level routes of varying lengths and degrees of difficulty, to cater for different weather conditions and abilities. A fit mountain walker will not find any of the routes particularly strenuous. Most of the routes are circular, include as few roads as possible and mainly explore less frequented areas.

For each route, the start point (including grid reference), distance, total ascent, grade, maximum elevation and map required are listed at the beginning of the route description. Routes are illustrated with extracts from 1:50,000 OS maps, with the main route marked in orange and any alternative routes marked in blue and extensions in green (alternative and extended routes are described at the end of the main route description). Features along the walk that appear on the map are highlighted in **bold** in the route description to help you follow your progress.

The route summary table and routes by interest table in Appendix A and Appendix B, respectively, are provided to help you choose a walk suitable for the weather, the time you have available, your fitness level and your interests. Once you have chosen a suitable walk from the table, you will find it summarised in the introductory box at the beginning of each route. Some of the valleys, especially the northern ones, offer a multiplicity of routes, and walks have been chosen using the ridges in a particular direction so as to present the best unfolding panorama. Valleys have been included to give shorter, less strenuous walks or as an alternative in bad weather when all but the most adventurous might eschew the high places.

### Walk grades

All the walks in this guide have been assigned a difficulty grade.

- **Grade 1:** easy and short low-level walk with easy navigation suitable for all walkers.
- **Grade 2:** easy but more demanding in terms of length and total ascent.

*Sunset over the Beacons from Cefn Cantref (Walk 2)*

Obvious route finding on mostly clear paths. A reasonable level of fitness is preferable.
- **Grade 3:** mountainous route with possible strenuous ascents with easy route finding.
- **Grade 4:** long mountainous route with possible strenuous ascents in a wilderness area.

### How long will a route take?
A general rule of thumb for calculating the minimum time that it might take to walk a particular route is to allow 1 hour for every 5km (3 miles) forward and an additional half-hour for every 300m (1000ft) of ascent. This formula, known as Naismith's Rule, is based on a fit hiker walking on typical terrain under normal conditions. Once you have walked a few of the routes in this guide, you should have a clearer idea of how much you need to tweak this rule for it to work for your own level of fitness.

Don't forget to add in time for rests, a break for lunch and for reading this book, to arrive at a rough indication of how long you'll be out on the hill.

### GPX tracks
GPX tracks for the routes in this guidebook are available to download free at www.cicerone.co.uk/1089/GPX. If you have not bought the book through the Cicerone website, or have bought the book without opening an account, please register your purchase in your Cicerone library to access GPX and update information.

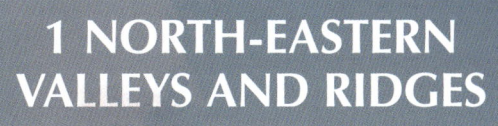

# 1 NORTH-EASTERN VALLEYS AND RIDGES

*Waterfall in Cwm Sere (Walks 2 and 3)*

# WALK 1
## Corn Du and Pen y Fan via Cwm Llwch

| | |
|---|---|
| **Start/finish** | Car park in Cwm Llwch (SO 006 245) |
| **Distance** | 10.75km (6.7 miles); ridge walk 12.5km (7.7 miles); valley walk 6km (3.7 miles) |
| **Total ascent** | 655m (2150ft); ridge walk 725m (2380ft); valley walk 335m (1100ft) |
| **Grade** | 3; ridge walk 3; valley walk 1 |
| **Max elevation** | 886m (2907ft); valley walk 266m (872ft) |
| **Map** | OL12 Western area |

This fine route heads into the most westerly of the northern Beacons valleys and has a number of options to suit all tastes and weather conditions. The final climb to the summits is steep, as is the upper part of the descent from Pen y Fan. Route finding is straightforward in good weather, but in mist or winter conditions the ability to use a compass and map is important. Points of interest include glacial geomorphology, plants and birdlife, and waterfalls and a lake, as well as good panoramic views and archaeological features.

An alternative start allows an anticlockwise ridge walk, and a pleasant valley walk can be taken to a waterfall and Llyn Cwm Llwch. A shorter alternative route returns to the start from the obelisk below Corn Du, dropping down Pen Milan ridge on the west of the valley.

Start at the end of the car park where there is a 'NO MOTORS' sign with the stream Nant Cwm Llwch on your left. Follow the track leading into the valley lined with beech, hawthorn, mountain ash and hazel. ◄

From here there are good views into Cwm Llwch with waterfalls in the foreground and a backdrop dominated by Corn Du straight ahead and Pen y Fan on the left.

> The woodland on the right contains the poorly preserved earthworks of an **Iron Age hill fort**, which is marked on the map as a dotted oval marked 'Settlement'. This is a small enclosure with widely spaced ramparts but its value as a hill fort is dubious as, although the land slopes away east to Nant Cwm Llwch, the land to the west and south rises gradually to the foot of Pen Milan.

## WALK 1 – CORN DU AND PEN Y FAN VIA CWM LLWCH

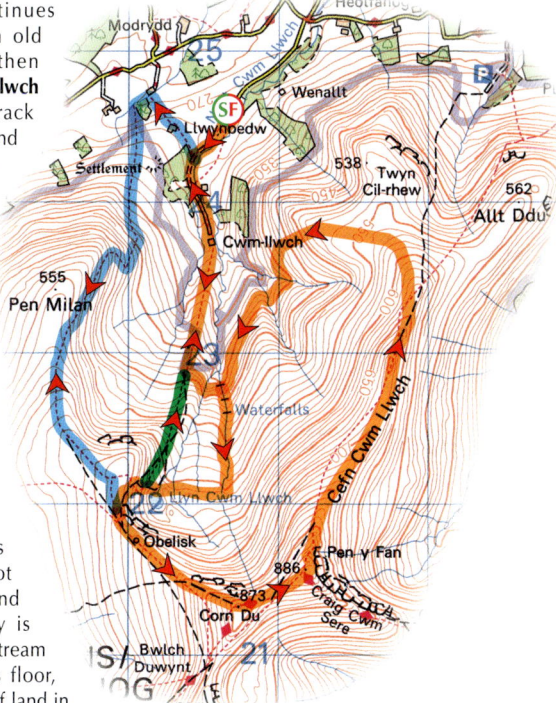

The track continues southwards between old stone walls and then detours around **Cwm-llwch Cottage**. Take the track ahead up a spur of land with stream courses on either side. Cross the hill fence and drop down to the stream on your left. This is a most interesting habitat as, after the birch woodland is left behind, the banks of the stream are lined with closely grazed grassy areas where there are many different species of wildflowers, such as lousewort, bird's-foot trefoil, red bartsia and eyebright. The valley is unusual in that two stream beds have eroded its floor, leaving a raised spur of land in the centre.

Notice that the valley slopes have a high density of hawthorn trees – a notable feature of Beacons valleys. For this reason, the number of **bird species** is more typically associated with woodland than an open valley. Keep a sharp lookout for the tree pipit, green finch, redstart, wren, whinchat, yellowhammer and chaffinch. Even the great-spotted woodpecker has been recorded. Do not be surprised if you see green woodpeckers often far from trees where they feed on ants. The falls and stream bed are good places to spot grey wagtail, heron and dipper.

*Cwm-llwch Cottage and sheep*

### GEOLOGY AND GEOMORPHOLOGY OF CWM LLWCH

Cwm Llwch was carved by glaciers during the last ice ages but its shape is different from many of the other glacial valleys in the Beacons. The upper section is relatively flat and contains a corrie lake, Llyn Cwm Llwch, but the gradient steepens in the middle section, where the waterfalls are found, before it eases again near Cwm-llwch Cottage. This may be due to a more resistant band of rock which is also responsible for the formation of the waterfalls. The characteristic U-shape of the glacial valley has been further modified in the middle section by two streams that have cut down into the valley floor leaving a ridge, which the main footpath follows.

Drop left down to the stream immediately after the hill fence is crossed. Continue upstream and follow the left branch when it divides. Just ahead is an impressive waterfall. The route climbs up on the right-hand side, arriving first at a small pool above the lower fall. If you prefer an easier route, walk up the hillside to the right of the lower fall.

The area is rich in **plant life**. The falls are shaded by a mixture of hawthorn, blackthorn, ash, rowan, willow and silver birch. Most of the trees are young or have grown from previously fallen trunks. Luxuriant mosses and ferns thrive on damp and wet rock faces surrounding the fall. Ferns include the rare Wilson's filmy fern and bryophytes include *Ulota crispa*, *Mnium undulatum*, *Hylocomium splendens*, *Atrichum undulatum*, *Neckera pumila*, *Fissidens taxifolius*, *Philonotis fontana*, *Hyocomium armorica*, *Frullania tamarisci* and several others. Several ungrazed tall herb ledges can be seen to the left and right of the fall. Interesting vascular plant species include valerian, wild angelica, meadow sweet, *Alchemilla vulgaris*, wood avens and Welsh Poppy.

Climb up the right-hand side of the upper fall to reach a series of smaller **waterfalls** from where there are magnificent views of Corn Du. Surprisingly, from this viewpoint the flat-topped summit of Corn Du at the head of the valley falsely appears higher than its neighbour, Pen y Fan, which is on the left. When the stream starts to break up into many smaller tributaries, leave the stream and head right, striking westwards to the corrie lake of **Llyn Cwm Llwch**. ▶ The Valley Walk option leaves on the right here and descends back down the obvious path to where you crossed the hill fence earlier on.

Llyn Cwm Llwch is a good place to have a break and appreciate this special place.

Legend has it that Llyn Cwm Llwch had an **enchanted island**, only accessible through a tunnel from the shore. The island would rise out of the water only on May Day, when visitors to the island would be presented with fairy flowers and enjoy enchanting fairy music. The flowers were so lovely that one sacrilegious visitor decided to take some away with him down the mountain. When they faded, the island disappeared below the waters and was never seen again.

### GLACIAL ORIGINS OF LLYN CWM LLWCH

Llyn Cwm Llwch is a small oligotrophic corrie lake that has a surprisingly shallow maximum depth of only 8m. The term oligotrophic means that nutrients are in poor supply and the water, therefore, remains crystal clear all year round. At first glance, Llyn Cwm Llwch appears to have been formed by glacial ice carving out a deep basin in the solid rock, but a closer inspection reveals this is not the case. The shallowness of the lake and the hummocky mounds that surround it are clues to its origins. The lake is situated at the head of Cwm Llwch in a spot that receives the most shade from the sun. Here one of the last remaining blocks of ice from the Ice Age lingered on. Rock fragments were plucked from the Brownstone crags above by freeze-thaw action, a process whereby water in fissures in rock freezes and expands, cracking the rock; the ice then melts, penetrating the rock even further before refreezing. These fragments tumbled over the wasting ice mass to accumulate in a ring around its edges. When the ice finally melted, a small lake dammed by the ring of moraine was left. Kettle holes are also formed through the same process.

Take the path which leads to the right (W) up the steep slope in a zigzag, climbing steeply to the lower end of the ridge of Craig Cwm Llwch. ◄

*The alternative shorter route which descends to Pen Milan leaves from here.*

The main route continues climbing along the edge of the ridge to **Tommy Jones' Obelisk**, a useful landmark in poor visibility. Looking back down to the left from the obelisk there is a fine view of the hummocky mounds of glacial moraine that dam the lake of Llyn Cwm Llwch.

The obelisk is a **memorial to Tommy Jones**, aged five, who died here in 1900 of exhaustion. Tommy and his father had taken a train to Brecon earlier in the day and were walking the last four miles to his grandparents' farm in Cwm Llwch. They stopped for a rest at an army camp at Login and were surprised by the arrival of Tommy's grandfather and his 13-year-old cousin who had come to meet them. While the two men greeted each other, Tommy's cousin Willie was sent ahead to the farm to let them know they would soon arrive. Tommy followed his cousin; however, perhaps being scared of the dark, he started to cry only halfway up the track. The two boys parted company and Tommy headed back towards the camp at Login. Sadly, he never arrived. His body wasn't found until 29 days later. The obelisk now serves as a useful landmark in poor visibility, marking a rapid descent route from Cefn Cwm Llwch to the safety of the valley below, ensuring that walkers today do not suffer the same fate.

Follow the ridge of Craig Cwm Llwch (SE) up the steep slope to the summit of **Corn Du**.

*Corn Du and Pen y Fan from Craig Gwaun Taf*

From here you may see buzzards, red kites, carrion crows and ravens wheeling overhead. Ravens nest nearby on the crags of Craig Cwm Sere. You will undoubtedly see or hear the meadow pipit and skylark, the commonest **birds** over hill grasslands. If you are especially observant you may see ring ouzels, as they breed in the vicinity of the crags. This area is near the limit of their British range.

The final 10m or so to the summit of Corn Du involves scrambling up the Plateau Beds, but a stepped path leading diagonally right will avoid further damage to these loose crags. An interesting path-cum-sheep-track avoids this and cuts east across the northern face of Corn Du below the crumbling cliffs to the col leading to Pen y Fan. From the top of the stepped path cross left (E) to the summit of the crags overlooking Cwm Llwch.

From the cairn follow the crags (E) and descend into the col. The path swings around (ENE) and climbs along a broad track, well marked by cairns. The final one is of Bronze Age origin and leads to the trig point on the summit of **Pen y Fan**, which at 886m (2906ft) is the highest mountain in South Wales. (For a description of the mountain see 'Geology and geomorphology of Pen y Fan', Walk 3.) ▶

Fforest Fawr is visible beyond Craig Cerriggleisiad to the west, with Swansea Bay to the south-west.

> Interesting plants on the rock face include rock stonecrop, mossy saxifrage, purple saxifrage, sea campion, Wilson's filmy fern, globe flower, green spleenwort and northern bedstraw.

Scramble carefully down the crags due north of the summit cairn. Look back at the north-east face of Pen y Fan, where in early spring you can see the brilliant colours of rare Arctic–alpines. ◀ Follow the ridge of **Cefn Cwm Llwch** for about 2km.

As you scramble down from the summit, look carefully at the upper surfaces of the near horizontal Plateau Beds for **ripple marks**. These are also present on the surfaces of rocks that form the summit. They were formed in exactly the same way as the ripples you see in the sandy beds of rivers today.

Take a small path which leaves the main track and bears left (NW) towards the pile of stones at the disused quarry of Cwar Mawr (SO 018 236). From here descend west-south-west down the spur of Twyn y Dyfnant to where the hill fence meets the mountain stream gully.

Turn left at the hill fence and follow it up the valley. Cross two gullies and descend to the stream bed where the hill fence meets it on the other side. Rejoin your earlier route back to the start.

### Alternative start

From the car parking area, continue along the main track into the valley of Cwm Llwch. After about 200 metres there is a wood on the right. Take the path to the right and follow this up the hill into the field. The path goes past deciduous woodland with alder trees on the left and comes to a stile near a large oak tree. Continue in a north-westerly direction, reaching a second wooden stile with a yellow waymark arrow and then head towards a renovated farmhouse at **Llwynbedw**, turning right to bypass it on your left. ◀

> On the left is the bulk of Pen Milan, over which this route climbs.

Skirting round the farm buildings cross a stile and the field ahead to a **house** in the trees, Clwydwaunhir. Cross a stile and walk down the left-hand side of the hawthorn hedge to a stile and stream. After crossing the stream, turn sharp left and follow the sign to Pen Milan.

Continue between holly trees, fording the stream again, and follow the track ahead to the gate with a yellow waymark arrow and the National Trust sign to Pen Milan. This is where you cross the hill fence. Head due south along an indistinct path, aiming for the left side of the spur of land

## WALK 1 – CORN DU AND PEN Y FAN VIA CWM LLWCH

ahead, and follow the land grooves up to the crest. A slightly sunken grassy track leads diagonally up the valley side to a path through gorse and bracken.

From here look up the valley to Pen y Fan on the left and Corn Du on the right. Far over to the east is the Cefn Cwm Llwch ridge, which will be your descent route. The route drops down this ridge to Twyn y Dyfnant on its left (N) edge.

Pass a group of hawthorn trees on the left and follow the old quarry track to a point where it swings sharply back to the right at the first zigzag. Continue south between small quarry spoils and keep on the main track to a flattened area of quarry debris. From here follow the path to the cairn. ▶

Walk through peat hags to a broader section of the ridge and on to **Tommy Jones' Obelisk**, where you join the main route.

From the cairn there are good views to the west to Craig Cerrig-gleisiad and Fan Nedd beyond.

### Alternative descent route

If the weather becomes unfavourable to continue to the peaks, or if you prefer a shorter route, turn north at the obelisk and follow the footpath which swings first right, left, then right again around the head of a side valley of Cwm Llwch, with steep slopes on the right. Just before the final spur of **Pen Milan**, the path changes into an old broad green quarry track. The hill vegetation comprises dwarf-shrub heath and grass heath, in which ling and bilberry are common. Purple moor grass is abundant on flatter areas.

*Craig Cerrig-gleisiad from Pen Milan*

The route descends to the right diagonally across the valley side. This track has obviously seen heavy use in the past and, in fact, was once used to transport Old Red Sandstone from a quarry on the left, now abandoned. The softer rock was used as road infill, whereas the harder stone was used in building.

The quarry track swings sharply right and then left, descending between grassy banks and heading due north again. The path becomes ill-defined in places but eventually the fences on either side funnel the path to a gate. Pass through the gate, ford a small stream and follow the tree-lined track to the yard with the **cottage** of Clwydwaunhir on the left.

Opposite the house are a small ford and a stile. Cross these and cut across some fields (SE) back to the start of the walk.

# WALK 2
*Pen y Fan via Cwm Sere*

| | |
|---|---|
| **Start/finish** | Cwm Gwdi car park (SO 025 248), postcode LD3 8LE |
| **Distance** | 10.75km (6.7 miles); valley walk 8.25km (5.1 miles) |
| **Total ascent** | 655m (2150ft); valley walk 275m (900ft) |
| **Grade** | 3; valley walk 1 |
| **Max elevation** | 886m (2907ft); valley walk 509m (1669ft) |
| **Map** | OL12 Western area |

This fulfilling mountain route explores one of the most spectacular and wildest valleys in the Beacons and includes sections that can be demanding in snow and ice conditions. The lower reaches of the valley are well wooded and lead into an amphitheatre created by the steep northern slopes of Cribyn and Pen y Fan. There is a steep ascent of the headwall, and the upper parts of the route can be quite challenging in poor weather or winter conditions but the valley route is a less demanding option. The main features of interest include geomorphology and glaciology, panoramic views and archaeological sites.

*Cribyn from Cwm Sere*

From the main car park follow the footpath down into the stream valley of Nant Gwdi, cross the bridge and climb up through woodland to the open hillside. Turn left and follow the path above the fence around the foot of Allt Ddu into the valley, to where it drops down to the stream. Pick an easy descent and work your way along **Nant Sere** to the head of the valley.

The spectacular north-east face of Pen y Fan is on the right and the north-west face of Cribyn is on the left. If you wish to just enjoy the valley, take your time to savour the most impressive glacially cut valley in the Brecon Beacons before retracing your steps back to the start.

Once in the basin below Cribyn, strike across towards the foot of the north-east face of Pen y Fan and from here climb the headwall on the track which starts from bottom right and continues to top left. You will cross piles of stones brought down the gullies by winter frosts. The

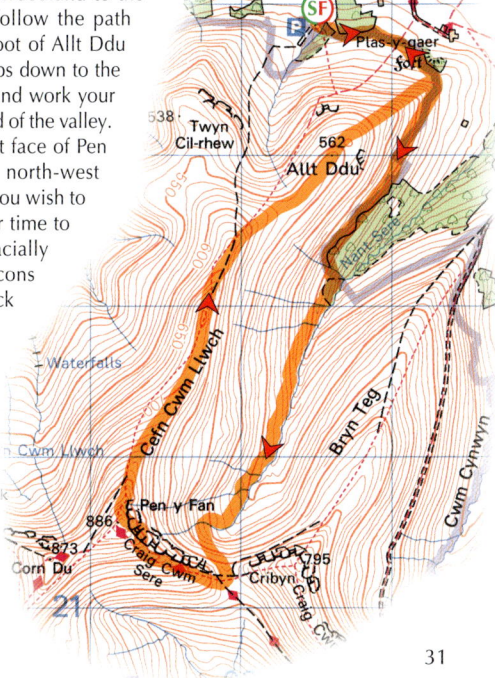

*There is a good view of Cribyn during the ascent.* headwall track rises at an easy angle, presenting no problems, and arrives at the unnamed col between Cribyn and Pen y Fan. ◀

From the col climb steadily (W), following the line of **Craig Cwm Sere** to the summit of Pen y Fan. In early spring the vibrant colours of rare Arctic–alpines may be seen on the most inaccessible crags.

## VEGETATION OF THE NORTH-EAST FACE OF PEN Y FAN

This steep, impregnable face protects one of Britain's true botanical treasures from grazing sheep. The combination of high altitude and a shaded northern aspect creates living conditions more akin to polar latitudes than to temperate southern Britain. Extensive ledges high up on the face are crammed full of interesting and unusual species that bring the otherwise bleak and foreboding crags alive with vibrant colour in spring. Interesting plants include roseroot, rock stonecrop, mossy saxifrage, purple saxifrage, vernal sandwort, sea campion, Wilson's filmy fern, globe flower, serrated wintergreen, green spleenwort, lesser meadow rue, brittle bladder-fern and northern bedstraw. These ledges also support an unusual collection of bryophytes and several upland invertebrate species, including a rare Arctic aphid. These plants and animals are highly specialised to be able to survive in these extreme conditions.

Looking back down Cwm Sere from the approach to Pen y Fan, you get an ideal view of its **geomorphology**. Cwm Sere was carved into a U-shape by ice, but this has been altered slightly since the last Ice Age. On the left there is a distinct step in the valley side, a post-glacial feature known as an antiplanation terrace, while Nant Sere has also been eroding away a notch at its base.

An **antiplanation** terrace is formed when a snowbed develops on a sheltered step in a valley side. This snowbed erodes into the hillside by freeze-thaw action, depositing material further downslope. In the case of the western side of Cwm Sere, a minor platform formed due to differences in the resistance to erosion of underlying rock types and, in fact, this antiplanation terrace may be related to the change from Brownstones to the underlying Senni Beds.

## WALK 2 – PEN Y FAN VIA CWM SERE

*Cloud spilling over the north-east face of Pen y Fan*

Looking up the slope, you will see the flat-capped summit of Corn Du, and to the left is Bwlch Duwynt, which means 'windy gap'. The final ascent to the summit of **Pen y Fan** is up a very stony area, and the National Trust has built a zigzag path, known as Jacob's Ladder, up this steep slope to the top. ▶

Walk across the flat surface of Pen y Fan to the trig point. This can be found in bad visibility by carefully following the north-east crag line, the trig point being located at the end of this on the left. The north-east face is very steep and care must be taken not to stray too near the edge, especially in strong south-westerly winds or when corniced in winter. The summit is the site of a Bronze Age cairn and there are good views from here, with the cliffs of a beautiful glacial cwm, Craig Cerrig-gleisiad, almost due west and Swansea Bay to the south-west. (For details of the geomorphology of Pen y Fan, see 'Geology and geomorphology of Pen y Fan', Walk 3.)

The crags here are made of Plateau Beds, which form a distinctive cap to the summits of Pen y Fan and Corn Du.

The slope of the summit surface is the key to the dip of the resistant Plateau Beds which cap the summit. The summit is, in fact, the **dip slope** of this rock formation, which lies unconformably on the Brownstones, but the general trend in dip of all the rock strata in this area is to the south. A slight component of the dip controls the drainage in the valley sides, favouring the eastern-facing slopes. A close look at the map reveals this to be true for the majority of the gullies in Cwm Sere and Cwm Cynwyn.

Leave the summit of Pen y Fan by carefully scrambling (NNE) down the exposed Plateau Beds. The rocks can be slippery but the route drops quickly to the fine ridge of **Cefn Cwm Llwch**. ◄

*As you scramble down from the summit, look carefully at the upper surfaces of the near horizontal Plateau Beds for ripple marks.*

Below to the left is the valley of Cwm Llwch and the lake of Llyn Cwm Llwch. Looking down to the right, you will see a large gully which holds a frothy white cataract after heavy rain.

Once on the flat section of the ridge, look across to the east for a magnificent view over the ridges of the Beacons and the triangular profile of Cribyn. Follow the path along the flat ridge, leaving it when it drops gradually to the valley of Cwm Gwdi. Keep to the eastern edge of the ridge, following a path through some areas of boggy heather moorland past the disused quarries and onwards to **Allt Ddu**.

From the spur of Cefn Cwm Llwch, which is very well populated with skylarks in spring and summer, there is a good view looking back to Pen y Fan with Cribyn on the left and Corn Du sticking up through the gap in the ridge. As you descend this route further, you can see the town of Brecon over to the left beyond the end of the ridge. There is an area of heather and bilberry with the odd pool in the peat. At the end of this ridge are a number of hummocks and hollows, part of an old quarry, and you can look down past a rowan tree growing out of the crags to Cwmcynwyn Farm. There is a rock outcrop here with bedding showing clearly.

From the pools on the summit of Allt Ddu, drop down (N) past the stones of the quarry to the path above the hill fence. Turn left and retrace your earlier route back to the car park.

The descent of this ridge provides a good view of the **Plas-y-gaer settlement** with the earth bank now planted with a line of large trees.

**Plas-y-gaer** is an Iron Age settlement some 2000 years old, *gaer* meaning 'fortress' and *plas* meaning 'place'. The site is unexcavated but was probably built to defend the surrounding fertile land. The surviving earthworks form an oval shape and the height of the main rampart varies between 2 and 3.2m. As there is no sign of an entrance, access was probably gained from the north. No ancient features are visible in the interior.

## WALK 3
*Cribyn via Cwm Sere*

| | |
|---|---|
| **Start/finish** | Cwm Gwdi car park (SO 025 248), postcode LD3 8LE |
| **Distance** | 10.75km (6.6 miles); with extension 12.5km (7.7 miles) |
| **Total ascent** | 600m (1970ft); with extension 815m (2670ft) |
| **Grade** | 3 |
| **Max elevation** | 795m (2608ft); with extension 886m (2907ft) |
| **Map** | OL12 Western area |

This classic route from the north side of the Beacons is well worth choosing for a first visit. It includes a superb valley walk with small waterfalls, a steep climb up the head wall, a detour to the highest peak of Pen y Fan and a return via Cribyn and the Bryn Teg ridge. There are good views of the Beacons themselves, the Black Mountains and even Cadair Idris to the north on a clear day. Route finding, as in all high places, may require a map and compass and the final climb to the summits can be hard going. The glacial geomorphology of the U-shaped valleys is of particular interest.

From the main car park follow the footpath down into the stream valley of Nant Gwdi, cross the bridge and climb up to the open hillside. Turn left and follow the path above the fence around the foot of Allt Ddu into the valley to where it drops down to the stream. Pick an easy descent and work your way along **Nant Sere** to the head of the valley.

*The minor platform on the western side of the valley, an antiplanation terrace, was formed due to differences in the resistance to erosion of the underlying rock types.*

You can expect to see dippers in the stream bed and, with luck, a buzzard wheeling overhead or a heron hunting its prey near the water. Cwm Sere was carved by ice into a U-shape, but this has been altered slightly by a snowbed eating away at its western side in post-glacial times and by Nant Sere eroding away a notch in its base. ◄

Once in the basin below Cribyn strike across towards the foot of the north-east face of Pen y Fan. The sheer immensity of this face can be fully appreciated from the head of the cwm.

## GEOLOGY AND GEOMORPHOLOGY OF PEN Y FAN

The north-east face of Pen y Fan rises some 380m (1200ft), becoming vertical near the top where the more resistant Plateau Beds form a distinctive cap to the summit. Units of the Lower Old Red Sandstone, Plateau Beds and Brownstones are well exposed in the face. The ribbed nature of the Brownstones is due to the alternation of sandstone with softer marls. The brown scars on the face of the mountain are testimony to the relentless onslaught of the elements and the processes of erosion. The deadliest of these is the freezing and thawing of water in cracks in the rocks, which literally shatters the stone along existing lines of weakness. The Brownstones are particularly well bedded and cleaved, and split apart forming regular blocks seemingly made for constructing drystone walls and buildings. Gravity then plays its part in transporting stone and soil downslope. Rainwater percolates into the ground and becomes concentrated along the upper surfaces of the less permeable marly layers. Eventually, it seeps out of the face, leading to the erosion of the soft marls. This undermines the sandstone blocks above, causing them to collapse. The water then collects in gullies, further eroding soil and rock that is then channelled to the bottom of the face where it spreads out to form talus cones. Look out for a distinctive white, frothy stream that forms in the large gully on the right of the face after heavy rain. In snow and ice conditions, the gullies provide spectacular winter climbing routes for daring climbers equipped with crampons and ice axes.

*The extension to the summit of Pen y Fan leaves from here, and there is also an exhilarating alternative route round the shoulder of Cribyn.*

From the foot of Pen y Fan take the track up the headwall which goes from bottom right to top left. Crossing piles of loose stones at first, the headwall track rises at an easy angle, presenting no problems, and arrives at the unnamed col between Cribyn and Pen y Fan. ◄

Turn left (E) up the steep, eroded slope to the summit of **Cribyn**. On a clear day the ascent of Cribyn is rewarded with an impressive panorama, with good views to the west of the north-east face of Pen y Fan and to the east of the

*The sun setting behind Corn Du*

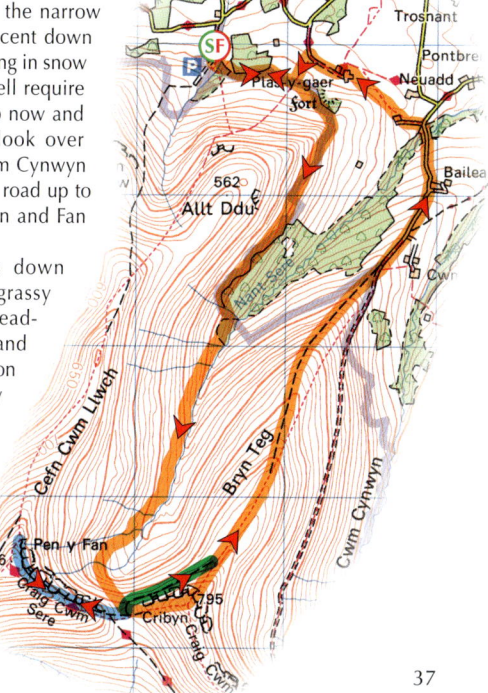

other Beacons valleys and ridges, Fan y Bîg and the Black Mountains beyond.

Descend (NNE) following the narrow prow of Cribyn. The steep descent down the nose of Cribyn can be exciting in snow and ice conditions and may well require crampons and an ice axe. Stop now and again to enjoy the views – look over into the adjacent valley of Cwm Cynwyn through which runs the Roman road up to Bwlch ar y Fan between Cribyn and Fan y Bîg.

The return route heads down **Bryn Teg** (NNE) on a wide grassy track to a gate past a sign reading 'Entry to National Trust Land (Bannau Brycheiniog – The Brecon Beacons)'. Follow the stony track, part of the Roman road, which becomes a tarmac road near **Cwncynwyn Farm**. Continue straight ahead and cross over Pont y Caniedydd. Turn left on the farm track near the crest of the hill and then right after some derelict

*An aerial view from Bryn Teg of Cwm Cynwyn and Cefn Cyff, with the Black Mountains in the distance*

buildings on the waymarked route across the fields to **Plas-y-gaer**. Turn left after the farm and then right onto the track heading west. Turn left onto a bridleway after two fields and up to the hill fence where you rejoin the earlier route. Turn right and retrace your steps back to the start.

### Extension
Climb W along **Craig Cwm Sere** to the summit of **Pen y Fan**. The final ascent of Pen y Fan is badly eroded, but the National Trust has built a zigzag path out of the Brownstones to reduce further damage. Now descend the same way back to the unnamed col between Pen y Fan and Cribyn and rejoin the main route.

### Alternative route
Traverse around the shoulder of **Cribyn** along a sheep track. This is the most exciting mountain route in the Beacons, with the narrowness of the path and the steep drops giving the walker a real taste of exposure. ◄ Look back now and again at the north-east face of Pen y Fan which dominates the skyline, making this one of the finest viewpoints in the Beacons. The final part of this traverse affords grand views of Cwm Sere and across Allt Ddu to the town of Brecon on the left. Rejoin the main route at the start of **Bryn Teg**.

Remember that great care must be exercised here in winter conditions, where crampons and an ice axe may well be the order of the day.

# WALK 4

*Cwm Sere ridge ascending Cribyn and Pen y Fan*

| | |
|---|---|
| **Start/finish** | Cwm Gwdi car park (SO 025 248), postcode LD3 8LE |
| **Distance** | 11.5km (7.1 miles) |
| **Total ascent** | 755m (2480ft) |
| **Grade** | 3 |
| **Max elevation** | 886m (2907ft) |
| **Map** | OL12 Western area |

One of the classic ridge walks in the Beacons, this route climbs the ridge on the east side of the valley and includes ascents of Cribyn and the highest peak in the Beacons, Pen y Fan. The route then descends via Cefn Cwm Llwch, the ridge on the western border of the valley. The ascents and descents in the upper reaches are steep, and a good level of walking fitness is essential. Interesting features along the route include a nature reserve and the mountain geology, and there are excellent views of all the high peaks and the valleys associated with them.

From the main car park follow the footpath down into the stream valley of Nant Gwdi, cross the bridge and climb up to the open hillside. Follow the path above the hill fence on your left to where a footpath crosses it just before the settlement at Plas-y-gaer. Turn left, crossing the hill fence, onto the bridleway and then turn right at the track that leads to the farm (**Plas-y-gaer**). At the farm turn left through a gate and right into a field at the blue waymark post.

From here head across the field to a line of pylons reached through a gap in the trees. Turn right at a line of trees and walk up to a gate and stile in the right-hand corner of the field. After crossing the stile, descend a shallow valley to another stile, which you will see in the field about 60 metres in front of you. Follow the wire fence on the right-hand side downslope to the derelict buildings. Walk to the left of these to a stile and onto a track. Turn left here and this brings you to a gate, beyond which is a tarmac road. Turn right on the road and drop down the hill to Pont Caniedydd.

*An aerial view from Bryn Teg of Cribyn and Pen y Fan, with Cwm Sere to the right*

The Roman road would have been a natural link between the fortress at Y Gaer and others to the south at Pen y Darren, Gelligaer and Cardiff.

Cross the bridge over **Nant Sere** and go up the lane ahead to where it swings sharp left and through a gate. Ignore this turning and follow the stony track straight ahead to a gate in the hill fence, on the far side of which is a National Trust sign for Cwm Cynwyn.

The stony track you have just walked along is part of the Roman road that leads to Bwlch ar y Fan. ◄ The Scots pines immediately on the left as you cross the hill fence may have been planted as route indicators for drovers and, if this is the case, would have signalled that shelter and grazing could be obtained from the farm nearby. This highway through the mountains was probably used long before the Romans or even the Celts came to the Brecon Beacons.

Nant Sere drains the vast cauldron formed by the headwalls of Cribyn and Pen y Fan. Water avens and mossy saxifrage grow on the banks of this mountain stream, which then flows on through ash, alder and birch woodland. Cwm Sere is extremely rich in **plants and wildlife**, with over 200 species of flowering plants and ferns, abundant fungi, birds and insects, of which at least two are rare Arctic–alpine species.

On the left is the ridge of Cefn Cyff, which leads down from Fan y Bîg, and straight ahead is the ridge of **Bryn Teg**, which you are about to ascend to the summit of Cribyn. On the right is Cefn Cwm Llwch, which leads down from Pen y Fan. This will be your descent route.

## Walk 4 – Cwm Sere ridge ascending Cribyn and Pen y Fan

Continuing from this point at the hill fence, ignore the stony track that goes off to the left and head straight for the ridge ahead of you. After a concentrated pull up the beginning of this ridge you arrive at a cairn. The ridge ascends in three main steps, and after the second major climb you arrive at a level section marked by a second cairn. The final step is the ascent of the prow of Cribyn. ▶

The alternative route to Pen y Fan leaves from here.

The step in the middle of the ridge has formed due to the underlying geology. This step is known as a **secondary scarp** and results from a change from Brownstones to Senni Beds.

Climb the narrow path to the summit of **Cribyn**, then descend west along a distinct path to the col. To the south is the Neuadd Valley where two small reservoirs dam the Blaen Taf Fechan, which is fed by surface run-off and groundwater collected in this basin.

From the col, climb steadily (W), following the line of **Craig Cwm Sere**, to the summit of Pen y Fan. The final ascent to the summit of **Pen y Fan** is up a very stony area, and the National Trust has built a zigzag path up this face to the top.

Walk across the flat surface of Pen y Fan, which is badly eroded, to the trig point. This can be found in bad visibility by carefully following the north-east crag line. The trig point is at the end of this to the left. The north-east face is very steep and care must be taken not to stray too near the edge, especially in strong south-westerly winds or when it is corniced in winter.

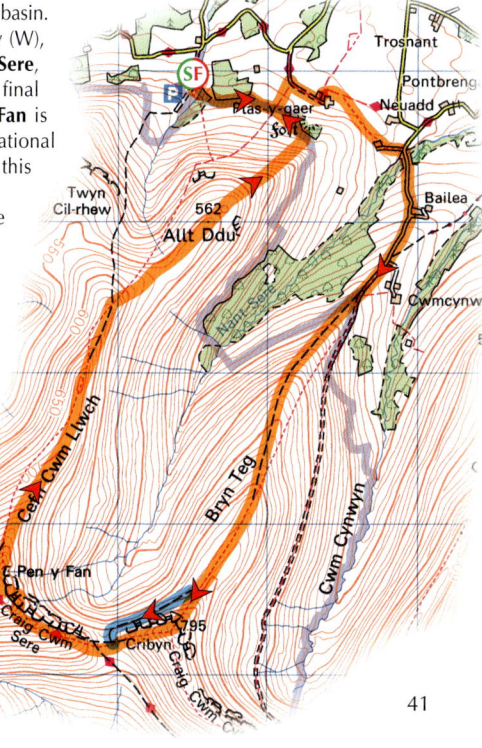

*Looking east from Pen y Fan*

Leave the summit of Pen y Fan by carefully scrambling (NNE) down the exposed Plateau Beds. The rocks can be slippery but the route drops quickly to the fine ridge of **Cefn Cwm Llwch**.

Follow the path along the flat section of the ridge, leaving it when it drops gradually to the valley of Cwm Gwdi. Keep to the eastern edge of the ridge, following a path through some areas of boggy heather moorland past the disused quarries and onwards to **Allt Ddu**.

From the pools on the summit of Allt Ddu drop down past the stones of the quarry towards the settlement at **Plas-y-gaer**. Just on the edge of this hill there is a distinctive furrow in the hillside, an old quarry path. Continue down this path towards the settlement, descending the front of the ridge. The descent of this ridge provides a good view of the settlement with the earth bank now planted with a line of large trees.

Drop down the slope to meet the path you used earlier and turn left, retracing your steps back to the start.

### Alternative route

Follow the path that breaks right, across the face of **Cribyn**, leading to the col between Cribyn and Pen y Fan.

On a still day you will often hear the sound of croaking ravens high above you.

The further you travel, the steeper the cliff becomes, with the Brownstones becoming more prominent up to your left. These are responsible for forming the red soil of the path. ◄

Towards the end of the path, as you cross a number of small gullies, there are quite steep drops away to the right and the path surface becomes uneven and stepped. As you are walking along this path the views of the main face of Pen y Fan change, becoming even more impressive (see 'Geology and geomorphology of Pen y Fan', Walk 3). This path can be dangerous in winter conditions and crampons and an ice axe may be needed.

### PLANT LIFE OF THE NORTH-WEST FACE OF CRIBYN

The ledges of this face are more accessible to grazing sheep than those of the north-east face of Pen y Fan, and so the interesting Arctic–alpine plants are not so prolific. Nevertheless, roseroot, mossy saxifrage, purple saxifrage and vernal sandwort are common. Rock stonecrop can be found but is more localised. Other species include cowberry, green spleenwort, brittle bladder-fern, limestone bedstraw, viviparous fescue, great woodrush, cowslip, common wild thyme and northern bedstraw. The wet ledges also support an excellent collection of upland bryophytes.

# WALK 5
*Cribyn via Cwm Cynwyn*

| | |
|---|---|
| **Start/finish** | Cwm Gwdi car park (SO 025 248), postcode LD3 8LE; alternative start: Cwmcynwyn Farm (SO 038 236) |
| **Distance** | 13.5km (8.3 miles) |
| **Total ascent** | 660m (2160ft) |
| **Grade** | 3 |
| **Max elevation** | 795m (2608ft) |
| **Map** | OL12 Western area |

The route enters Cwm Cynwyn and crosses the stream to the other side of the valley, avoiding the busy and rather monotonous walk along the Roman road. An ascent of Cribyn via Craig Cwm Cynwyn is followed by an exciting descent along the prow of Cribyn and an easy walk back along Bryn Teg ridge. The headwall ascent to Cribyn and the first part of the descent to Bryn Teg are steep. In adverse weather conditions a map and compass are mandatory, and if there is snow and ice on the ground, crampons are desirable. The glacial nature of the valley, the views from Cribyn and the Roman road are the main points of interest.

From the main car park follow the footpath down into the stream valley of Nant Gwdi, cross the bridge and climb up to the open hillside. Follow the path above the hill fence on your left to where a footpath crosses it just before the settlement at Plas-y-gaer. Turn left, crossing the hill fence, onto the bridleway and then turn right at the track that leads to the farm (**Plas-y-gaer**). At the farm turn left through a gate and right into a field at the blue waymark post.

From here head across the field to a line of pylons reached through a gap in the trees. Turn right at a line of trees and walk up to a gate and stile in the right-hand corner of the field. After crossing the stile, descend a shallow valley to another stile, which you will see in the field about 60 metres in front of you. Follow the wire fence on the right-hand side downslope to the derelict buildings. Walk to the left of these to a stile and onto a track. Turn left here and this brings you to a gate, beyond which is a tarmac road. Turn right on the road and drop down the hill to Pont Caniedydd.

Cross the bridge and head south up the road, passing **Bailea Farm** on the way. At the head of this valley is the north-east face of Pen y Fan and to the left is Bryn Teg ridge. Ignore the turning on the left to Bailea Farm and follow the road up the hill to where it swings sharp left and through a gate to Cwmcynwyn Farm. The field on the left is the alternative start, where the farmer has kindly left an honesty box.

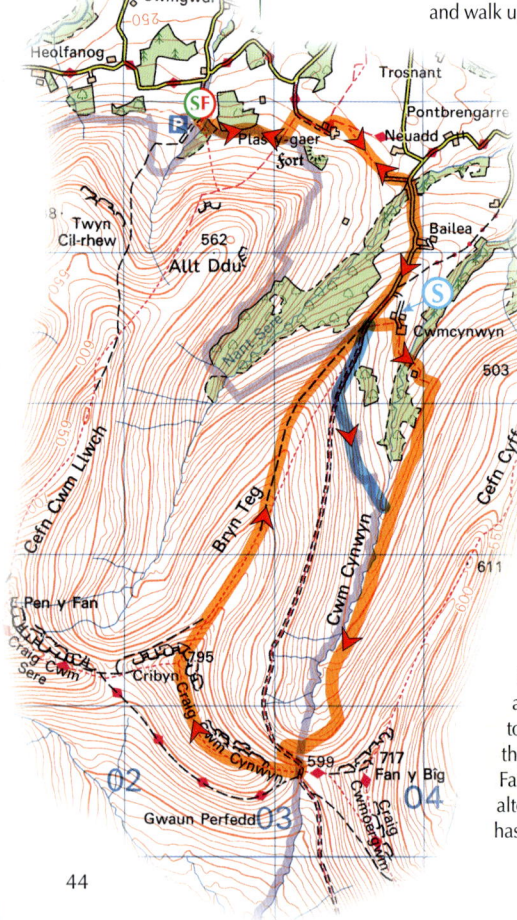

## WALK 5 – CRIBYN VIA CWM CYNWYN

Follow the stony track straight ahead to a gate in the hill fence, on the far side of which is a National Trust sign for Cwm Cynwyn. ▶

If rivers are in spate, you might struggle to ford Nant Cynwyn so carry on along the bridleway that runs above the hill fence and then follow the hill fence down to the stream. Cross over at the earliest opportunity to rejoin the main route.

If water levels are low, then pass through a gate in the hill fence on the left after fifty metres, which leads into a walled enclosure at the end of which is a second gate. Follow through these and down the rough track to another gate and on to **Cwmcynwyn Farm** via the lane to the right. Pass through the farmyard to a gate and continue through this to a stony lane; ahead there is a fine view of Fan y Bîg. At the bottom of this stony lane the track bears to the right up the valley. Ignore this and continue dropping down left alongside the green moss-covered stone wall to Nant Cynwyn. Cross the river, aiming for the gate opposite.

> This stony track is popularly known as the Roman Road, and once linked the fortress at Y Gaer with others at Pen y Darren, Gelligaer and Cardiff via Bwlch ar y Fan.

*Old Cwmcynwyn Farm*

Once you have crossed the ford, pass through the gate and keep left up the hill to the top and round to the right into the grounds of Old Cwmcynwyn Farm. The fireplace still has its oak lintel in place and a surprisingly large tree emerges halfway up the front of the chimney breast. Its roots have penetrated through the stones and into the ground below.

From the ruins turn left by the wire fence and head up the track to a stile and so to the path running along the hillside 50m above. Turn right (SSW), following the path towards the head of the valley. The hill fence turns right and drops down to the riverbed. ◄

*In front of you on the right is the prow of Cribyn, and the ridge descends to the left to the gap through which the Roman road passes.*

Continue along the east side of the valley above the stream down to the right. Eventually, the indistinct path you are following meets the stream bed at a hawthorn tree and old stone enclosures (*hafodydd*).

> The ruined stone enclosures in this area were originally small buildings and pens, **hafodydd**, used when flocks were moved to higher pastures in the spring. One stone is inscribed 'GH', the initials of the Gwynne Halfords of Buckland, a large landowning family in Victorian times.

Leave the stream course here and strike up left onto the lower reaches of Fan y Bîg, on which there is a double row of small rock outcrops that should be passed on the left-hand side. Traverse right above the lower outcrops and climb steadily to the Roman road.

You will want to catch your breath after this sustained climb and there are plenty of interesting features to see from this good viewpoint. Down below in the head of the valley the hummocky terrain is a remnant from the last Ice Age. Up above to the west is the impressive crag of Craig Cwm Cynwyn, formed from resistant Brownstones. Finally, you may well be resting on a once busy Roman thoroughfare.

### HEAD OF CWM CYNWYN

The hummocky terrain in the head of Cwm Cynwyn is an interesting glacial feature. Deposited by melting glaciers, it consists of angular and rounded boulders in a sandy, clayey matrix known as boulder clay. Below the headwall crags is a marshy area where the corrie lake would once have been. Hare's tail grass, soft rush and sphagnum now thrive in the wet conditions.

## WALK 5 – CRIBYN VIA CWM CYNWYN

*Cribyn from Craig Cwm Cynwyn*

Turn left at the Roman road and make your way to Bwlch ar y Fan, 'the Gap' between the peaks. ▶ From here climb west up **Craig Cwm Cynwyn** to the summit of **Cribyn**. The lower part is the steepest pull but the slope becomes easier as you approach the summit.

From Cribyn descend steeply along the **Bryn Teg** ridge northwards down to the National Trust sign and along the lane back down to Pont y Caniedydd, from where you retrace your steps back to the start. The steeper section in the middle of the ridge is a secondary scarp formed by the transition from Brownstones to underlying Senni Beds.

This is an ideal place from which to appreciate the almost perfect U-shape of this glacial valley.

# WALK 6
## *Fan y Bîg via Cwm Cynwyn*

| | |
|---|---|
| **Start/finish** | St Brynach Church, Llanfrynach (SO 075 257), postcode LD3 7AZ |
| **Distance** | 16km (10 miles) |
| **Total ascent** | 570m (1870ft) |
| **Grade** | 3 |
| **Max elevation** | 719m (2359ft) |
| **Map** | OL12 Western area |

On this moderate walk you can enjoy the beautiful valley of Cwm Cynwyn and return via the ridge of Cefn Cyff. Deciduous woodland fills the lower reaches, giving a natural, timeless atmosphere. The valley provides easy walking but a degree of exertion is required for the final climb up to 'the Gap' (Bwlch ar y Fan) and to Fan y Bîg. Interest is sustained by the plants and birds of the valley, the river scenery, the geological features and the views from Fan y Bîg, which are among the most impressive in the Beacons.

Start at the entrance to the church on the corner and follow the sign for 'Taff Trail 8'. Take the next left, signposted 'Cantref', and follow the lane out of the village and turn left onto a bridleway marked on the map as the 'Three Rivers Ride'. Follow this across the fields alongside **Nant Menasgin** and cross straight over a lane and onto another path across two fields. Turn left when you meet the next road and take the lane to the cottages at Pen-yr-heol. Bear right up the obvious stony track to a gate that leads to the open hillside.

Cross over the hill fence and follow the path, which keeps close to the hill fence on the right at first and then rises slightly when the hill fence drops away below. It then meets the hill fence again and contours into the valley. ◄ Straight ahead you can see Pen y Fan with Cefn Cwm Llwch leading up to it.

*Look back from here for a great view of the Black Mountains stretching up to Hay-on-Wye.*

## WALK 6 – FAN Y BÎG VIA CWM CYNWYN

Cross a small **stream** and come to a group of hawthorn trees. There is a good view up to Cribyn on the left and Pen y Fan to the right.

The view south-west to the head of the valley shows its ice-sculpted U-shape and the steep headwall. The notch in the col, called Bwlch ar y Fan, or 'the Gap' between the peaks, is where the Roman road reaches its highest point before dropping into the Taf Fechan Valley.

Continue contouring across the slope and into the stream bed.

Across the valley to the right is the Bryn Teg ridge with its secondary scarp and the Roman road running beneath it. This ridge leads up to the prow of Cribyn. On your left as you look up the Cwm Cynwyn Valley is your return route along the ridge of Cefn Cyff.

The walk up the valley is most enjoyable. Hawthorn trees are dotted around on the grassy slopes of the upper valley, and the level sheep tracks make a criss-cross pattern with the steep gullies created by water run-off. The head of the valley is formed by the steep slope of Fan y Bîg to the left and the higher crags of Cribyn to the right.

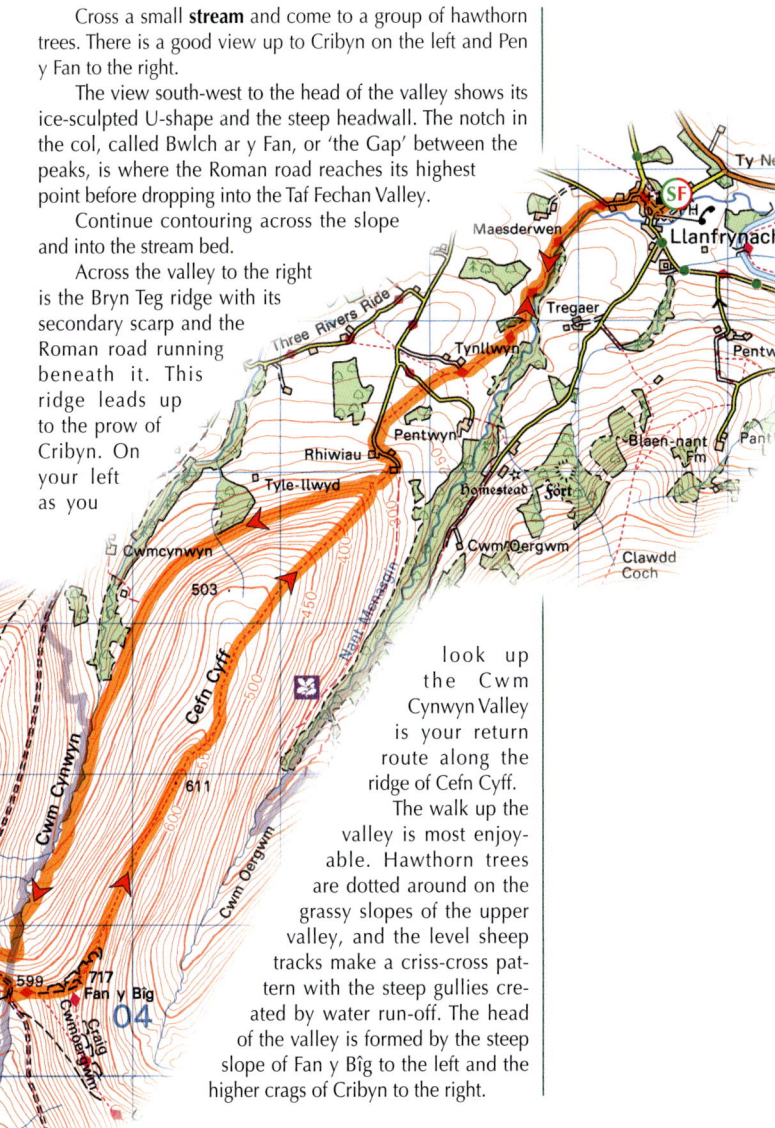

*Looking towards Cribyn and the Black Mountains*

Leave the stream at the head of the valley and strike up left onto the lower reaches of Fan y Bîg, on which there is a double row of small rock outcrops that should be passed on the left-hand side. Traverse right above these and climb steadily to the Roman road and onto 'the Gap' (Bwlch ar y Fan).

There is nothing specifically Roman about this **road**, but it is likely to be of Roman origin as the fortress at Y Gaer is near the mouth of this valley and the road would have been the natural link with other fortresses to the south at Pen y Darren, Gelligaer and Cardiff.

There are many features to be seen from this good viewpoint. Down in the head of this U-shaped valley is an interesting glacial feature: the hummocky terrain formed from boulder clay deposited by melting glaciers. Up above to the west is the impressive crag of Craig Cwm Cynwyn, formed from resistant Brownstones. Finally, you may well be resting on a once busy Roman thoroughfare.

The step in the ridge is a result of the underlying rock formations and is a secondary scarp formed by the transition from Brownstones to underlying Senni Beds.

Head east up the steep slope, following the line of the crags, to the summit of **Fan y Bîg**. Descend gradually (NNE) along the obvious ridge of **Cefn Cyff**, which drops more steeply after 1.5km. ◄

The path becomes steeper again after another 1.2km of fairly flat ground and drops north-east to the gate in the hill fence, which is where you crossed earlier on. Retrace your steps back to the church.

# WALK 7
## *Cwm Cynwyn ridge ascending Fan y Bîg and Cribyn*

| | |
|---|---|
| **Start/finish** | St Brynach Church, Llanfrynach (SO 075 257), postcode LD3 7AZ |
| **Distance** | 17.5km (10.9 miles) |
| **Total ascent** | 770m (2530ft) |
| **Grade** | 3 |
| **Max elevation** | 795m (2608ft) |
| **Map** | OL12 Western area |

This high-level clockwise circuit of the ridges around Cwm Cynwyn climbs steadily along Cefn Cyff and then more steeply to the summit of Fan y Bîg. A short descent is followed by a sustained climb to the impressive summit of Cribyn, before one of the steepest descents in the Beacons to the ridge of Bryn Teg. Two high peaks are included, demanding reasonable fitness. The glacial valleys and panoramas from the summits provide interest throughout the walk. The ford at Cwm Cynwyn may not be passable if Nant Cynwyn is in spate, and it will be necessary to make a detour and cross the stream higher up the valley.

Follow the sign for 'Taff Trail 8' from the entrance to the church on the corner and take the next left, signposted 'Cantref'. Follow the lane out of the village and turn left onto a bridleway marked on the map as the 'Three Rivers Ride'. Follow this across the fields alongside **Nant Menasgin** and cross straight over a lane and onto another path across two fields. Turn left when you meet the next road and take the lane to the cottages at Pen-yr-heol. Bear right up the obvious stony track to a gate that leads to the open hillside.

Head straight up the ridge ahead, **Cefn Cyff**, eventually picking up a distinctive path marked by two cairns. Continue along the ridge to **Fan y Bîg** and look out for the 'diving board' on the right just as you reach the summit. This is a slab of red sandstone that protrudes out into space; it is possible to reach the slab and stand on it.

## CEFN CYFF

Towards the northern end of Cefn Cyff, the view south-west is of the valleys and ridges leading up to the summits. The steeper section in the middle of the ridge is a secondary scarp formed by the transition from Brownstones to underlying Senni Beds. The top of the ridge is covered in heavily grazed blanket mire, which is mostly hare's tail grass with some ling, deer grass and bilberry. The sides of the ridge are covered in heath rush/mat grass grassland, which grades into mat grass on lower slopes and then into bracken.

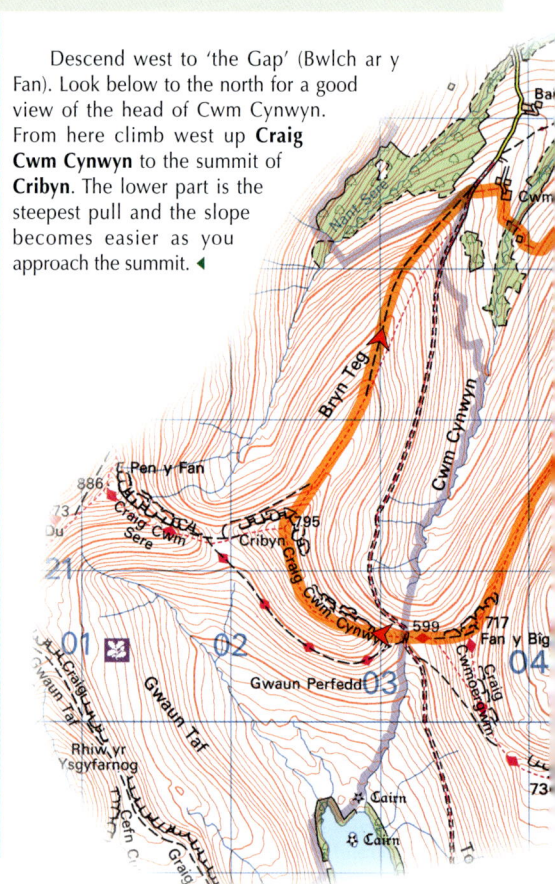

From this ridge you have a superb view north of the perfectly U-shaped glacier-cut valley of Cwm Cynwyn.

Descend west to 'the Gap' (Bwlch ar y Fan). Look below to the north for a good view of the head of Cwm Cynwyn. From here climb west up **Craig Cwm Cynwyn** to the summit of **Cribyn**. The lower part is the steepest pull and the slope becomes easier as you approach the summit. ◄

## WALK 7 – CWM CYNWYN RIDGE ASCENDING FAN Y BÎG AND CRIBYN

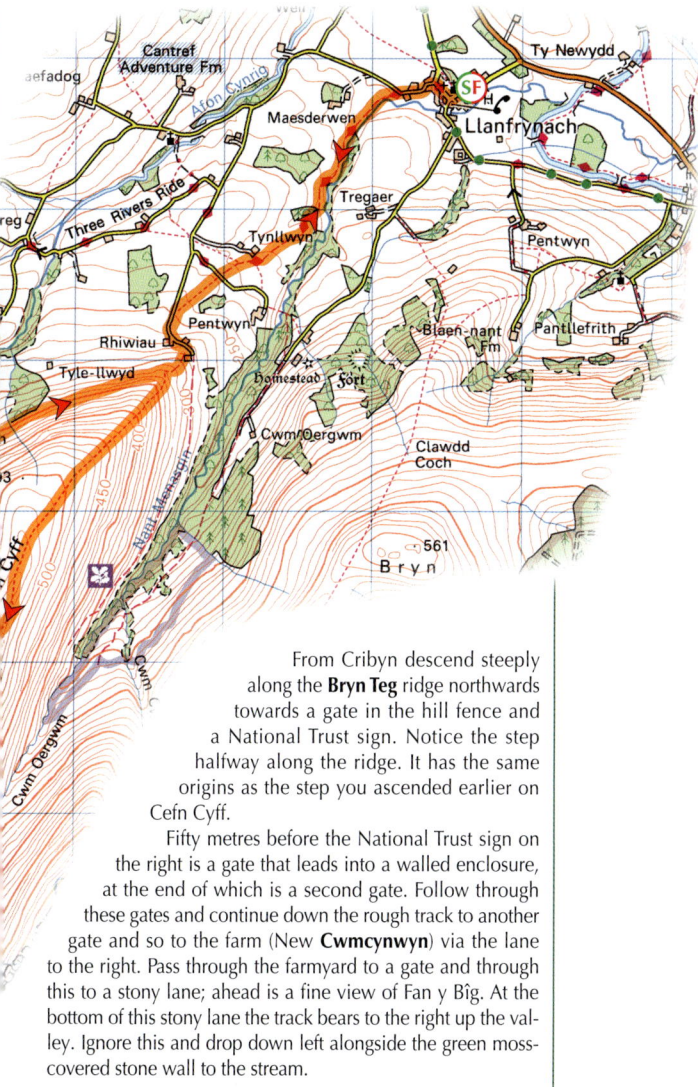

From Cribyn descend steeply along the **Bryn Teg** ridge northwards towards a gate in the hill fence and a National Trust sign. Notice the step halfway along the ridge. It has the same origins as the step you ascended earlier on Cefn Cyff.

Fifty metres before the National Trust sign on the right is a gate that leads into a walled enclosure, at the end of which is a second gate. Follow through these gates and continue down the rough track to another gate and so to the farm (New **Cwmcynwyn**) via the lane to the right. Pass through the farmyard to a gate and through this to a stony lane; ahead is a fine view of Fan y Bîg. At the bottom of this stony lane the track bears to the right up the valley. Ignore this and drop down left alongside the green moss-covered stone wall to the stream.

*Hawthorn trees in the Cwm Cynwyn Valley*

### CRAIG CWM CYNWYN

The crags beneath Craig Cwm Cynwyn are accessible to grazing sheep and so are not as botanically interesting as the Pen y Fan and Cribyn headwalls, especially the highest ledges of the sheer north-east face of Pen y Fan. The vegetation consists mostly of mixed acidic grassland and purple moor grass heath on the slopes and ledges between the rock faces. The most inaccessible ledges are oases for herb-rich communities, including Scabiosa columbaria, mossy saxifrage, viviparous fescue, brittle bladder-fern and limestone bedstraw.

Cross the stream aiming for the gate opposite and, keeping left, go up the hill to the top and round to the right into the grounds of Old Cwmcynwyn Farm. From the ruins turn left by the wire fence and head up the track to a stile and so to the path running along the hillside 50m above. Turn left along this and follow it above the hill fence to the point where you crossed it on the ascent. Retrace your steps back to the start.

After heavy rain Nant Cynwyn may be impossible to cross at the ford. To avoid a long trek around the roads to your start, it is best to climb back up to the farm track and turn south up the valley. Follow the track to enable you to cross Nant Cynwyn at an easier spot. Turn north down the stream to Old Cwmcynwyn Farm and follow the route from here back to the start.

# WALK 8
*Fan y Bîg via Cwm Oergwm*

| | |
|---|---|
| **Start/finish** | St Brynach Church, Llanfrynach (SO 075 257), postcode LD3 7AZ |
| **Distance** | 16km (10 miles); alternative 17km (10.6 miles) |
| **Total ascent** | 600m (1970ft); alternative 740m (2430ft) |
| **Grade** | 3 |
| **Max elevation** | 717m (2352ft); alternative 740m (2428ft) |
| **Map** | OL12 Western area |

Following the western side of Cwm Oergwm, this walk passes through fields and some woodland to emerge onto open hillside at the hill fence. From here it drops to the stream below and a scenic waterfall and then continues up the stream course to the head of the valley. The headwall is climbed via a steep ascent to the lowest point of the ridge, which is then followed north-west to Fan y Bîg. A long, gentle descent along Cefn Cyff brings the mountain part of the walk to an end. Following the stream provides easy route finding and the ascent of the headwall is straightforward but steep; the alternative route ascending Craig Cwareli is even more strenuous. The flowers and birdlife in the valley are extremely varied and complement the waterfall and mountain scenery.

Follow the sign for 'Taff Trail 8' from the entrance to the church on the corner. Take the next left, signposted 'Cantref', and follow the lane out of the village and turn left onto a bridleway marked on the map as the 'Three Rivers Ride'. Follow this across the fields alongside **Nant Menasgin** and cross straight over a lane and onto another path across two fields. Turn left when you meet the next road and take the lane to the cottages at Pen-yr-heol. At the end of the tarmac road, follow the footpath that passes in front of the buildings on your right. After 100 metres it rejoins the track.

There are two Iron Age hill forts, Coed y Brenin and Coed y Caerau, marked on the map on the opposite side of the valley. ▶

The woodland occupying the valley floor is managed as a nature reserve.

# WALKING IN THE BRECON BEACONS

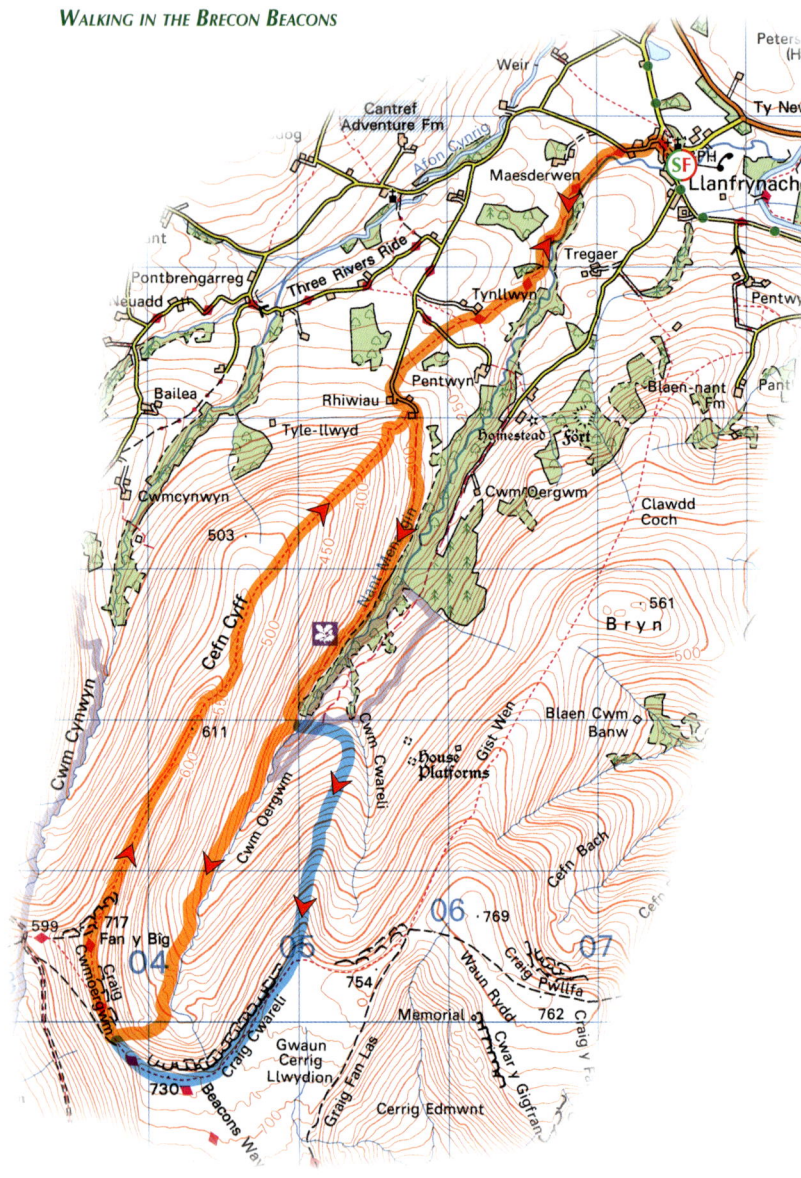

56

## WALK 8 – FAN Y BĪG VIA CWM OERGWM

### IRON AGE HILL FORTS

The poorly preserved defences of the almost rectangular Coed y Brenin hill fort overlook the entrance to Cwm Oergwm. The fort is marked on the map as 'homestead'. Natural protection is afforded by deep stream gullies to the east and the west and by the slope dropping away to the north-west; however, the fort is vulnerable to the south-east, where the slope rises steeply.

Just to the east of the 'homestead' is a 'settlement' – Coed y Caerau hill fort. This is another Iron Age hill fort, again naturally protected by stream gullies on either side but overlooked by ground rising steeply to the south-west. The highest fortifications, which are well preserved, face uphill to defend this weakest point. Charcoal debris has been found inside the ramparts on a level oval platform: an ancient charcoal-burning hearth. Other platforms have been discovered in nearby woodland.

---

Continue for 200 metres and cross a stile. The route follows a clearly defined, slightly sunken, track between mainly hawthorn, alder and ash. Coming to a gate, you will get a good view into Cwm Oergwm. From here follow the overgrown track between trees, with an old stone wall on the left, to a gate and a stream bed. Below, on the left, are the remains of buildings but the track continues and divides 200 metres further on.

Leave this hut on your right and after 20 paces take the track down to the left and continue along the upper edge of deciduous forestry and into woodland. This part of the route is difficult to follow as there is no obvious path and care in route finding must be taken.

Once in the woodland, head straight towards **Cwm Cwareli** to a gate in a stone wall. Beyond is open hillside and from here navigation is straightforward. Drop down left to the stream bed and proceed upstream to a waterfall. Buzzards are often found soaring on thermals overhead. ▶

> The alternative route to Craig Cwmoergwm via Craig Cwareli leaves from here.

To continue on the main route, scramble upstream from the main fall, encountering many smaller waterfalls on the way. Towards the head of the valley the stream has cut through mounds of glacial moraine left behind after the last Ice Age. From the base of the headwall climb steeply to the lowest point of **Craig Cwmoergwm** (SO 038 199).

This small col on the ridge is easily identified by piles of Brownstones and a number of drystone structures, including a bothy built by the army. From the col turn right

*A waterfall in Cwm Oergwm*

(NNW) as the route gently climbs along the eroded path to the summit of **Fan y Bîg**. ◄ Fan y Bîg has a distinctive sandstone block, known as the 'diving board', protruding from the north-west side.

> There are fine views looking westwards to Cribyn and Pen y Fan.

Descend (NNE) on a distinct path along **Cefn Cyff** to a prominent cairn constructed from Brownstones. Continue (NNE) along the ridge path, which is now quite wide. Keep to the path along the top of the ridge to some old quarry spoils, where a distinctive track to the left of these descends the end of the ridge. If you miss this track, a good reference point to aim for is the church tower at Llanfrynach. The old quarry track winds its way downslope to a gate in the hill fence. Pass through this and follow a stony track, bordered on either side by stone walls with hazel, birch and holly, to where you rejoin your inbound route at Pen-yr-heol. Retrace your steps back to the start.

## WALK 8 – FAN Y BIG VIA CWM OERGWM

*Crybin and Pen y Fan from Craig Cwmoergwm*

### Alternative route
Follow the directions above to the waterfall. Climb south-east to the spur that separates the side valley of Cwm Cwareli from Cwm Oergwm. The ridge high above is gained by a steep, strenuous ascent of this spur and may well require crampons and an ice axe in winter conditions.

Turn right (SSW) along **Craig Cwareli** to the col, marked by piles of Brownstones. ▶ Rejoin the main route on the ridge at the head of the valley.

The crags below have interesting plant life, including rock stonecrop, mossy saxifrage, purple saxifrage and limestone bedstraw.

# WALK 9
## Cwm Oergwm and Gist Wen

| | |
|---|---|
| Start/finish | St Brynach Church, Llanfrynach (SO 075 257), postcode LD3 7AZ |
| Distance | 17.25km (10.7miles); alternative 13.5km (8.4 miles) |
| Total ascent | 710m (2330ft); alternative 640m (2100ft) |
| Grade | 3 |
| Max elevation | 754m (2474ft); alternative 740m (2428ft) |
| Map | OL12 Western area |

The route follows the eastern side of Cwm Oergwm through woods and fields to a waterfall. It then continues along the valley bottom to the headwall, where a steep ascent is required to gain the col. The walk then follows the level ridge around the eastern sides of Cwm Oergwm and Cwm Cwareli before returning to the hill fence. Route finding is straightforward and the highest peaks are avoided so that only low mist would require recourse to the map. The walk provides a great deal of interest, ranging from wetland vegetation and birdlife to glacial scenery and two hill forts. The eastern ridge of Cwm Oergwm provides some of the finest panoramic views in the Beacons.

Follow the sign for 'Taff Trail 8' from the entrance to the church on the corner. Take the next left, signposted 'Cantref', and follow the lane out of the village and turn left onto a bridleway marked on the map as the 'Three Rivers Ride'. Follow this across the fields alongside **Nant Menasgin** to **Tynllwyn**.

Go through the gate and follow the footpath arrow that points diagonally left across the field to where it crosses a field boundary. Continue in the same direction across the next field to a gate where you turn left onto a lane. Take the next footpath on the left down to the bridge across Nant Menasgin. Cross over the stone bridge, turn left then right up the bridleway, waymarked in blue. Follow the conspicuous track, which winds first left, then diagonally right, up the hillside. ◄ The sunken path leads up on the edge of a field between two banks lined with mature trees to the road, where you turn right. Up on the hillside to the south-east are two archaeological sites – a homestead and a settlement. Unfortunately, there does not appear to be a public right of way to either site.

*The woodland here has an understorey of hazel with the odd oak, ash, holly, birch, beech, hawthorn and blackthorn tree.*

## WALK 9 – CWM OERGWM AND GIST WEN

The route continues along the road to a gate and the start of a bridleway. Pass through the gate and follow the bridleway to the hill fence. Pass through a gate and turn right, following a ditch down to the stream below. Cross the ditch using a few stones and follow the eastern bank of Nant Menasgin to a picturesque waterfall (SO 050 219).

Look out for an old ruin at SO 058 228, which was probably once used for making charcoal.

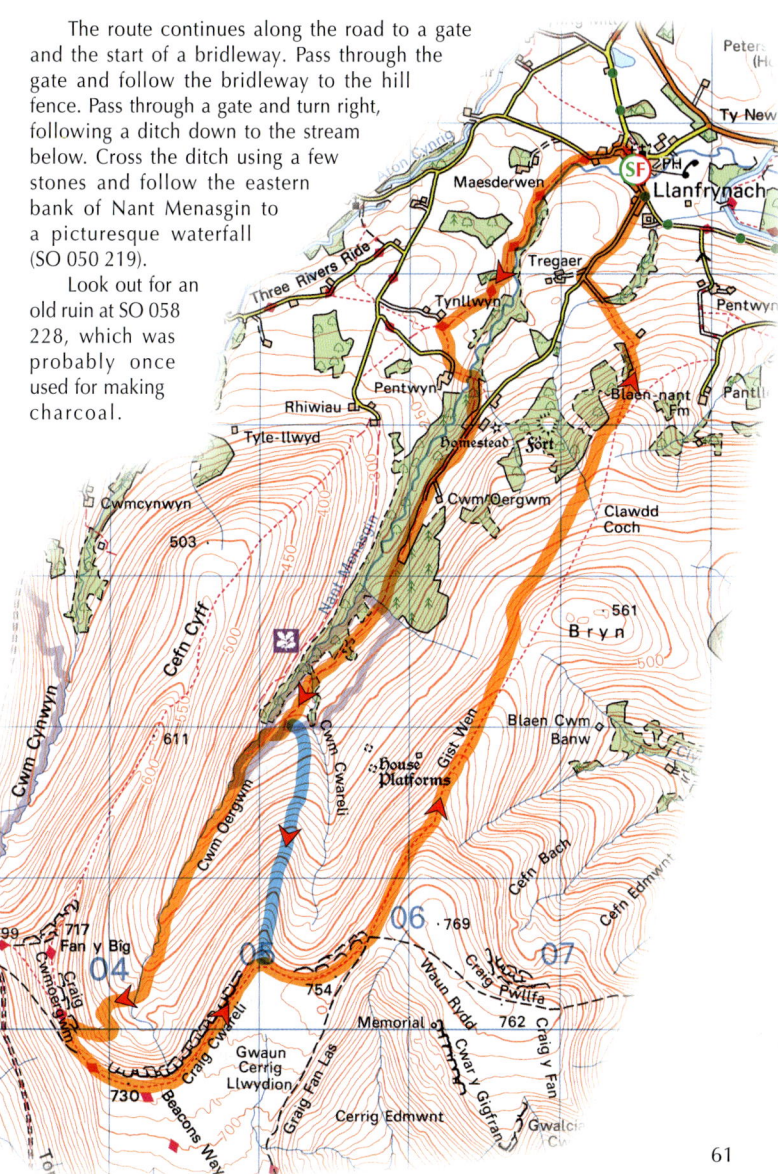

*The easily recognisable fly agaric mushroom*

In this area you may see herons, ravens, meadow pipits, skylarks, buzzards, ducks, finches and robins.

**Nant Menasgin**, which tumbles over a number of small waterfalls created by the more resistant bands of sandstone, is a misfit in this valley because the classic U-shape was carved by glacier ice and not scoured away by the stream. Look out for birds, such as dippers and wagtails, darting low over the water and, if you are very quiet, you might be able to watch a heron stalking fish. Buzzards and red kites are often found soaring on thermals overhead.

*The alternative route to Craig Cwareli leaves from here.*

Further on there is a picturesque waterfall. ◄
Continue following the stream to the head of the valley, where the stream has cut through mounds of glacial moraine left behind after the last Ice Age. The ruddy-brown crags high up to the left and right are formed by resistant bands of Brownstones.

*Shelter can be found here for a well-earned rest, snack and warm drink, especially if the weather is inclement.*

Climb steeply to the right to the lowest point of **Craig Cwmoergwm** (SO 038 199). This small col is easily identified by piles of Brownstones and a number of drystone structures, including a bothy built by the army. ◄

Turn left (SE) and follow the ridge path around the head of the valley to **Craig Cwareli** and on to Bwlch y Ddwyallt, Rhiw Bwlch y Ddwyallt and **Gist Wen**. Follow the obvious path, Ffordd Las or Bwlch Main, passing below the rounded summit of **Bryn** on your right. The disused sandstone quarries on Bryn were once worked for local building stone.

*Nant Menasgin in Cwm Oergwm*

Continue along the well-worn path descending Rhiw and **Clawdd Coch**, which then passes along the fence above Coed Tyle-du. Make sure you do not stray too far to the right and inadvertently reach the wrong gate in the hill fence. Once the fence above the woodland of Coed Tyle-du drops to the left, make for the gate and stile in the hill fence just to the right of Coed Cae-rebol.

Drop through the clearing, with denser woodland on the left and sparser woodland on the right, and then swing to the right to a gate in the corner of the field. Leave the farm of Tir Hir on the right and follow the track that swings down to the left along a line of trees, cross the ford and follow the farm lane to the road.

Turn right and then left at the T-junction, which brings you back to the start in **Llanfrynach**.

### Alternative route

Follow the main route to the hill fence. Strike south and ascend the spur of land that separates the side valley of **Cwm Cwareli** from **Cwm Oergwm**. This is an exciting and strenuous route and may well require crampons and an ice axe in winter conditions. Below to the left is the glacial cirque of Cwm Cwareli. ▶ The steep inaccessible crags on the eastern side of the valley are an interesting Arctic–alpine habitat. Rejoin the main route at the start of Bwlch y Ddwyallt.

*The disused stone pens are hafodydd or sheep pens.*

# WALK 10
## Cwm Oergwm ridge ascending Fan y Bîg

| | |
|---|---|
| Start/finish | St Brynach Church, Llanfrynach (SO 075 257), postcode LD3 7AZ |
| Distance | 16.75km (10.4 miles) |
| Total ascent | 695m (2280ft) |
| Grade | 3 |
| Max elevation | 754m (2474ft) |
| Map | OL12 Western area |

This route follows the last two ridges of the north-eastern valleys. A fairly easy ascent brings you to Bryn, where you can enjoy one of the finest panoramic views in South Wales. The route is easy to follow along the ridges; however, map and compass skills are essential if the weather closes in on the higher sections. Height is gained and lost without undue exertion. The inclined geology of the Beacons can be fully appreciated from the eastern aspect and some of the finest views in the area are to be found here.

From the entrance to the church on the corner, cross over the junction, following the sign 'Taff Trail', and head out of the village, crossing over **Nant Menasgin**. Take the next right up a lane with a dead-end sign, keeping left when it splits at **Tregaer Farm**. Turn left shortly afterwards where a lane leaves the road to the south-east. Follow this track south-east, climbing gently for a while, and then drop into a wooded gully and cross a ford. Turn first to the left, up the hillside, along a track that soon bears to the right along the left side of the field, following a line of trees and an old sunken track on the left.

There is a good view over to the right of Pen y Fan, half hidden by the ridge of Cefn Cyff leading down from Fan y Bîg. Halfway up the hill there is a track off to the left to the farm. Ignore this and continue up the hill alongside the line of trees. The Black Mountains can be seen well over to your left.

At the apex of the field, with the buildings of Tir Hir Farm on your left, turn right to a gate and then left up the hill. The

## Walk 10 – Cwm Oergwm ridge ascending Fan y Bîg

path winds through widely spaced small oak trees diagonally right up the slope to a more open area. Head straight up the hill, with the boundary of the deciduous woodland of Coed Cae-rebol on your right, to the hill fence. This is crossed by a stile and the route joins a farm track rising from the left. The wall on the right swings further away to the right and the path steepens as it climbs the hillside to **Clawdd Coch**. ◄ The woodlands of Coed y Caerau and Coed y Brenin down to your right contain two Iron Age hill forts.

> There are good views here of Pen y Fan, Cribyn and Fan y Bîg.

The path skirts to the right of the summit of **Bryn**, reaching a somewhat flatter section. On the opposite side of the valley is Cefn Cyff, which leads down from the summit of Fan y Bîg. Make a mental note here that this will be your descent route. ◄

> The deciduous woodland in the valley floor is a nature reserve.

From here climb along Ffordd Las, which ascends first **Gist Wen** and then Rhiw Bwlch y Ddwyallt, meeting a junction of paths ascending from Carn Pica and Craig Fan-las. Continue round the spectacular ridge, which swings around the head of **Cwm Cwareli** and **Cwm Oergwm**.

The path is eroded and route finding is simple, but care must be taken in icy conditions or in strong winds, as the route has precipitous drops immediately on the right.

**Craig Cwareli** and the flat lunar landscape of Gwaun Cerrig Llwydion provide some of the best locations for views of the Beacons' highest summits. The dip slopes of the Plateau Beds, which cap Corn Du and Pen y Fan, clearly parallel each other from these viewpoints. The bedding of the underlying Brownstones exposed in the faces of Cribyn and Fan y Bîg are also in step.

### PLANT LIFE OF CRAIG CWARELI, BWLCH Y DDYWALLT AND CRAIG FAN-LAS

Craig Cwareli, Bwlch y Ddywallt and Craig Fan-las have interesting vegetation. Situated below the ridge path, these steep crags are inaccessible to grazing sheep in places and have some interesting species. Rock stonecrop, mossy saxifrage, purple saxifrage and limestone bedstraw have been recorded here.

Just around the head of Cwm Oergwm, the broad path drops into a small col, marked by a military bothy. From the col, climb (NNW) to the summit of **Fan y Bîg**. From here there are magnificent views of Cribyn and Pen y Fan.

*The Beacons from Fan y Big*

The summit has a block of sandstone, known as the 'diving board', protruding from its western side.

Descend almost due north from the summit on an obvious path along **Cefn Cyff** to old quarry spoils, where you will meet and descend a quarry track to the left of these. ▶ The old track winds its way downslope to a small copse and a gate and stile in the hill fence, marked by a blue bridleway indicator. Walk down the stony lane to a gate leading to Pen-yr-heol, the beginning of a road. Descend this and take the next footpath on the right, signposted 'Llanfrynach'. A path waymarked by two arrow posts crosses the field to a stagger in the hedge. The right of way marked on the map follows the right-hand side of the hedge but in fact the waymarked route passes through the gate, keeping the hedge on the right. Look back the way you have just come for one of the last views you will have of the summit of Pen y Fan. ▶

Follow the track curving to the right to a gate and cross straight over the road on the national park waymarked route, which is now part of the Three Rivers Ride. Continue along this through the fields alongside **Nant Menasgin** to a road where you turn right and then right again at the next junction to return to the start in Llanfrynach.

The steeper section in the middle of the ridge is a secondary scarp formed by the transition from Brownstones to underlying Senni Beds.

The field is improved grassland used to fatten ewes just after they have given birth in spring.

# WALK 11
## Cwm Oergwm Valley

| | |
|---|---|
| Start/finish | St Brynach Church, Llanfrynach (SO 075 257), postcode LD3 7AZ |
| Distance | 11km (6.8 miles) |
| Total ascent | 285m (930ft) |
| Grade | 1 |
| Max elevation | 393m (1290ft) |
| Map | OL12 Western area |

The low-level route in Cwm Oergwm heads along the eastern side of this classic U-shaped glacial valley to a waterfall and returns along the western side. Once beyond the hill fence feel free to choose how you explore this delightfully quiet area. The wildlife and history throughout this walk provide more than enough interest. As this is a valley walk, the gradients are easy but route finding can be more difficult through the fields and woods on the western side. This area is particularly interesting because of its woodland and bird nature reserve.

From the entrance to the church on the corner, cross over the junction following the sign 'Taff Trail' and continue out of the village, crossing over Nant Menasgin. Take the next right up a lane with a dead-end sign, keeping left when it splits at **Tregaer Farm**.

The route continues along the road until it ends at a gate and the start of a bridleway. Pass through the gate and follow the bridleway to the hill fence. Pass through a gate and turn right, following a ditch down to the stream below. Cross the ditch using a few stones and follow the eastern bank of **Nant Menasgin** to a picturesque waterfall (SO 050 219). ◀

Look out for birds such as dippers and wagtails darting low over the water and, if you are very quiet, you may well be able to watch a heron stalking fish.

*WALK 11 – CWM OERGWM VALLEY*

## CWM OERGWM WOODLAND

The narrow strip of deciduous woodland found in Cwm Oergwm is similar in character to that found in Cwm Sere. The nature reserve comprises some 20 acres of deciduous woodland extending for almost 1.5km along the steep eastern bank of Nant Menasgin. The valley bottom is wet and the species that grow here reflect these boggy conditions. Species found in these swampy conditions include alder trees and wetland plants such as great horsetail, king-cups and broad-leaved cotton-grass, the latter found in more open calcareous flushes. This reserve is also blessed with woodland birds typical of the north-eastern valleys. You may well see redstarts and pied flycatchers here.

Climb out of the stream bed, to the west, to a stone wall (the hill fence) with a stream gully running parallel to it and to a gate to return down the opposite side of the valley.

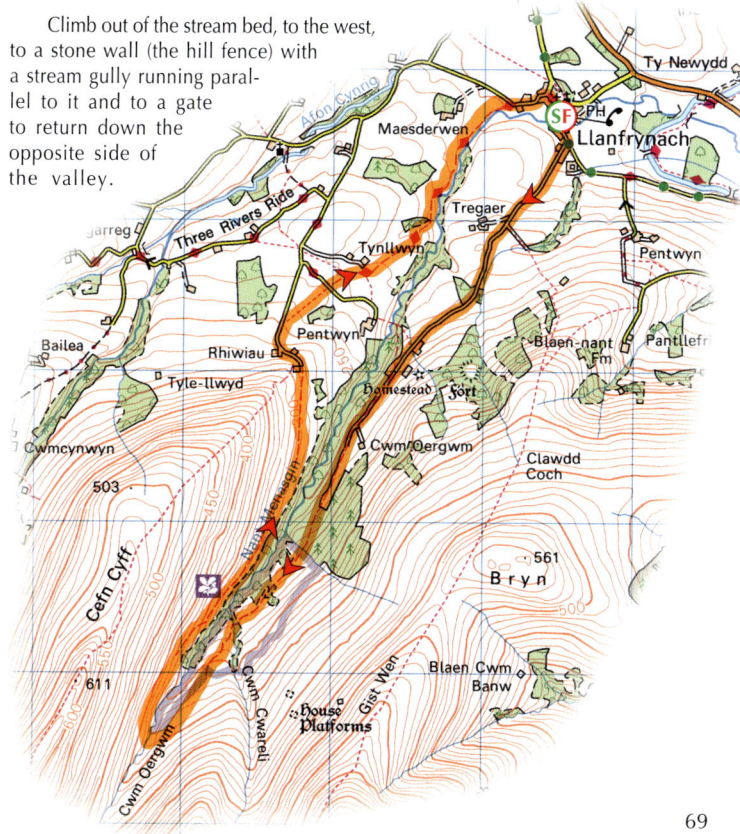

*The northern end of the Cwm Oergwm Valley*

Pass through the gate and follow a path through woodland and then along the edge of deciduous forestry, eventually climbing diagonally to the left.

Continue to a gate and a stream gully. Below to the right are the remains of old buildings. The path climbs gently from here, following an overgrown track lined by remnants of a drystone wall. Pass through the gate at the top and follow a slightly sunken path to sheep pens, beyond which is a metal road. The old path is blocked by a gate some distance before the farm buildings, but the route makes a detour into the field below, skirts below the sheep dip, passes through a gate and so to the road.

Shortly the road swings down to the right, with a lane leading to **Rhiwiau Farm** on the left. Take the first gate on the right, signposted with a yellow fingerpost and a sign to Llanfrynach. The path crosses the field to a stagger in the hedge. The right of way marked on the map follows the right-hand side of the hedge but in fact the waymarked route passes through the gate, keeping the hedge on the right.

*The field is improved grassland used to fatten ewes just after they have given birth in spring.* ◀

Look back the way you have just come for one of the last views you will have of the summit of Pen y Fan. ◀

Follow the track curving to the right to a gate and cross straight over the road on the waymarked route, which is now part of the **Three Rivers Ride**. Continue along this through the fields alongside **Nant Menasgin** to a road where you turn right and then right again at the next junction to return to the start in Llanfrynach.

# 2 EASTERN VALLEYS AND RIDGES

*Waterfalls in Blaen-y-glyn (Walk 15)*

*WALKING IN THE BRECON BEACONS*

# WALK 12
## Bryn

| | |
|---|---|
| **Start/finish** | St Meugan's Church (signposted 'Llanfeugan Church') (SO 087 245), postcode LD3 7DR |
| **Distance** | 8km (5 miles) |
| **Total ascent** | 400m (1310ft) |
| **Grade** | 1 |
| **Max elevation** | 561m (1841ft) |
| **Map** | OL12 Western area |

This varied walk initially passes through farmland before making an excursion above the hill fence to one of the best viewpoints in the Beacons. The circular route then winds its way through picturesque woodland, with photogenic views of the River Usk and the Black Mountains beyond. The beginning and end of the walk require care in path finding but the height gain is moderate, making the route safe and fairly gentle. The main interest lies in the exceptional view from Bryn of the northern valleys and in the solitude of the approaches.

*The canal at Pencelli*

Start at the end of the road where it widens at St Meugan's Church. On the left is a lane which is the end of the return route. Take the footpath to the left of the church and after a few metres bear left onto a rough track and walk to a house. The church is surrounded by yew trees, a species traditionally found in churchyards, and in early spring snowdrops can be found at the side of the church.

Turn right in front of the house and walk down the steps to the river bridge. Follow the path up the slope and bear right through a gap in the line of trees ahead. Look for a gate in the hedge on the right and go through this, turning left onto the tarmac road and on up the hill.

# WALK 12 – BRYN

At the crest of the hill take the track off to the right, which is marked by a national park sign.

Pass through the gate and along a track between hazel trees. ▶ Cross over a stile and continue towards conspicuous Scots pines. Just past these is a good view of the north face of Pen y Fan (WSW). Continue up the slope and cross over the stile in the hill fence.

Keep close to the fence on the right. When this drops down to the right, head straight up left to the summit of **Bryn**. ▶

The rounded, pool-covered summit of Bryn is a superb vantage point for views and photographs, especially of the northern ridges and summits of the Brecon Beacons. To the west the first ridge is Cefn Cyff leading to Fan y Bîg, the middle ridge is Bryn Teg leading to Cribyn and the final ridge is Cefn Cwm Llwch. Llyn Syfaddan and the rolling wave-like front of the Black Mountains can be seen to the north-west.

At the summit turn north-east to a new cairn and head down left of the coniferous forestry with a bearing (060°) slightly to the right of Llangorse Lake, which you can see in the distance. Keep the coniferous forestry on your right and follow the track down the ridge. The track then cuts back to the left towards deciduous woodland, meeting this at a **wall**. Turn right along the wall and climb the stile into the wood.

Look back for a superb view of the Black Mountains.

Red grouse are thought to breed in this area.

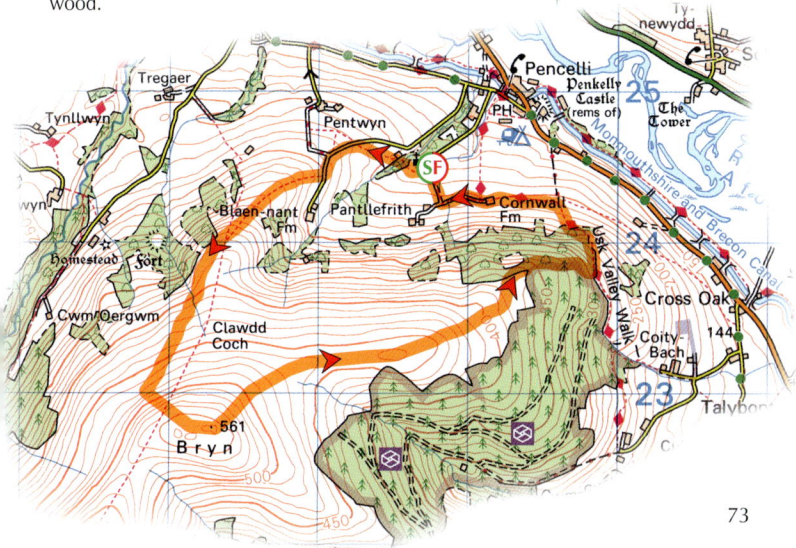

*The Beacons from Croftau*

Once in the wood, follow the path down Allt Feigan. The path curves round to the right through oak and beech woodland. Follow the track along the left of the wall, which is now broken down, and on to a gate and stile. Ignore the path that leads straight ahead and swing left down the hill. The wood is on the left and looking right over the fields, you will get a wonderful view of the River Usk meandering in the valley floor with the Black Mountains beyond.

The track continues north-west along the northern edge of the wood to a gate and on to a second gate at the beginning of a wide track.

Turn left through the second gate and along the stony track but be careful not to miss this turn as it is easy to continue on down the hill. Follow the track and pass through the farmyard at **Cornwall Farm**. Stay on the bridleway, cross a small ford and turn right following the bridleway down the hill back to the church.

# WALK 13
*Cwm Tarthwynni circuit*

| | |
|---|---|
| **Start/finish** | Talybont Reservoir car park (SO 100 197) |
| **Distance** | 8.5km (5.2 miles); with extension 11.5km (7.1 miles) |
| **Total ascent** | 595m (1950ft); with extension 720m (2360ft) |
| **Grade** | 2 |
| **Max elevation** | 750m (2461ft) |
| **Map** | OL12 Western area |

This fairly strenuous walk involves a continuous ascent of 480m (1500ft) over the first 2.5km. A short walk to a col is followed by an airy ascent up a narrow rib to the southern end of Craig y Fan. From this vantage point a panorama unfolds of the beautiful valley below and of the mountains to the east. A worthwhile extension to the route around Waun Rydd provides superb views of the northern summits, ridges and valleys of the Brecon Beacons. Most of the route is easy to follow but you may need to rely on compass bearings as you reach the high plateau. As well as enjoying the quality of the views, you can visit a Bronze Age funerary mound and a memorial to the crew of a crashed bomber on the extension.

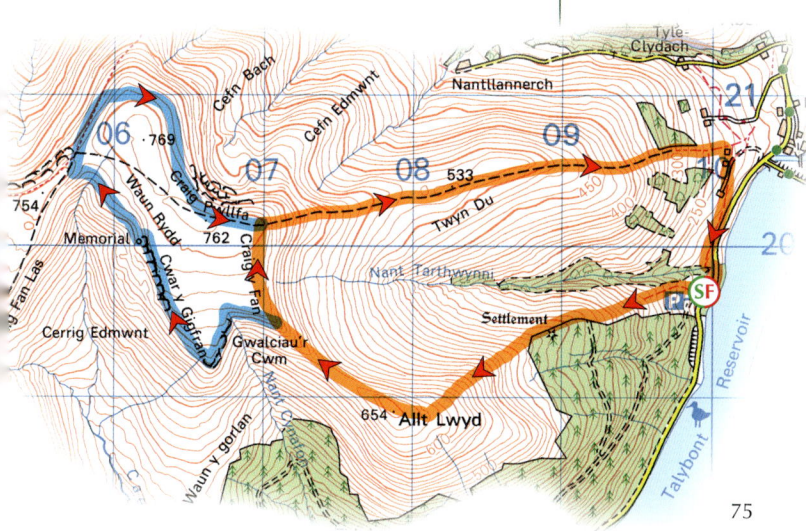

*Straight up the valley you can see Carn Pica, the large cairn on the top of the summit.*

Leave the car park, cross the main road onto a lane for about 50 metres and cross a stile on the right. Follow a grassy track between two fences, with the stream of **Nant Tarthwynni** down in the valley to the right. ◄

Climb this grassy track, with rushes on either side, to another gate and stile. Crossing over this, you reach a steep field with stone walls on both sides and the coniferous forestry plantation up to the left. Walk up this field with the wall on the right until it drops away and take the path across the slope to the end of the coniferous forestry. Walking up the valley, you get a good view of the cliff at the end (Craig y Fan) with the stream running straight into its head. Looking back down the slope, you can see the head of the Talybont Reservoir and beyond to the main ridges of the Black Mountains.

> The two **settlements** marked on the Ordnance Survey map were once Iron Age hill forts that may have formed part of a settlement complex. The northern perimeters of both forts lie in the field you are crossing, but the majority is situated in the coniferous forestry plantation, which has damaged and obscured most of this archaeological site.

### TALYBONT RESERVOIR

*Talybont Reservoir*

## WALK 13 – CWM TARTHWYNNI CIRCUIT

> This is the largest reservoir in the Beacons and serves the Newport area. It was completed in 1938, flooding the valley and affecting 25 farms and 2875 acres of land, which was a compulsory purchase. Land around the reservoir was also included and subsequently leased to the Forestry Commission. The creation of the reservoir made the surrounding hillside less viable for agriculture, and the comparative fertility of the 'bottom land' was reduced; without it the higher rougher pasture cannot support stock. Forestry was favoured by the Water Authorities, as it was thought to be less of a pollution threat to water supplies than livestock. The area became a Local Nature Reserve in 1975 in recognition of its ornithological importance, in particular, as a wintering area for migrant birds. The reserve covers 490 acres and was set up by the National Park Authority through an agreement with the Welsh Water Authority and the Forestry Commission.

From the gate and stile in the hill fence, make straight for the summit of **Allt Lwyd** ahead of you (bearing 235°). Just to the right are the col and the ridge that leads up to Craig y Fan.

> **Vegetation** on the rounded summit of Allt Lwyd is dominated by hare's tail grass, heath rush and bilberry. Localised patches of ling occur, as well as common cotton-grass and wavy hair-grass.

Cross north-west over to the col and ascend the steep prow to the top of the ridge, the last bit of ascent to gain the high Beacons plateau. Surprisingly, the face to the right is at a much shallower angle than it appears from the approach walk. It is made up of erosion-resistant Brownstones that form the spectacular crags to the west and, if you look carefully in this direction, you can just see the two highest summits in South Wales, Pen y Fan and Corn Du. ▸

To continue on the main route turn north to follow the head of this valley along **Craig y Fan**. From here there is a good view down the valley, with deciduous woodland at the bottom, Tor y Foel in the middle ground and the distinctive shape of the Sugar Loaf Mountain in the distance. The top of the crag leads you to the distinctive landmark of Carn Pica, a large cairn made of sandstone.

*The extended walk around Waun Rydd leaves from here.*

*Carn Pica*

**Carn Pica** is a modern cairn marking the site of a Bronze Age funerary mound. Pottery urns containing the remains of human cremations were placed in an excavated pit and covered with large flat stones. A cairn was then built on the site. Radiocarbon dating has determined that these sites in the Beacons date back to the early Bronze Age, around 2200–1400BC.

From the cairn, descend the obvious eroded path (E) down a steep slope to the col and climb slightly to **Twyn Du**, an area covered in bilberry with a little heather, on the northern side of the valley. Halfway along this ridge you meet a rutted track – follow this down. This turns into a wide grassy track that drops down the side of the hill to the left (N) of the ridge and through a boggy area. Just to the left of this is the corner of the fence and an old drystone wall. Keeping the wall on your left, follow the grassy track down the hillside to a gate and a stile. If you miss the track, head straight for the reservoir dam and you will easily find the stile as the fences on either side funnel you to it. From here the path becomes obvious again.

The path follows a gully carrying a stream on the right. Follow this downslope and, after a few hundred metres, cut across the stream to the right-hand bank. You are now on a raised bank with ditches on either side with a field on the right. Cross the small stream that joins from the right and continue to a gate on the right.

Through the gate and immediately on the left is a barn. Continue straight ahead towards a house called Berthlwydfach. The route passes through the field below the house.

## WALK 13 – CWM TARTHWYNNI CIRCUIT

Turn left after the cattle grid through a gate and head for the fence at the bottom of the garden. Walk across the slope to a stile in the hedge.

The route drops to the bottom left-hand corner of the field to a very old track lined with hazel and the odd oak tree. Pass through a gate and along a line of coppiced hazel trees parallel with the road. Go through another gate and along the track. In the next field drop to a gate where there is a stream and a series of old tank traps. Turn right at the road, cross over the bridge and walk a short distance back to the **car park** on the left.

### Extension

Turn left (W) along the top of the crags around the head of **Gwalciau'r Cwm** to the end of **Cwar y Gigfran**. From the southern end of Cwar y Gigfran the valley of Blaen-y-glyn and Blaen Caerfanell comes into full view. This is a glacial hanging valley with a stream plunging in a series of waterfalls into the valley below. The cliff was formed when the stream below cut into the valley bottom.

Follow the top of the crags (NNW) and descend when they finish, to the wreckage of the Wellington bomber. ▶ Continue on the path at the top of the slope to Rhiw Bwlch y Ddwyallt, the ridge above Cwm Oergwm. The inaccessible crags below provide an unusual plant habitat. Look out for the interesting shapes created by the eroding peat hags on the plateau area of **Waun Rydd**, which is covered mainly in hare's tail grass together with common cotton-grass, heath rush and scattered bilberry, mat grass and crowberry.

The views from the ridge of Rhiw Bwlch y Ddwyallt are some of the finest in the Beacons and really capture the essence of the area. The valley immediately below is Cwm Cwareli. It has been deeply cut by the stream, which later joins with Nant Menasgin in Cwm Oergwm.

Turn right (NNE) along the obvious path and when it begins to drop, contour around to the right (E). Gradually, the slope above Cwm Banw (the valley to the north) becomes steeper until it forms the steep slopes of **Craig Pwllfa**.

The glacial cirque below is the most sheltered area from the sun's rays in the whole valley and so was most susceptible to freeze-thaw action. The resulting moraine, known as a nivation ridge, is now bisected by a stream.

Continue contouring the top of these to Carn Pica, where you pick up the main route once more.

> There is a memorial nearby commemorating the crew of the bomber, which crashed during a training exercise in 1941.

# WALK 14
## Blaen-y-glyn and Allt Forgan

| | |
|---|---|
| Start/finish | Blaen-y-glyn Isaf car park (SO 063 170) |
| Distance | 8.75km (5.4 miles); alternative 9.25km (5.7 miles) |
| Total ascent | 530m (1740ft) |
| Grade | 2 |
| Max elevation | 729m (2392ft) |
| Map | OL12 Western area |

This route combines the beautiful waterfall scenery of Blaen-y-glyn with a classic view of the Brecon Beacons' highest peaks. The walk gains height as it follows the course of the Caerfanell, which plunges in a series of waterfalls. This popular area is soon left behind as the route enters the glacial hanging valley of Cerrig Edmwnt. Finally, the ascent along the mountain stream of Blaen-y-glyn brings you to one of the finest vantage points in the whole of the Central Beacons. Route finding is simple as long as you follow the river, but care should be taken as you climb up to the high ridges. Waterfalls, superb mountain views and a war memorial to a crashed bomber provide plenty of interesting features along the route.

From the car park, walk back to the main road, turn left down the hill and cross the bridge over the **Caerfanell**. Cross over the stile on the left and follow the distinctive path north-west on the right-hand bank looking upstream.

The initial stretches of the Caerfanell are quite wide as the water tumbles over a boulder-strewn bed.

Keep glancing at the stream bed for a chance to see the specialist bird of this habitat, the **dipper**. On a quiet day you are likely to chase a pair upstream until they reach the end of their territory. At this point they will either hide or make a quick dash back downstream. Their companions, yellow and pied wagtails, are also abundant here.

The **woodland** on your right is composed of alder because the area is very wet, being fed by a number of springs issuing from the hillside above.

## WALK 14 – BLAEN-Y-GLYN AND ALLT FORGAN

Alder thrives in wet ground conditions and is characteristically found in boggy areas and along watercourses. The best time to explore this area is early in the morning when the woodland is full of birdsong.

The riverbed soon changes character as the stream course narrows and you will come across a small waterfall, which has a man-made rim, and the water then tumbles over a natural exposure of Brownstones. The stream is soon forced to run in a very narrow chute and just above this, beyond a right-hand bend in the stream, there is the first glimpse of the largest fall in the lowest section of the valley. You can explore the fall by crossing the bridge just before it and proceeding up the left bank.

After exploring the fall, rejoin the path which continues above the gorge on the right-hand side of the stream. Looking back down the river, you will see the high ground of Pant y Creigiau in front of you and below this is the line of the old railway cutting through the forestry.

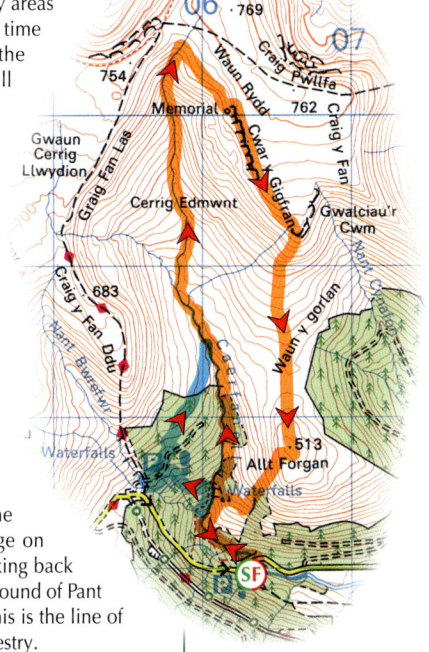

### BRECON AND MERTHYR JUNCTION RAILWAY

A continuous break in the forestry on the eastern side of the Talybont Valley is not a firebreak but the course of the old Brecon and Merthyr Junction Railway. Opened in January 1863, it tackled some very steep gradients, but it was closed a century later in 1962. The narrow-gauge line carried coal from Merthyr to Brecon as well as lime for agricultural purposes, made from limestone removed from extensive quarries between Pontsticill and Dowlais. The return trains hauled pit wood and other timber, cattle, sheep and pigs, cereals, beer and cider. The most difficult engineering task was the construction of a 666yd tunnel at Torpantau, through the ridge separating Glyn Collwn and Taf Fechan. Excavation began in March 1860 from both sides of the ridge, with nine men in action, night and day, at each end of the tunnel bore. The final breakthrough was achieved on 11 January 1862 and, amazingly, the two centres coincided within two inches of each other.

Continue following the path along the stream valley, which, after a short distance, straightens to give good views of the mountains ahead. In front is the slope of Cerrig Edmwnt, which leads up to the southern end of Cwar y Gigfran. This crag was formed by a massive landslide that was caused by the stream undermining the stability of the valley side. On the right-hand side, in the near foreground, the valley sides are covered in oak and alder. Continue up the path to the stile in the hill fence near the stream.

> There is an unusually large **stone block** immediately on your right above the hill fence, which has been carefully inscribed with the initials 'GH' and the year '1845'. The initials may well be those of the Gwynne Halfords of Buckland, a large land-owning family in Victorian times (a similar stone can be found on the wall of a sheep pen on Walk 5).

The path now works its way high above the stream, which flows in a steep-sided wooded gorge and culminates in the last waterfall in this section. The path passes close by this and it is worth making a short detour to stand at the top of the fall and look back down the gorge.

From the waterfall the route keeps close to the stream, passing a ruin where there is a good exposure of sandstone. Continue along the stream and follow the right-hand fork (N) up **Cerrig Edmwnt** towards the head of the valley. It is easier to climb up the left-hand side of the stream gully where there appears to have once been a man-made cutting, possibly associated with the disused quarry. The spoils of this can clearly be seen above to the right below the line of Cwar y Gigfran.

Finally, you join the main path and ridge of Rhiw Bwlch y Ddwyallt.

> Your long climb is rewarded with a breathtaking **view** of the north-eastern valleys and ridges. The valley below is Cwm Cwareli, which joins the classic U-shaped Cwm Oergwm. To the west are the three highest summits of the Beacons. Cribyn lies in front of Pen y Fan with Corn Du to the left, separated from the major summit by a small col. To the north is a green and yellow patchwork of fields and the town of Brecon. This scene is particularly

## WALK 14 – BLAEN-Y-GLYN AND ALLT FORGAN

dramatic after a light snowfall, which picks out the relief in the steep faces of the mountains.

Turn right and contour south-south-east along a path that winds its way through the peat hags. Continue to the war **memorial** just below the crest line at SO 062 200.

*The memorial to the crashed bomber crew*

The **memorial** commemorates the crew of a Wellington bomber that served with 214 Squadron in 1941, which took part in raids on Hamburg and Rotterdam. Tragically, the plane crashed while undertaking a training exercise. It is likely that the mountain was covered in cloud and the pilot was flying low, trying to pinpoint his position. Each Armistice Day, wreaths of poppies are placed on the memorial, which is situated close to the remains of the crashed aircraft.

From here, climb to the end of the crags and walk (SSE) along **Cwar y Gigfran** to where it turns sharply north.

The slopes below Cwar y Gigfran have a hummocky topography characteristic of a **landslide**. Here the rock and soil are slumping, due to gravity, on curved slippage planes. This was a massive event that resulted in the backward tilting of upper bedding plane surfaces. Notice how well cleaved the Brownstones are in the cliffs here, making them break apart easily to expose their bright-red surfaces.

The ridge is a fine vantage point affording views to the south of the hidden valley of Blaen-y-glyn and of the Talybont Valley and its reservoir, the largest in the Beacons. To the west are the limestone escarpments of Mynydd Llangynidr and Mynydd Llangattock.

From this high point one can truly appreciate the decimation of this area by the **coniferous forestry plantations**. During the winter months the larch loses its greenery and it becomes clear that it is often planted on the periphery and as linear tracts within the forestry. The reason for this is that larch is less combustible and so acts as a firebreak.

Descend the steep slope (S) to the col where you will notice a conspicuous furrow dropping straight down the slope. This was once used to transport stone down from the quarry. Head for a gate in the hill fence ahead where a drystone wall drops away from it. This gate might be locked but can be climbed as this is open access land. Keeping above the boggy area, go through the gate and strike up left to the summit of **Allt Forgan**.

This is a fine viewpoint for the ridges on the western side of the Talybont Valley. ◄ You have one of the best views

> The vegetation here is largely purple moor grass together with ling and crowberry.

### HANGING VALLEY

*A glacial hanging valley*

The upper half of Blaen-y-glyn has been left 'hanging' above the main Talybont Valley. During the Ice Age, Blaen-y-glyn would have contained a small glacier that fed the main glacier responsible for carving out the Talybont Valley. This glacier in turn fed one of the major glaciers of the Beacons that flowed down the Usk Valley. The stream that now drains the classically ice-sculpted, U-shaped hanging valley has cut a small 'V' notch in the valley floor. The stream plunges over the overhang in a series of waterfalls.

of the glacial hanging valley when looking back up Blaen-y-glyn. Look out for buzzards wheeling overhead.

From the summit descend due west to pick up the line of the drystone wall. Cut down the zigzag path (W) to where a stream gully drops to the right. On a clear day you will be able to see some stone ruins down to the right, which is where you pick up a track. If you cannot see these, follow the gully downslope, keeping to the right-hand fork, and after passing the third large alder, turn left and pass above a group of silver birch. Continue diagonally downslope to some stone ruins and pick up a track here that leads back to the main waterfall. Retrace the path along the bank of the river to the road bridge. Turn right up the road and back to the **car park**.

### Alternative starting point: Torpantau-Talybont Car Park (SO 056 176)

The car park at Torpantau-Talybont is an alternative starting point for the upper parts of Walk 14 and Walk 15. It is useful for those not wishing to include the waterfalls in their route, making for shorter walks, but still with the opportunity of reaching the high Beacons plateau.

The upper parts of Walk 14 and Walk 15 can be followed by joining them in the upper half of the valley. This can be reached from the **Torpantau-Talybont car park** by continuing (NNE) along the forestry track. Turn left up a forestry ride and then right, finally coming to a stile in the hill fence (SO 059 182). Cross over the stile and turn right (NNE) across the hillside to meet the stream above the last area of deciduous woodland and the last waterfall. This is where you join Walk 14 and Walk 15.

Your return route for Walk 14 begins at the bridge over the **Caerfanell** after the descent from **Allt Forgan**. Cross over the bridge and climb up, ignoring the path that joins on the right at the crest. At the next T-junction turn right and, if you are feeling adventurous, immediately left up the slope through the woodland. Nant Bwrefwr has incised a deeply cut valley and there are many waterfalls to explore on the ascent back to the start. Otherwise, continue on the well-maintained wide track uphill to the start.

# WALK 15
## Blaen-y-glyn and Craig y Fan Ddu

| | |
|---|---|
| Start/finish | Blaen-y-glyn Isaf car park (SO 063 170) |
| Distance | 9.25km (5.7 miles); with extension 12.75km (7.9 miles); valley-head alternative 9.75km (6 miles); valley walk 4km (2.5 miles) |
| Total ascent | 525m (1720ft); with extension 640m (2100ft); low-level walk 220m (720ft) |
| Grade | 2 |
| Max elevation | 735m (2411ft); with extension 754m (2474ft); low-level walk 460m (1509ft) |
| Map | OL12 Western area |

This route is similar in character to Walk 14, but it returns along the western side of Blaen-y-glyn and then follows another stream with a spectacular waterfall. Numerous alternatives can be followed, bringing great variety to the length and character of the walks. This area of the Brecon Beacons can satisfy all interests and abilities. The route is easy to follow along the riverbed, but map-reading skills are required in the higher reaches. The whole walk is moderately strenuous but your efforts are rewarded with the waterfalls, some of the finest views in the Central Beacons and spectacular glacial features.

*Waterfall on Caerfanell stream*

## WALK 15 – BLAEN-Y-GLYN AND CRAIG Y FAN DDU

From the car park, walk back to the main road, turn left and cross the bridge over the **Caerfanell**. Cross over the stile on the left and follow the distinctive path on the right-hand bank looking upstream.

The stream is soon forced to run in a very narrow chute and just above this, beyond a right-hand bend in the stream, there is a first glimpse of the largest fall in the lowest section of the valley. The first of the waterfalls is encountered just after a wooden bridge crosses the stream, and you can explore it by crossing the bridge and making your way up the left bank.

After exploring the fall, retrace your steps to rejoin the path which continues up the stream above the gorge. Continue following the path along the stream valley to the stile in the hill fence near the stream. The path now works its way high above the stream, which flows in a steep-sided, wooded gorge that culminates in the last waterfall in this section. The path passes close by and it is worth making a short detour to stand at the top of the fall and look back down the gorge.

Follow the stream past the waterfalls, taking the right fork (N) where it divides, and continue all the way up the valley to the ridge of Rhiw Bwlch y Ddwyallt and the junction of four paths at SO 058 206. ▶ To continue on the main route turn left (SSW, bearing 200°) and follow the path along the edge of **Craig Fan Las** and cross the stream of Blaen Caerfanell at SO 050 192 where it disappears over the cliff edge and falls to the valley below.

The extended walk around Craig Cwareli leaves from here.

Looking back along Craig Fan Las, you will notice that the peat hags of Waun Rydd take on a surreal appearance in the low afternoon light. The area to the right is **Gwaun Cerrig Llwydion**, also composed of eroding peat hags.

Take a close look at the exposed surfaces of Brownstone blocks for evidence of **ripple marks**. Particularly good examples can be found on rock surfaces where the path crosses the stream, which then tumbles over cliffs to the valley below. These ripples were formed in the beds of streams during the Devonian Period of geological time.

### GWAUN CERRIG LLWYDION

The flat lunar-like landscape of Gwaun Cerrig Llwydion and the ridge of Craig Cwareli provide some of the best locations for views of the Beacons' highest summits. From these viewpoints, the dip slopes of the Plateau Beds (which cap Corn Du and Pen y Fan) and the bedding of the underlying Brownstones (exposed in the faces of Fan y Bîg, Cribyn and Pen y Fan) align. Peat hags interspersed with areas of frost-shattered Brownstones provide plenty of foreground interest, and this horizontal plateau helps to balance the tilt of the Beacons' ridges. These rock fragments were produced by freeze-thaw action at the end of the last Ice Age and have recently been exposed by erosion of the peat cover, which developed in post-glacial times on poorly drained, flattish areas. This area is covered in badly eroding blanket mire, which results in islands of peat becoming stranded among peaty channels or stone. Their tops are covered in hare's tail grass and common cotton-grass, together with occurrences of bilberry, heath rush, wavy hair-grass and deer grass.

*From this ridge the Mumbles Lighthouse can be seen on a clear day to the south-west, the sea sometimes glowing a deep red under a setting winter sun.*

◀ Keep to the edge which now turns south-south-east (bearing 152°) along **Craig y Fan Ddu**. The obvious path tends to cut across to the right but following the crag line is more interesting, even though the path is not so obvious. Descend the steep prow of the mountain (S) to the edge of the forestry (SO 055 179).

Dense coniferous **woodland** was planted in the Blaen-y-glyn valley in the late 1950s and originally consisted of Norway spruce. Much of it was replaced later by Sitka spruce, and Japanese larch was planted instead of larch.

From the corner of the forestry, continue on the path which now follows the streamway of **Nant Bwrefwr** to the entrance of a car park. The steep banks of the small stream gorge are covered mainly in hazel, ash, alder and birch. Be careful not to miss a number of surprisingly high waterfalls on your right.

Cross the cattle grid into the car park (Torpantau-Talybont) and turn immediately right and descend the track with the stream on your right.

If you are feeling adventurous, take a path off to the right for an exploration of the steeply incised valley. This is rewarded with many waterfalls but requires scrambling up and down steep slopes. Eventually, you are forced away from the bank of the stream but be careful not to miss the largest fall, which is accessed by dropping down a steep slope and then walking back up the riverbed for a little way. Continue downstream along a path that arrives at a track where you rejoin the main route. Turn right and follow this back to the start.

Otherwise, descend through the woodland and follow the well-maintained stone track back to the start, ignoring a turning on your left.

*The view south-east from Craig y Fan Ddu*

### Extension

From the ridge of Rhiw Bwlch y Ddwyallt at the head of Blaen-y-glyn follow the northern-facing crag line around the head of Cwm Cwareli along Bwlch y Ddwyallt and then along **Craig Cwareli**. A cairn marks the point where a footpath, the Beacons Way, leaves to the south-east. Take this and cut across Gwaun Cerrig Llwydion to where the Blaen Caerfanell stream disappears over the cliff edge and falls to the valley below. Rejoin the main route here.

### Alternative route: waterfall walk combined with a circuit of the head of the valley

Follow the main route to the top of the waterfalls, where the gradient becomes gentler and the forestry has been left behind. Leave the stream course near where a small tributary joins on the right and a wall meets the main stream on the left. Head north-east, guided by a straight furrow in the hillside, and climb to the southern end of **Cwar y Gigfran**. ◄ The summits of Pen y Fan and Corn Du are just visible over the headwall of the valley to the west from the end of Cwar y Gigfran. Notice how well cleaved the Brownstones are in the cliffs here, making them break apart very easily to expose their red surfaces.

Follow the crag line (NW) to rejoin the main route at the beginning of Bwlch y Ddywallt.

*This furrow was once used for transporting stone from the quarry above and to the right.*

### Alternative route: low-level waterfall walk

Follow the main route to the top of the waterfalls. Cross the stream just above the last fall and walk up the slope to a gate in the hill fence around the coniferous forestry plantation. This is being logged and replanted, so the forest roads are continuously changing in character. Walk along the forestry ride and turn left at the next junction and then right onto a track that leads to the car park, where you join the main route just before the cattle grid.

# WALK 16
*Torpantau circuit*

| | |
|---|---|
| **Start/finish** | Torpantau-Talybont car park (SO 056 176) |
| **Distance** | 13.75km (8.5 miles) |
| **Total ascent** | 505m (1660ft) |
| **Grade** | 3 |
| **Max elevation** | 754m (2474ft) |
| **Map** | OL12 Western area |

An initial short, steep climb to Craig y Fan Ddu is all that is needed to reach the high Beacons plateau and a spectacular upland walk. The route follows the ridge around the head of Blaen-y-glyn and then continues around another ridge that forms the head of Cwm Oergwm. From the summit of Fan y Bîg, the route drops to the gap and a circuit of Torpantau brings you back to the start. The initial ascent is strenuous but once you have gained the ridge, the day's hard work is complete. Even in poor visibility, the route can be followed easily by keeping to the ridges; however, compass bearings may be needed at the highest point. The geomorphology of the Beacons can best be seen from this walk and the views are spectacular.

*The Beacons from Craig Cwareli*

## WALKING IN THE BRECON BEACONS

Many plants can be found along the banks of the stream and interesting species include bog pimpernel, lesser valerian and marsh arrow-grass.

Walk out of the car park, recrossing the cattle grid, and climb immediately right up the path on the right-hand bank of **Nant Bwrefwr** with the coniferous forestry plantation on the right. ◀

At the corner of the forestry the route leaves the stream and heads directly up the wide eroded path for the southern end of **Craig y Fan Ddu**. From this viewpoint the decimation of the Talybont Valley by conifer plantations is fully visible.

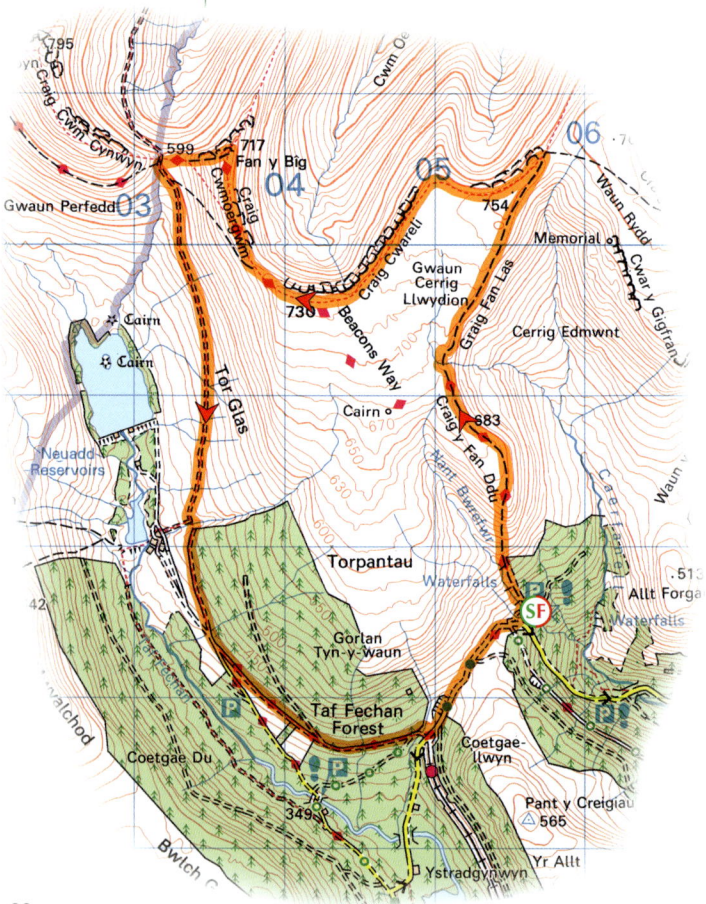

92

## CONIFEROUS FORESTRY

Conifers that are planted tightly together on hillsides throughout the national park in this area are alien to this area, having been imported for commercial reasons. They were planted closely together to produce what is called a closed canopy, so that they produce straight stems with a minimum of branching. This technique has a disastrous impact on wildlife in that it entirely suppresses growth on the forest floor and prevents any natural regeneration. There is a total absence of ground vegetation, partly due to the intense shade and partly due to the carpet of conifer needle leaves, which produce an acidic surface layer. The humic acid produced from the breakdown of the needles contaminates streams and lakes and, if the receiving waters cannot buffer this acidic solution, fish and other life die, resulting in a sterile environment. The trees are all of the same age and are clear-felled at maturity, leaving the area prone to soil erosion and leaching. The end result is an area of land where the topsoil is either sterile, as no fertile leaf mould has been produced, or it has been washed away after felling.

Keep to the eastern edge of Craig y Fan Ddu and follow the line of crags north to where the small stream of Blaen Caerfanell cuts the path and disappears over the cliff edge, falling to the valley below. Cross the stream and continue along **Craig Fan Las** (NNE) to a junction of paths on Rhiw Bwlch y Ddwyallt. ▶

Notice the classic U-shape of the hanging valley.

## PEAT HAGS

These islands of peat are all that remain of a once continuous cover that has been eroded by water-cut channels. Peat is formed in boggy conditions when dead plant material accumulates. The process began in this area around 6000 years ago and continued for about 4000 years. The present climate is drier and this may account for the absence of peat formation in this area today. Man has not contributed to this decay by peat cutting at this site, but grazing animals have had a detrimental effect. Peat erosion has been further accelerated by excessive drying due to the wind and the sun and by the action of rain, frost, ice and snow. The cusp-shaped margins of the peat hags provide essential shelter from the elements for sheep. Unfortunately, this striking topographical feature will eventually disappear completely.

Turn left (SW) and follow the ridges of Bwlch Ddwyallt and **Craig Cwareli** to the col, where there is a bothy. Continue following the ridge path along **Craig Cwmoergwm** to the summit of **Fan y Bîg**. The path is eroded and route

*The Beacons from Craig Cerrig Llwydion*

finding is simple, but care must be taken in icy conditions or in strong winds as the route has precipitous drops immediately on the right.

As you walk to the summit of Fan y Bîg, there are fine **views** westwards towards Cribyn and Pen y Fan. Fan y Bîg is easily identified by a distinctive sandstone block known as the 'diving board', which protrudes on the north-west side. The steep scarp faces of these ridges and summits are formed from resistant Brownstones.

Descend west to 'the Gap' (Bwlch ar y Fan). Down below in the head of this U-shaped valley is an interesting glacial feature: the hummocky terrain formed from boulder clay deposited by melting glaciers. Up above to the west is the impressive crag of Craig Cwm Cynwyn.

Turn left and take the Roman road south across the slopes of **Tor Glas**. ◄

*You may well be walking in the footsteps of Roman legionnaires.*

Do not turn right on the track descending to the valley bottom but stay on the track that skirts the lower edge of the forestry on your left. When the track meets the road at SO 035 174, continue along the edge of the forestry on a track that contours around the base of **Torpantau** and eventually meets the Pontsticill to Talybont road. Here you will see signs of the old railway line (see 'Brecon and Merthyr Junction Railway', Walk 14), which ran from Pontsticill to Talybont. Walk north-east along the road back to the car park.

# 3 SOUTH-WESTERN VALLEYS AND RIDGES

*Morning mist on Pentwyn reservoir*

# WALK 17
## Neuadd Horseshoe: Corn Du, Pen y Fan and Cribyn

| | |
|---|---|
| **Start/finish** | Taf Fechan car park (SO 036 171) |
| **Distance** | 13.25km (8.2 miles); extension 14.5km (8.9 miles) |
| **Total ascent** | 640m (2100ft); extension 835m (2735ft) |
| **Grade** | 3 |
| **Max elevation** | 886m (2907ft) |
| **Map** | OL12 Western area |

This is one of the most popular circular walks in the Beacons, taking in the three highest peaks in South Wales: Cribyn, Pen y Fan and Corn Du. The route is reasonably strenuous and the time required to complete it is deceptively long, but route finding is straightforward. It is worth doing this classic walk on quieter days. The most difficult sections are the initial climb to the ridge and the ascents of the main peaks. It is difficult to exaggerate the beauty of the views from this walk and the varied geology of the area can be well appreciated.

From the car park, head north along the road to what was the Lower Neuadd reservoir. Follow the waymarked path across the valley to the hill fence on the other side.

*Beacons from Pentwyn reservoir*

## WALK 17 – NEUADD HORSESHOE: CORN DU, PEN Y FAN AND CRIBYN

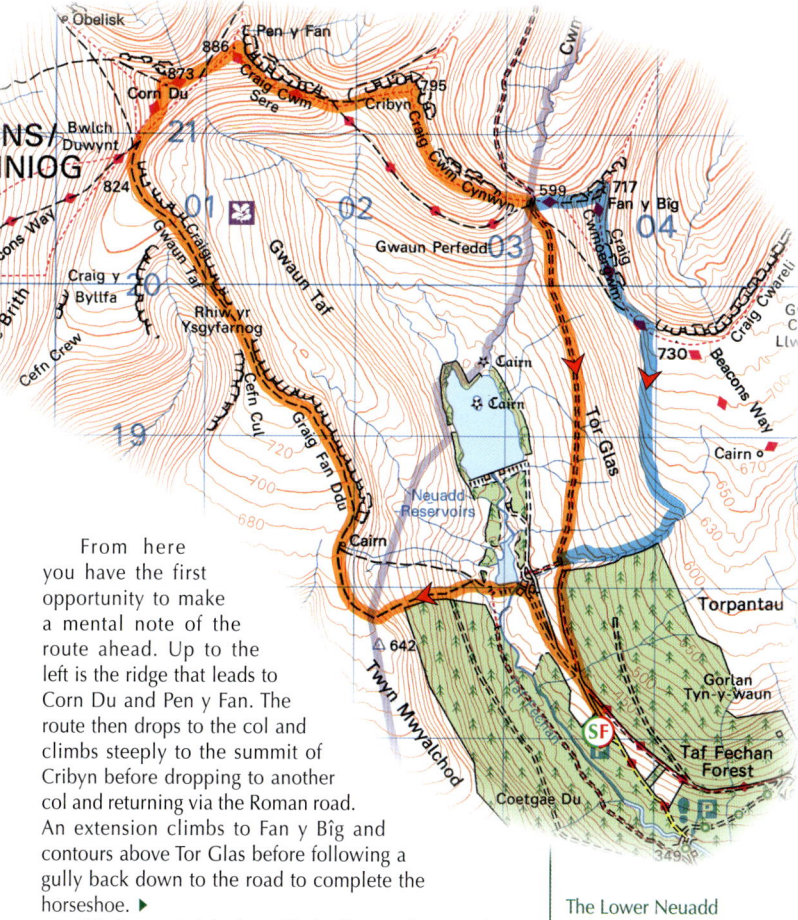

From here you have the first opportunity to make a mental note of the route ahead. Up to the left is the ridge that leads to Corn Du and Pen y Fan. The route then drops to the col and climbs steeply to the summit of Cribyn before dropping to another col and returning via the Roman road. An extension climbs to Fan y Bîg and contours above Tor Glas before following a gully back down to the road to complete the horseshoe. ▶

Climb steeply left alongside the forestry fence and so up to the ridge above. There is a good view during the ascent looking up the valley, with Graig Fan Ddu to the left. Notice that the hillslope leading up to **Graig Fan Ddu** has a pronounced step. This is a well-developed antiplanation terrace, a post-glacial feature that came about due to differences in the resistance to erosion of the underlying rock types.

The Lower Neuadd reservoir was decommissioned in 2019–20 and the original course of the Taf Fechan has been restored.

The steep cliffs of **Graig Fan Ddu** have interesting crag plant communities, including the southernmost occurrence of the dwarf willow in Britain, its only locality in the Beacons. The crags have mostly ungrazed Vaccinium grass heath with a good population of sea campion. In general, the ledges are rather dry and less species-rich than those of Pen y Fan and Cribyn.

Once on the ridge there is a magnificent **view** west to the Carmarthen Fan, to the Rhigos and to the heads of the valleys. To the east are the Neuadd Valley and the headwaters of the Taf Fechan. South is the Taf Fechan reservoir. Southeast is the distinctive shape of the Sugar Loaf near Abergavenny. And to the north, through Bwlch ar y Fan where the Roman road passes, you can see the Black Mountains.

Continue north along the ridge to **Cefn Cul**. Across the valley is the Roman road crossing over the gap between Fan y Bîg and Cribyn and so on to Brecon. On a clear day Mumbles Bay can be seen to the left (SW) down the Neath Valley, as can the lighthouse on Mumbles Head and the smoke rising from the stacks of Baglan Bay.

The track continues along the crest of the ridge, close to the steep drop on the right, and care should be taken in winter. Towards its northern end the ridge falls off to the west and becomes the headwall to Cwm Crew.

The rocks that make up the ridge are the **Plateau Beds** and these are well exposed in the northern crags of Cwm Crew. These have been eroded where the path drops to the col at Bwlch Duwynt but remnants are still left as distinctive flat caps to the summits of Corn Du and Pen y Fan.

*The rocky steps up to the flat-topped summit of Corn Du are formed by a resistant cap of Plateau Beds.*

At the end of **Craig Gwaun Taf** descend to the col at **Bwlch Duwynt** where the track from the left comes up from Pont ar Daf. Ascending **Corn Du** brings you up the rock steps to the summit plateau. This is best crossed at its western edge and so to the summit cairn. ◀

## WALK 17 – NEUADD HORSESHOE: CORN DU, PEN Y FAN AND CRIBYN

Corn Du is the best vantage point for **views** west of Fforest Fawr and Bannau Sir Gaer, otherwise known as the Carmarthen Fans. Beyond the cairn is a superb view down the steep northern face into Cwm Llwch.

The path that skirts below to the right of Corn Du can be taken if the weather conditions deteriorate. This rejoins the route at the col before Pen y Fan.

Now strike east, by a flattened cairn, and descend to the col and the well-worn track up to the summit of **Pen y Fan**. ▶ From the summit cairn of Pen y Fan, leave at the southern end of the plateau on a well-worn artificially stepped path. The path swings round to the east and drops steeply at first to the col.

Pen y Fan is the highest point in South Wales and, on a clear day, provides one of the finest vistas in Wales, with views of Fforest Fawr beyond Craig Cerrig-gleisiad and of Swansea Bay between the stacks of Port Talbot and Llandarcy. As you descend **Craig Cwm Sere**, look to your left for a fine view of the north-east face of Pen y Fan. The National Trust, which owns this land, has carried out extensive path restoration here and keeping to the made-up path will prevent further erosion problems.

The col is a natural place to stop and learn about the geological history of the northern Brecon Beacons (see 'Geology of the Brecon Beacons', Introduction). Looking north down Cwm Sere you can see a perfect example of a glacial U-shaped valley.

Ascend **Cribyn** steeply to another cairn. Then descend following the path along **Craig Cwm Cynwyn**, which swings first south and then east down to 'the Gap' and the Roman road. Stop at 'the Gap' and take in some of the interesting features in this area. You may well be resting where Roman legionnaires once marched. To the north is the head of Cwm Cynwyn and up to the left is Craig Cwm Cynwyn. Down below in the head of this U-shaped valley is an interesting glacial feature: the hummocky terrain from boulder clay deposited by melting glaciers. ▶

To continue on the main route, turn right (S) and follow the Roman road across **Tor Glas**. When you come to the stream gully of Nant y Gloesydd, cross over and continue on

---

*This col can be heavily corniced in winter and it is advisable to keep well back from the edge.*

*The extended route via Fan y Bîg and Craig Cwmoergwm starts from here.*

*Looking back down the Taf Fechan Valley from Craig Gwaun Taf before the Lower Neuadd Reservoir was decommissioned*

*Below to the north is Cwm Oergwm, the last of the north-eastern glacial U-shaped valleys.*

the track along the bottom edge of the **forestry** to the road. Continue (S) down the road back to the start.

### Extension

For those who still feel energetic, climb **Fan y Bîg** from the Roman road. This summit is easily identified by a distinctive sandstone block known as the 'diving board', which protrudes on the north-west side. The steep scarp faces of these ridges and summits are formed from resistant Brownstones.

From the summit, turn due south and follow the ridge path along **Craig Cwmoergwm** to the military bothy at the low point of the ridge. ◄

Leave the main ridge path just past here and contour south along the top of the slope of **Tor Glas**. When you meet a stream gully (Nant y Gloesydd), just before the conifer plantation, descend following the right bank to the **Roman road** and rejoin the main route.

# WALK 18

*Cwm Llysiog and Waun Wen*

| | |
|---|---|
| **Start/finish** | Layby north of Pont Nant Gwinau (SO 008 128) |
| **Distance** | 10.5km (6.5 miles) |
| **Total ascent** | 345m (1130ft) |
| **Grade** | 2 |
| **Max elevation** | 528m (1732ft) |
| **Map** | OL12 Western area |

This short walk is based on Cwm Llysiog, a valley that has a bleak and isolated atmosphere as it is probably the least visited of all the valleys in the Central Beacons. The head of the valley has a number of picturesque waterfalls. No great height is reached so the walk is not strenuous, but sections of the route require very careful route finding in bad weather. The main features of interest are the waterfalls.

From the layby walk north along the road, taking care as traffic travels very fast here. After 50 metres a conspicuous forestry track leaves to the right. Take this and climb up to the left and left again at the next junction (the track on the right is your return route) and follow this to the hill fence. Drop straight down to your left (NW) into the bottom of **Nant Wern-ddu**.

*Cwm Llysiog*

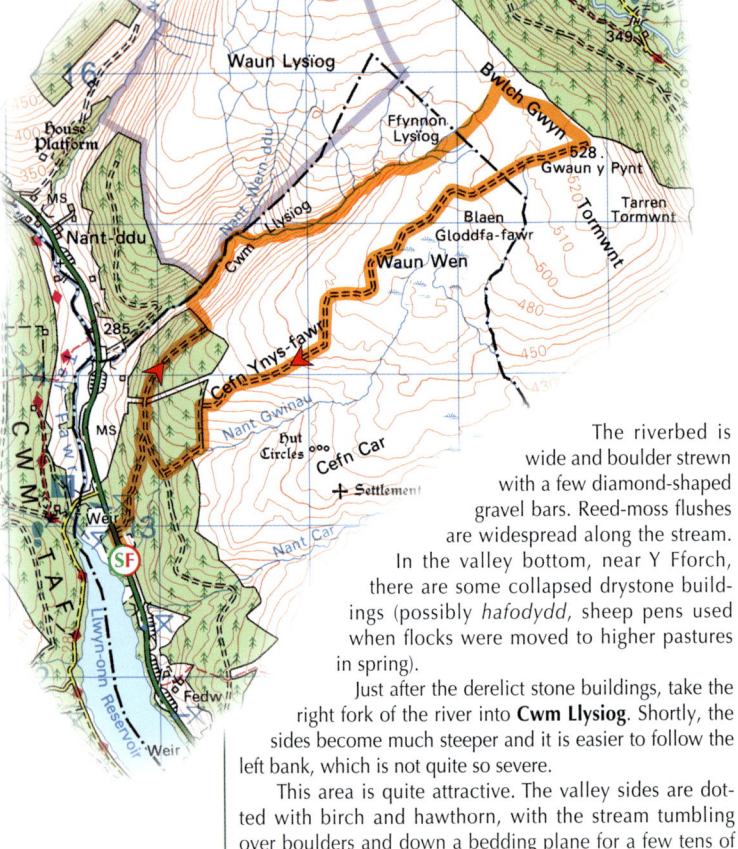

The riverbed is wide and boulder strewn with a few diamond-shaped gravel bars. Reed-moss flushes are widespread along the stream. In the valley bottom, near Y Fforch, there are some collapsed drystone buildings (possibly *hafodydd*, sheep pens used when flocks were moved to higher pastures in spring).

Just after the derelict stone buildings, take the right fork of the river into **Cwm Llysiog**. Shortly, the sides become much steeper and it is easier to follow the left bank, which is not quite so severe.

This area is quite attractive. The valley sides are dotted with birch and hawthorn, with the stream tumbling over boulders and down a bedding plane for a few tens of metres. On the right are Old Red Sandstone exposures with red marls below. These are interbedded with thinner units of sandstone, with rowan growing out of them.

Look out for flattened rushes and large amounts of rock debris brought down by small rivulets on either side of the stream, evidence of the Jekyll and Hyde character of this valley. Towards the upper reaches of this valley the stream bed narrows and twists between interlocking spurs.

## WALK 18 – CWM LLYSIOG AND WAUN WEN

### FLASH FLOODS

Nant Wern-ddu has a reputation for producing flash floods, and a number of measures have been taken in the past to combat this danger. A large stone embankment was constructed in the 1950s in the lower reaches of the valley in order to divert and slow down flood waters. A dam was also built halfway up the valley at around the same time. The reason this valley is prone to flash floods is that it is a strike valley, which means it lies at right-angles to the south-south-easterly dip of the rocks. You will notice from the map that there are more streams on its north-western bank, where the rocks dip towards it, than on the south-western sides, where the rocks dip away from the stream. These tributaries drain an extensive upland area that rapidly supplies relatively large quantities of water to a small valley with a straight watercourse. These are the ideal ingredients for flash floods.

Continue to an area of deciduous trees lining outcrops of Brownstones on the right of the stream. Just upstream is a small fall, about 3m high. The crags to the left are covered in ivy and numerous species of mosses and ferns.

The valley splits again just after this fall. The smaller tributary on the left is well worth exploring, with two small falls in a narrow gorge. ▶ Return to the confluence and follow the right-hand tributary to an impressive fall (3–4m high), with another a little further on. Both these falls are formed by thick beds of resistant sandstone: the first of Plateau Beds and the second of Grey Grits. Climb up to the left of these falls.

*The banks are covered in heather, bilberry, mosses, ferns and lichens.*

Nant Llysiog

From this vantage point there is a fine view looking back, the valley in the foreground having interlocking spurs with the larger, more U-shaped valley beyond. A spring, **Ffynnon Lysiog**, flows from the base of the Grey Grits along the banks of the last northern tributary, which meets the main streamway between the last two falls. At this point the stream is covered in a film of orange iron hydroxide precipitated by bacteria. The waters issuing from the spring further up the tributary are rich in iron and are reputed for their healing properties.

Just above the falls, the stream disseminates into flat open moorland: an expanse of bog with eroded peat hags dominated by purple moor grass, with hare's tail grass and deer grass in places. The ridge along the southern side of the valley is the line of a geological fault that lies along the northern boundary of the Neath Disturbance. The rocks to the south have been downthrown just enough to bring the Plateau Beds into direct contact with the Brownstones.

From immediately above the waterfall walk south-southeast (bearing 150°) across Twyn y Groes. This is a wet area of purple moor grass. Shortly (after about 500 metres) you meet and turn right (SW) onto two parallel drainage ditches about 10 metres apart and marked on the map as a track. These meander south-westwards across **Waun Wen**, a large featureless area where there are patches of common cottongrass and heather among purple moor grass. ◄ The ditches become indistinct for short stretches but eventually appear as double parallel-tracks, periodically marked by concrete fence posts with barbed wire wrapped around them.

*This open moor is quite a challenge from a route-finding point of view and when there is a covering of snow, navigation has to be done purely by compass or GPS.*

Gradually lose height crossing this moor and the coniferous forestry plantation you walked through on the way up eventually becomes visible. The route crosses a rivulet by a bridge of railway sleepers. Straight ahead a gate leads into the coniferous forestry. Pass through this and turn left after a short distance along a wide forest track to **Nant Gwinau**. The track swings right, following the bank to a T-junction with a well-used forestry track.

Turn right to the next junction, then left and retrace your steps back to the start.

# WALK 19
*Corn Du and Pen y Fan via Cwm Crew*

| | |
|---|---|
| Start/finish | Entrance to forestry plantation off A470 (SN 992 171) |
| Distance | 8.5km (5.3 miles); with extension 11.5km (7.1 miles) |
| Total ascent | 495m (1620ft); with extension 505m (1660ft) |
| Grade | 3 |
| Max elevation | 790m (2592ft) with extension 886m (2907ft) |
| Map | OL12 Western area |

This interesting walk is centred on Cwm Crew, a valley with an isolated feel even though it is adjacent to the busiest area of the Brecon Beacons National Park. Access is not easy and perhaps for this reason it is a very quiet and secluded area. From various vantage points during the walk a great deal of the surrounding countryside can be viewed and the route can easily be extended to take in Corn Du and Pen y Fan, the highest summits in South Wales. The geological history of Cwm Crew is interesting and there are fine views from the top of the valley.

This walk starts north of Nant Crew Bridge at the entrance to a forestry plantation. Walk up the road, cross the hill fence and head onto National Trust land. Ascend the hillside along the edge of the plantation and over the brow of the hill. Drop down to the valley bottom, picking up a distinctive sheep track just above the stream.

Looking up the valley, keep to the left-hand (NW) side, passing numerous hawthorn trees. After a short distance, drop down past these and follow the riverbed itself. There are two sheep *hafodydd* (pens used when flocks were moved to higher pastures in spring) in the valley bottom and a path rises up above these, necessitating the crossing of numerous side valleys as they drop steeply to the river.

*A grey heron in Cwm Crew*

In high winds the funnelling effect of the valley can cause the water to be blown vertically into the air in a large spout.

Continue past more stone *hafodydd* and just after these drop down to the stream bed to a small waterfall with a rowan tree. Keep in the riverbed and examine small cliffs with unusual mosses and ferns on them. Below the next fall is a willow and the highest fall has to be bypassed on the right. ◄

Keep close to the river above the fall and aim for the end of a 'tongue' of moraine that divides the stream course in two where the valley narrows before it changes direction to the north and becomes Blaen Crew. The tributary to the right soon disappears in a boggy area.

Climb up the prow of the moraine and continue diagonally up to the right to **Rhiw yr Ysgyfarnog**. Turn along the ridge (NNW) to **Craig Gwaun Taf** at the head of Cwm Crew.

From Rhiw yr Ysgyfarnog look back across the valley you have just ascended and you will notice another **moraine rib** that runs down the slope from the southern end of Craig y Byllfa. Both this moraine and the lateral moraine you have just walked along were formed at the end of the last Ice Age, when a lingering block of ice survived in the most shaded area of Cwm Crew. Rock debris from the steep slopes above the ice tobogganed down its slippery slope and accumulated around its edge.

The upland area around Cwm Crew, together with a very narrow strip along Rhiw yr Ysgyfarnog and the ridge south, still has its protective resistant cap of Plateau Beds. From the ridge you have excellent views of the Beacons summits. The peak on the left (due north) is Corn Du, followed by Pen y Fan, Cribyn and Fan y Bîg to the east. Blaen Crew very nearly became part of the Taf Fechan Valley during the Ice Age, and all that separates them today is Rhiw yr Ysgyfarnog. ▶

*Cwm Crew from A470*

The extended walk to Pen y Fan leaves from here.

### CWM CREW

This very secluded valley has a truly wild feel with hawthorn and birch scattered around, but in the upper reaches these disappear, giving way to a barren landscape.

For much of its length, Nant Crew is confined to a 15m-wide straight channel within which it meanders. The dip of the rocks is to the south-south-east, which has resulted in the northern and western valley sides eroding faster than the more stable southern and eastern sides where the rocks dip into the hillside. A few *hafodydd* are found on the valley floor and these derelict stone-walled pens were once used when sheep flocks were moved to higher ground in the summer. Upstream from these pens the stream changes character, becoming ever smaller, and the watercourse is forced to twist its way around interlocking spurs of land. The stream bed now consists of exposed red sandstone bedrock instead

*Cwm Crew from Craig y Byllfa*

of boulders and gravel. Small waterfalls and pools are found where the confined stream tumbles over more resistant bands of Brownstone. Here you will find interesting rock exposures of micaceous red sandstone, particularly on the right (SE) bank. The valley changes character when it becomes narrower and swings around to the north.

Cwm Crew is a classic U-shaped valley, which indicates that it was cut by a glacier. Much of the sides and floor are covered in unconsolidated sediments of glacial and periglacial origin. This 'head' moved downslope over the permanently frozen subsoil during the periglacial conditions that existed after the main Ice Age. The stream left in the valley, known as a 'misfit', began to cut a sharp 'V' down through these deposits, resulting in the abrupt change of slope on either side of the stream. In places the stream has washed away all these superficial deposits, exposing Old Red Sandstone bedrock underneath. Waterfalls result when the stream encounters a more resistant band of sandstone.

To continue on the main route turn left (W) and follow the ridge of **Craig y Byllfa**, which curves around to the south. The crags of Craig y Byllfa are an impressive sight and are steep enough for snow to avalanche in winter. A detached block of Plateau Beds at the head of the valley is slowly creeping downhill, leaving a well-developed landslip scar.

Keep to the high ground and follow the eastern side of **Cefn Crew** (SW) to where the ridge ends. Lose height steadily by dropping down the prow of the mountain towards the forestry and make your way down to the gate in the hill fence at the road and back to the start.

*Bwlch Duwynt*

### Extension

A worthwhile extension to the route is to visit the two highest summits in South Wales.

Continue (NNW) along **Craig Gwaun Taf** and sweep around north to **Bwlch Duwynt** (windy gap), which certainly lives up to its name. Ahead of you is a well-worn path leading up to the flat-topped summit of **Corn Du**. From the summit descend (E) to the col and then climb gently to the top of **Pen y Fan**.

> The resistant Plateau Beds that cap Corn Du and Pen y Fan have been eroded away on the intervening **ridge**, which is composed of softer Brownstones. The ridge is eroding at a faster rate than the summits and is a good example of differential erosion.

Retrace your steps to the col but do not climb back up to Corn Du. Instead, follow the distinctive path that skirts along Corn Du back to Bwlch Duwynt. Follow the ridge back to the head of Blaen Crew and rejoin the main route where you began your excursion to the high summits.

*View of the Usk Valley with Pen y Fan and Corn Du the highest peaks*

# WALK 20

*Corn Du and Pen y Fan from Pont ar Daf*

| | |
|---|---|
| **Start/finish** | Pont ar Daf car park (SN 988 199) |
| **Distance** | 7.5km (4.7 miles) |
| **Total ascent** | 520m (1700ft) |
| **Grade** | 3 |
| **Max elevation** | 886m (2907ft) |
| **Map** | OL12 Western area |
| **Note** | There is a national trust car park at Pont ar Daf that has charging points for electric vehicles and a visitor centre |

This is the quickest route to the two highest peaks in the Beacons but by far the busiest, with the car parks becoming full early in the morning at weekends and during holidays. Route finding is easy in good weather but the conditions can change dramatically if the wind picks up and the cloud comes down. Pen y Fan is just short of 3000ft high and temperatures drop with altitude. In addition, the prevailing south-westerly winds become accelerated with height on the mountain slopes. Make sure you are well equipped for this high excursion, the rewards of which include some of the best mountain views in Wales.

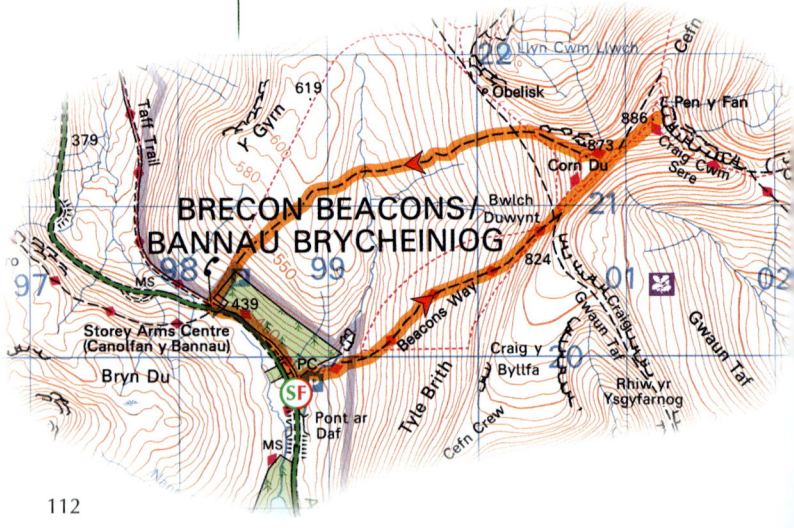

*Track to Corn Du*

Leave Pont ar Daf car park to the east, about halfway along the car park. The track descends to a bridge crossing one of the sources of the Taff Fawr. Follow the well-marked track up the hillside to **Bwlch Duwynt**. The route has been reinforced with local sandstone to reduce erosion. Turn left at the high point from where you have a view down into the valley of Blaen Taf Fechan. Take the path that skirts across the slope below Corn Du to the col before **Pen y Fan** and climb to the summit.

> At first sight, **Pen y Fan's summit** is rather flat and uninteresting, but walk carefully to above the north-east face where the precipitous nature of the mountain becomes all too obvious. This face can be ice-climbed in rare severe winters when the conditions are perfect. At other times the rock is loose and friable. Your efforts are rewarded with awe-inspiring panoramic views from the highest point in southern Britain. The cairn on the summit plateau is a Bronze Age burial chamber; a bronze brooch and spearhead were discovered here during an excavation in 1991.

## PEN Y FAN VISTA

The summit of Pen y Fan is one of the finest vantage points in Wales. On an exceptionally clear day Cadair Idris can just be distinguished to the north and Exmoor to the south. Almost due west are the cliffs of a beautiful glacial cwm, Craig Cerrig-gleisiad, and beyond is Fforest Fawr, a relatively unvisited part of the park that possesses many interesting features. To the south-west the plumes from the stacks of Port Talbot and Llandarcy can be seen when there is good visibility, and between these is the wide sweep of Swansea Bay, which culminates in the west with the Mumbles Lighthouse.

Retrace your steps back to the col and follow the path to the summit of **Corn Du**, which also has a Bronze Age burial cairn. The lake below is Llyn Cwm Llwch.

## CORN DU

Corn Du is the site of a Bronze Age cairn, and the stones near the edge are the remains of an excavated funerary mound. The steepest part of the northern face comprises the Plateau Beds, which are covered in grazed purple moor grass heath, some awnless sheep's fescue being the only plant species of interest. Corn Du is a fine vantage point with views to the west of the Fans and, in particular, of the finely sculpted headwall of Fan Fawr to the south-west. In the valley just below to the west is Blaen Taff Fawr, the headwaters of the River Taff. The south-east presents a quite different aspect down into the valley of Neuadd with its reservoir and a continuing view towards the South Wales coast in the distance. The peak lies at the head of Cwm Llwch with its glacial lake.

Descend the steep section on the western end down to Craig Cwm Llwch. You will be able to pick out Tommy Jones' Obelisk on the ridge below, a memorial to a young boy who died here in 1900. Turn left on the path that descends the slope to cross Blaen Taf Fechan. Cross the stream and climb to the gate on **Y Gyrn**. ◄ Continue on the path down to **Storey Arms**, turn left and take the track back to the start.

*This moorland habitat is managed for upland birds such as red grouse.*

# 4 FFOREST FAWR

*The cliffs of Craig Cwm-du (Walks 23 and 24)*

# WALK 21
*Craig Cerrig-gleisiad*

| | |
|---|---|
| **Start/finish** | Layby off A470 (SN 971 222) |
| **Distance** | 4km (2.4 miles) |
| **Total ascent** | 330m (1080ft) |
| **Grade** | 2 |
| **Max elevation** | 620m (2034ft) |
| **Map** | OL12 Western area |

The route of this short walk, which is packed full of interest, passes through the hollow of a periglacial cwm that is overshadowed by steep craggy cliffs, the habitat of rare alpine and Arctic–alpine plants. This area is part of a National Nature Reserve and must be respected as such. There is a relatively short but steep ascent and the main features of interest are the glacial features of the crags and the wildlife. Early spring to mid summer is the best time to see the wildflowers and excellent birdlife, while in August and September the mountain slopes are painted purple with heather. The walk provides no difficulty in route finding, but there is a steep descent that can be slippery.

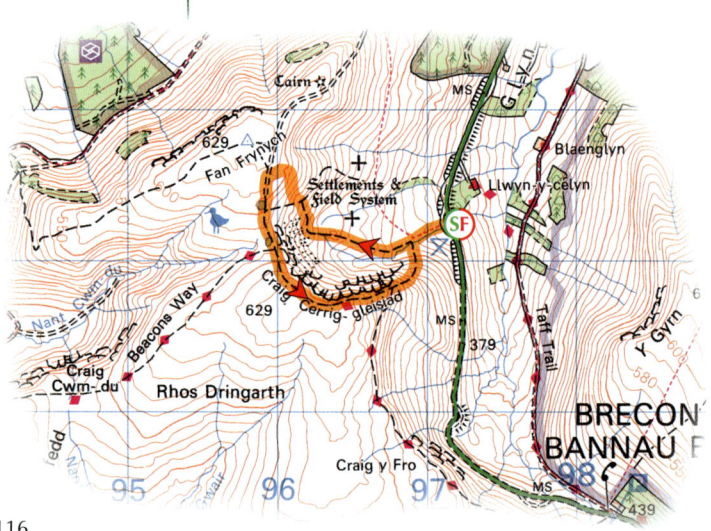

Cross the stile to the right of the stream and follow the path west into the cwm to a stone squeeze and a wooden gateway through the wall. Stop and read the information board after crossing the stile as it explains the purpose and code of conduct for the area. ▶

To the left of the stream is a laid-out picnic area with trestle tables.

> It is believed that the cwm was occupied by a small **glacier** during the Loch Lomond Stadial, the last period of glacial activity in the Brecon Beacons, when small glaciers developed and perennial snow patches formed in the shadows of northern-facing scarps. Periglacial conditions existed beyond the glacier margins. This was the last cold period and it ended around 10,000 years ago. Persistent erosion at the base of the western wall by glacial and freeze-thaw action on the wall itself led to slumping and rockfalls. The hummocky terrain left in the hollow was produced by the last small glacier, but some of it may have been left by the earlier Late Devensian ice sheet, which covered the entire Brecon Beacons around 20,000 years ago.

Take the waymarked route into the cwm. Here there are botanically interesting boggy areas that contain extraordinary species such as the carnivorous sundew, which flowers between June and August. The rocks exposed in the main crag are Senni Beds of Devonian Old Red Sandstone, topped with Brownstones.

> The flat area of land on your right was once a **Bronze Age settlement** with a field system that was farmed 4000 years ago. In 2013 a carved stone was discovered here; it measured 1.45m by 0.5m, and the exposed face contained rock art: 12 cup (hollow) marks of different shapes and sizes joined by connecting lines. The stone lies flat now, but it is thought to have once stood upright as a waymarker, making it unique in a Welsh context.

*Craig Cerrig-gleisiad in winter*

Ascend the steep slope, along a path in a north-westerly direction, crossing a number of stiles, to a small cairn. Cross another stile and continue diagonally left across a bilberry-covered slope to the top of **Craig Cerrig-gleisiad**, where there is a stile in a fence that runs north–south.

Cross the fence and walk parallel to it (S) to a **pool** at SN 960 221. A short distance further on there are two stiles near a T-junction of fences. Cross the stile on the right and continue along the path, keeping the fence on your left, following around the top of the crags. Take care when the path descends steeply east down a grassy slope. Cut north through a hole in the wall at SN 971 220 and continue north, walking parallel to the fence. Cross the stream and join the path again on the opposite side. Retrace your steps (E) to the start.

## CRAIG CERRIG GLEISIAD A FAN FRYNYCH NATIONAL NATURE RESERVE

The mountainous area of Craig Cerrig-gleisiad and Fan Frynych is of special botanical and geomorphological interest and is managed as a National Nature Reserve.

Rare Arctic–alpine plants are found mainly in the gullies of the steep crags, where a cold, damp microclimate exists and where they are protected from grazing animals. This special microhabitat allows them to exist at or near the southern limit of their range in Britain. Interesting species include purple saxifrage, mossy saxifrage, green spleenwort, lesser meadow rue and northern bedstraw. Moorland vegetation consists largely of dwarf-shrub heathland comprising heather, bilberry and crowberry, and associated grasses, such as wavy hair-grass and mat grass.

*Sundew*

Around 80 bird species can be found in the reserve, of which nearly 30 breed here. The skylark and meadow pipit are constant companions when walking over heathland, while buzzards, red kites, kestrels, peregrine falcons and ravens are often sighted wheeling overhead. Look out for the wheatear on boulder-strewn slopes, the whinchat among bracken and heather, the redstart and tree pipit in hawthorn scrub and the dipper and wagtail darting along streams. This is the best place in the park to see the ring ouzel, a rare summer migrant that flies here from Africa. Known as the mountain blackbird, its preferred habitat is the gullies and craggy cliffs where it nests and forages on worms, insects and berries. The management objectives of the reserve are to re-establish a diverse dwarf-shrub heathland dominated by heather and bilberry and to encourage the development of scattered hawthorn on mid-slopes and a denser cover of trees and shrubs on the lower slopes. These will be achieved primarily by controlling the numbers of grazing stock and by selective tree planting.

# WALK 22
## *Fan Fawr*

| | |
|---|---|
| **Start/finish** | Car park off A4059, Beacons Reservoir (SN 988 181) |
| **Distance** | 6km (3.7 miles) |
| **Total ascent** | 340m (1110ft) |
| **Grade** | 2 |
| **Max elevation** | 734m (2408ft) |
| **Map** | OL12 Western area |

This route to the summit of Fan Fawr, the highest peak in Fforest Fawr, avoids the busier direct approach from Storey Arms. The walk gains height gradually by following the crest of the glacial cwm. A circuit of the summit gives fine views in all directions, including the Carmarthen Fan to the west and the Tarell Valley to the north. No great exertion is required and there are good views across to the highest of the Beacons and down into a glacial cwm and moraine.

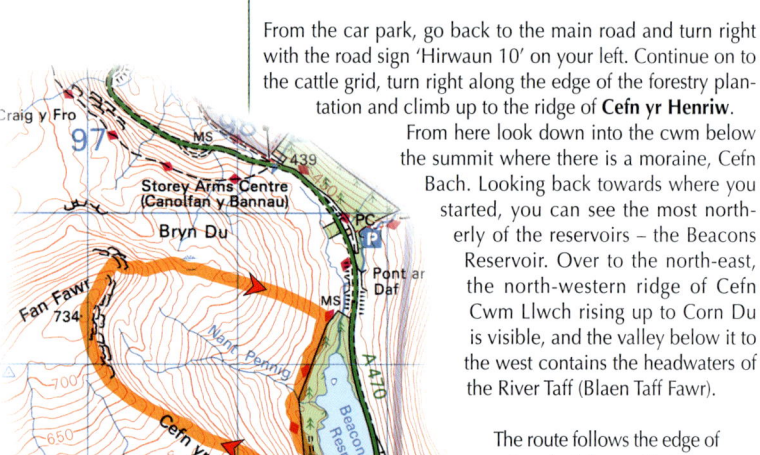

From the car park, go back to the main road and turn right with the road sign 'Hirwaun 10' on your left. Continue on to the cattle grid, turn right along the edge of the forestry plantation and climb up to the ridge of **Cefn yr Henriw**.

From here look down into the cwm below the summit where there is a moraine, Cefn Bach. Looking back towards where you started, you can see the most northerly of the reservoirs – the Beacons Reservoir. Over to the north-east, the north-western ridge of Cefn Cwm Llwch rising up to Corn Du is visible, and the valley below it to the west contains the headwaters of the River Taff (Blaen Taff Fawr).

The route follows the edge of the glacial cwm that gives Fan Fawr its character. A most interesting feature lies in its base:

*Fan Fawr from Bryn Du*

a **linear moraine** marked on the map as Cefn Bach, which runs parallel to the ridge. This was probably formed when scree material from the back wall of the cwm slid down the surface of a snow bed which formed because it was sheltered from the sun's rays. This is called a nivation ridge or protalus. Another theory is that the moraine is of glacial origin and was formed when ice occupied the cwm.

Follow the ridge along a sheep track up to the **Fan Fawr** summit cairn, which lies to the north-east of the trig point.

To the east the summit of Corn Du obscures Pen y Fan, which at 886m (2907ft) is the highest point in South Wales. Due west is a superb **view** of Bannau Sir Gaer, with the ridges of Fan Dringarth, Fan Nedd and Fan Gyhirych in the foreground. Due north is the buttress that hides Craig Cerrig-gleisiad, part of a National Nature Reserve, in the valley beyond.

Descend north-north-east from the summit cairn, following the top of the crags, on the path that heads up the hill from Storey Arms. Use this to descend the steep slope from the summit and then leave it to cross over to **Bryn Du**, heading for the top of the Beacons Reservoir where you join the **Beacons Way**. Head south with the forestry plantation on your left above the hill fence at first and then cross into the woodland and back to the start.

# WALK 23
## Craig Cwm-du and Fan Frynych

| | |
|---|---|
| **Start/finish** | Brecon Beacons National Park Visitor Centre (SN 978 263), postcode LD3 8ER |
| **Distance** | 13.75km (8.5 miles) |
| **Total ascent** | 380m (1250ft) |
| **Grade** | 2 |
| **Max elevation** | 623m (2044ft) |
| **Map** | OL12 Western area |

This medium-level walk takes in a relatively quiet part of the park. A flat approach along Sarn Helen, a Roman road, brings you to the entrance of Craig Cwm-du – a place of outstanding beauty that may remind you of a miniature Scottish glen. Being part of a National Nature Reserve, the area is of exceptional nature conservation interest. An easy climb through slopes covered in heather and bilberry brings you to the top of Fan Frynych and fine views of the Brecon Beacons. The walk presents no great route-finding difficulties, except care should be taken on the climb to the summit of Fan Frynych. The area is quiet and unspoilt and presents a different character to other parts of the National Park.

Leave the visitor centre and head back to the road junction. Carry straight on to the track across the moor, with **Daudraeth Illtyd Nature Reserve** on your right. The chances are you are now walking on the Roman road of Sarn Helen, although this is marked on the map as being further northwest. This track, however, runs in a straight and level line, continuing past Cwm-du where Sarn Helen is marked on the Ordnance Survey map. Heading in the opposite direction is the most direct route to the Iron Age hill fort at Twyn y Gaer, an obvious high-ground site due to its panoramic views of the surrounding countryside and its defensive potential.

The wetland bog on your right is **Traeth Mawr**, which means 'big beach', a clue to the fact that this area was once a basin containing a large lake. Known as a 'dead-ice hollow', it formed when a melting glacier left behind a block of ice that later

# WALK 23 – CRAIG CWM-DU AND FAN FRYNYCH

became covered in rock fragments and soil. The ground appeared to subside as the ice eventually thawed, and the depression left in the ground then filled with water. Natural succession has resulted in the formation of a raised mire, and no open water can be seen today. In the seventeenth and eighteenth centuries peat was heavily cut in this area, which was probably a factor in the creation of such a wide variety of habitats in a relatively small area, making it unique in Wales.

Ignore any footpaths or bridleways that meet the track and carry straight on across when you meet a road onto a minor tarmac road to a right-angled bend near **Forest Lodge Cottages**. Continue on the stony track to a gate, just after which there is a footpath signed 'Coed Ty Mawr'. Ignore this and carry on for a short distance and pass through a second gate. Continue to a third gate where a track leaves to the left.

The mountains ahead of you are the westerly 'Fans' and in the very far distance you can see Bannau Sir Gaer. You are looking over Fforest Fawr.

Continue along the bridleway, passing a sign that indicates you are entering Craig Cerrig Gleisiad a Fan Frynych National Nature Reserve. The track divides after crossing a gully.

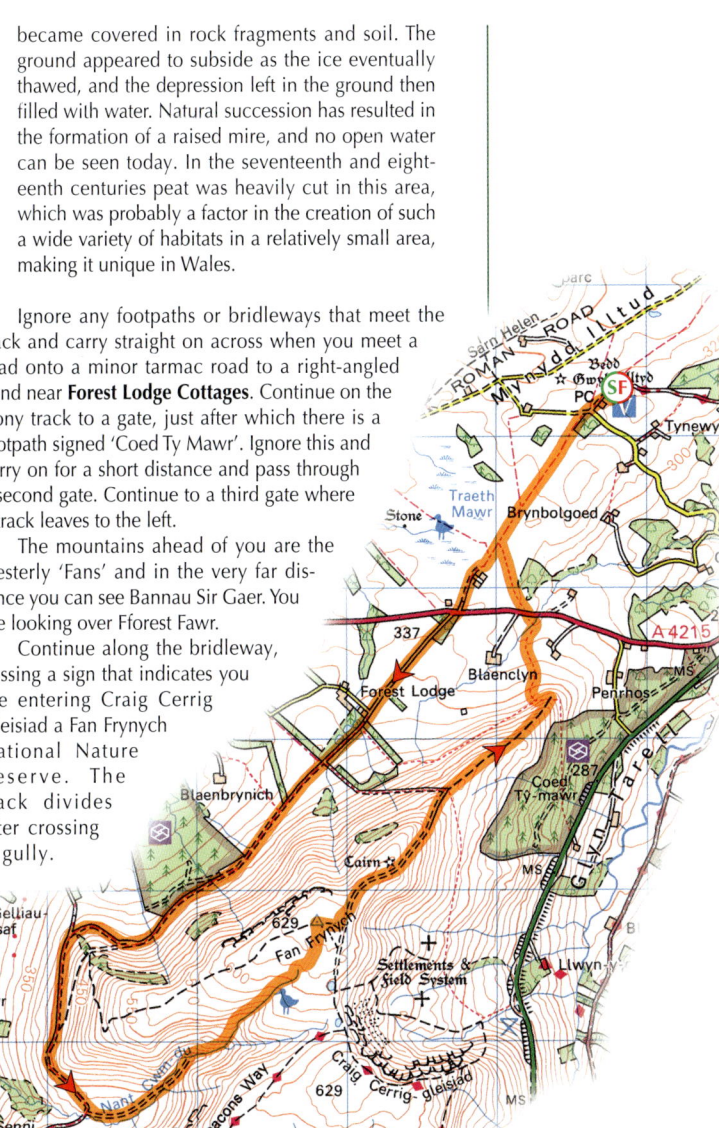

The left fork passes through a gate and disappears over the skyline. Take the right fork, continuing along Sarn Helen. The left fork is an old drovers' road. Clumps of Scots pines were loosely planted on the bare hillside as an indication of the drovers' route, to show where cattle and sheep might graze and where their drovers might obtain refreshment. As you round the next bend in the Roman road there is a good view of the end of the Senni Valley, with Fan Nedd to the left and Fan Gyhirych to the right.

### SARN HELEN

This Roman road linked Neath and Brecon and eventually connected with the coast road running from Chester to Segontium. It is named after Helen, Welsh wife of the Romano–British emperor Magnus Maximus. Also known as St Helena, she is celebrated as being the discoverer of the True Cross and mother of the Emperor Constantine, who was first declared emperor by the army in Britain. A 14th-century Welsh story in the Mabinogion tells how Macsen Wledig – the Roman usurper Magnus Maximus – dreamt of a girl whom he later discovered in Arfon and married. As a wedding gift Helen asked for the three strongholds built at Caernarfon, Caerleon and Carmarthen to be joined by roads, known as the 'Roads of Elen of the Hosts'. A 12th-century tradition, however, remembers Helena as the daughter of the founder of Colchester. The Romans struggled to seize control of the Silures, a warlike Welsh tribe that ruled this mountainous part of South Wales. In fact, from the time of the Roman invasion of Britain in AD43, it took the Romans around 25 years to subdue the Silures. The Romans ruled Britain for nearly 300 years, finally leaving, their empire in ruins, in AD400. Sarn Helen continued to be an important road and was used for many centuries by drovers taking their cattle and sheep to market.

Craig Cwm-du

## WALK 23 – CRAIG CWM-DU AND FAN FRYNYCH

Continue along Sarn Helen to where a track leaves to the left just before the bridge, where there are ruins of an old toll house at the entrance to Cwm-du. ▶ Leave Sarn Helen by turning left up the track at the apex of the right-hand bend before the bridge.

The pool at the entrance to Cwm-du would have been used by drovers to water their cattle.

**Craig Cwm-du** is part of a National Nature Reserve comprising 493 hectares of heathland and crags. The southern side of the valley was steepened by the action of ice, which formed 150m high crags. It was left 'hanging' above the main U-shaped Senni Valley below. Here a rich plant life thrives, including Arctic–alpine species. In June and July rare yellow Welsh poppies can be found on the cliffs and stream banks.

Follow the track into the cwm to the fork in **Nant Cwm-du** and take the left-hand branch. Towards the top, near the small waterfalls, a sign indicates a left turn. Follow this, working up left slightly away from the stream to avoid impassable waterfalls in the stream bed. When the stream forks again, take the left branch up a small side valley on its left flank. Follow this to a bed of cotton-grass and reeds. Continue north-north-east, arriving at the summit of **Fan Frynych** where you will meet the track from Craig Cerrig-gleisiad coming up from the right. ▶

From the trig point aim north-north-east, with the Brecon Beacons at about two o'clock, and pass close to small quarry spoils, leaving them on your right. Keep to this stony track as it drops along the spur and continue following the ridge across Twyn Dylluan-ddu down to the hill fence, ignoring the track that turns left just after the larch trees. Turn left and then cross the hill fence on the waymarked path through the fields to the road. Turn left, cross over and take the signposted footpath on the right across the fields back to the track that you used earlier. Turn right and retrace your steps to the start.

*Craig Cwm-du in winter*

Fan Frynych is a fine vantage point for views to the east of Corn Du and Pen y Fan.

# WALK 24

*Fan Frynych, Fan Dringarth and Fan Llia*

| | |
|---|---|
| **Start/finish** | Blaen Llia car park (SN 927 164) |
| **Distance** | 18km (11 miles) |
| **Total ascent** | 515m (1690ft) |
| **Grade** | 2 |
| **Max elevation** | 632m (2073ft) |
| **Map** | OL12 Western area |

Packed full of interest from both the past and the present, this walk takes in the Roman road of Sarn Helen, which passes in front of Cwm-du, the Black Valley, part of a National Nature Reserve. From the head of the cwm there are superb views of the rest of the reserve and the crags and gullies of Craig Cerrig-gleisiad. Both of these cwms have an astonishing variety of birdlife, including buzzards and peregrine falcons. The return route crosses over Fan Frynych, Fan Dringarth and Fan Llia before dropping into the Llia Valley. The walk, which is not too strenuous nor difficult to follow, takes in a rarely visited area of the national park. If you enjoy seclusion, this is a walk well worth considering.

Head upstream along the right-hand bank of **Afon Llia** to Rhyd Uchaf where you join Sarn Helen, a Roman road (see 'Sarn Helen', Walk 23). After 2.5km pass through a gate to the entrance to Cwm-du. This valley has the feel of a Scottish glen and at any moment one expects to see a red deer moving among the Scots pines. It is the western half of a National Nature Reserve, home to a rich variety of plants and birdlife (see 'Craig Cerrig Gleisiad a Fan Frynych National Nature Reserve', Walk 21). The pool at the entrance to Cwm-du would have been used by drovers to water their cattle.

### DROVERS

Many old tracks in the Brecon Beacons were used by drovers over the centuries. These men transported livestock from agricultural areas to markets in England. Cattle were shod to protect their feet on the long journeys, and geese had their

## WALK 24 – FAN FRYNYCH, FAN DRINGARTH AND FAN LLIA

feet dipped in tar. The drovers returned from the markets with various goods for the farmers. Interestingly, they brought back gorse seed, which was sown on the ffridd land, the steep hillside, often enclosed, up to 300m. Young gorse shoots are, apparently, a delicacy to sheep, but they also provide shelter for seedlings such as thorn. A hard winter may well kill off old gorse but the thorn seedlings may have grown just enough to survive grazing. A notable feature of the Brecon Beacons today is the dotted thorn trees on the valley sides, which provide good nesting sites for merlins.

Continue to a stone bridge, Pont Blaen-cwm-du, where there are ruins of an old toll house. The Roman road swings away to the left here and ascends the hill. A few metres further on take the track that leaves on the right and heads into the cwm to the fork in the stream. Take the left-hand branch. Towards the top, near the small waterfalls, a sign indicates a left turn. Follow this, working up left slightly away from the stream to avoid impassable waterfalls. When the stream forks again, take the left branch up a small side valley on its left flank, following this to a bed of cottongrass and reeds. Continue north-north-east, arriving at the summit of **Fan Frynych**.

From the summit head south, past the old quarry workings, and join the path by the side of the fence above **Craig Cerrig-gleisiad**. Follow this to a stile where another fence meets it from the west. Craig Cerrig-gleisiad is the eastern part of the National Nature Reserve and is similar in character to Cwm-du. ◄ Cross over the stile, turn right and follow the fence to the west. Continue, with the slope on the right becoming steeper all the time, until you reach the high point of **Craig Cwm-du** above the steepest crags.

> This is a good vantage point for looking down into Craig Cerrig-gleisiad or for views of Corn Du and Pen y Fan in the distance to the east.

From this vantage point above the crags there are good **views** of Corn Du and Pen y Fan to the east and Fforest Fawr to the west. The bowl-shaped hill is Fan Gyhirych, and to its right and beyond is Bannau Sir Gaer. The summit on its left with the trig point is Fan Nedd.

Leave the top of the crags and follow the track due south, keeping to the crest of the hill, now along the **Beacons Way**, arriving at a cairn just short of the summit of **Fan Dringarth**.

## WALK 24 – FAN FRYNYCH, FAN DRINGARTH AND FAN LLIA

*Pen y Fan and Cribyn from Fan Dringarth*

Below on the left there is evidence of a massive landslide where the side of the summit of Brownstones has broken away leaving a bulge of rocky debris. ▶

Continue following the ridge (SSW) to the slightly higher summit of **Fan Llia**. A little further on are a number of peat pools and the site of an ancient cairn. Looking due south, you will see the prominent ridge of the Rhigos in the distance. Fan Llia is covered by purple moor grass together with mat grass and heath rush. Soft rush is common towards the southern end of the ridge.

The **cairn** provides a reference point to start the descent (SSW) to reach the stream of **Afon Llia**, where the coniferous forestry fence drops down the hillside to the stream bed. Cross the hill fence via a stile and walk back to the start.

Look out for a variety of upland birds.

# WALK 25
## Fan Gyhirych and Fan Nedd

| | |
|---|---|
| **Start/finish** | Devil's Elbow, top of the Senni Bends (SN 923 196) |
| **Distance** | 13km (8 miles) |
| **Total ascent** | 580m (1900ft) |
| **Grade** | 2 |
| **Max elevation** | 725m (2379ft) |
| **Map** | OL12 Western area |

These mountains, which form part of Fforest Fawr, are more rounded and gentler than the high peaks of the Brecon Beacons. The walk includes the summits of Fan Gyhirych and Fan Nedd and, although of reasonable length, is not too strenuous. Ascents and descents are gentle, but there may be some difficulty in route finding in bad weather as the tracks are unfrequented. This area is recommended if you like solitude and there are some fine views to be enjoyed in clear weather.

Start at the top of the Senni Bends and climb over the stile in the hill fence on the right. Follow the path that runs across the face of **Fan Nedd**, ignoring the path that climbs up to the left.

*The valley lying before you is called Blaen Senni. This area is part of Fforest Fawr.*

◀ As you turn the corner, the head of the valley becomes quite steep with a number of Brownstone crags leading down from the summit of Fan Nedd on the left. Before you reach the crags there is a fine panorama with sandstone blocks in the foreground, the head of the U-shaped valley in the middle ground and Fan Gyhirych in the background. Looking back to the north, you will see a patchwork landscape of fields and natural woodland.

As you traverse the slope, the impressive cliff and cusp of Fan Gyhirych can be seen. Look back occasionally for views of the summits of Corn Du and Pen y Fan in the distance.

The slope on the left eases and just before the col, join the permitted route that drops from the summit of Fan Nedd. Continue to the col between the valleys of Blaen Senni and the Nedd. From the col follow the fence on your right. ▶ At the end of the col is a fence and gate with a white arrow indicating a permitted footpath. Follow this sign up to the left.

*The Senni Valley*

This area can be boggy and very wet after a rainy period.

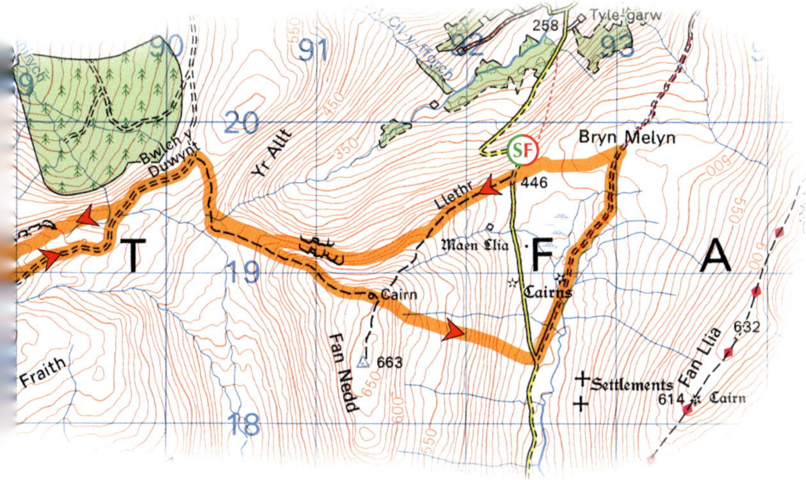

From this point, looking back down the Blaen Senni Valley, there are fine **views** into Cwm-du, the western half of Craig Cerrig Gleisiad a Fan Frynych National Nature Reserve. The line at the top of the green fields is, more or less, where the Roman road of Sarn Helen runs, and to the right of this the two highest peaks of the Brecon Beacons are clearly in view: Corn Du (Black Horn) to the right and Pen y Fan to the left.

## FFOREST FAWR, THE GREAT FOREST OF BRECKNOCK

The broad upland area between Pen y Fan in the east and Carmarthen Fan in the west is known as Fforest Fawr, the Great Forest. The term 'forest' is a legal definition and denotes an area of land set aside for royalty for hunting. Fforest Fawr came under Forest Law after the Norman Conquests of the Welsh Princes in 1066. The formerly wooded valleys provided good cover for game and, in particular, red deer, a truly royal beast and an important source of fresh venison during the winter. The semi-fortified enclosure of Castell Coch, at the confluence of Afon Dringarth and Afon Llia, was located in the heart of the Forest and may well have been the site of the Forest Court, where offenders were tried. By the beginning of the 18th century the last deer had disappeared due to poaching and grazing competition with commoners' flocks of sheep and herds of cattle. Fforest Fawr was divided up by the 1815 Act of Enclosure, and of the original 39,390 acres, 21,484 acres were withdrawn from the common and sold to private landholders. The funds raised by the Crown were supposedly to finance wars but, in fact, were used for the building of Regent Street in London.

About 15 metres past the gatepost, cross a derelict stone wall. Cut across the field, climbing diagonally up the slope to a wire fence. Follow this to the apex of fences. ◄ Nearing the apex of this field, climb over the brow of the hill and directly ahead is a gate in the fence leading to an obvious track. This gate is signposted with a white permitted footpath arrow. Beyond is the impressive sweeping cliff of Fan Gyhirych on the extreme western edge of the Central Brecon Beacons map.

Go straight across the track as the route is made more interesting by skirting around the cwm above the headwall. Rising above the brow of the hill is the fine profile of Bannau Sir Gaer, the Carmarthen Fan. Below to the right is the Cray reservoir and in the foreground is a private forestry

*The Rhigos Mountain forms the skyline to the left.*

## WALK 25 – FAN GYHIRYCH AND FAN NEDD

*A red kite high above the Senni Valley*

plantation. The upper third of the back slope of the cwm in front of Fan Gyhirych is marked by a resistant rock band which marks an abrupt change of slope.

Overgrazing by sheep has resulted in a loss of **heather moorland**, which has been replaced by bent and fescue grassland, often intermixed with mat grass. Britain's only deciduous grass, purple moor grass, grows in wetter areas, such as the moor between Penderyn and the Mellte. Its dead leaves can be found trapped on wire fences after winter storms. Sadly, the Forestry Commission has attempted to drain the land and plant conifers here in the past, causing considerable damage to the peat bog habitat.

As you follow the edge of the cwm, the ground to the right becomes much steeper as you climb the summit of **Fan Gyhirych**.

The surface on this side of the **headwall of Fan Gyhirych** has a crenulated appearance caused by the myriad sheep tracks that have crossed it horizontally; combined with soil creep, this creates a kind of ripple effect. Some of the uppermost ledges are partly inaccessible to grazing sheep and are home to interesting plant life. Green spleenwort, brittle bladder-fern, northern bedstraw, northern beech fern and cliff meadow rue are found here, together with a collection of uncommon bryophytes found only in rocky upland areas.

From the rounded summit of **Fan Gyhirych** look south-west, down to the Neath Valley with Pontneddfechan in the middle ground and the Rhigos massif in the background. On the far horizon, to the south of Fan Gyhirych, is the conspicuous smokestack at Baglan Bay. The stretch of water to the right of this is Mumbles Bay. To the east is Fan Nedd, which has a steep slope to the left. Beyond, in the distance, are the Black Mountains to the left of Pen y Fan. Further to the left of Pen y Fan, you may see the town of Brecon.

From the top of the headwall, cross west to the trig point, which is about 400 metres away. Once at the trig point, look west for a good view of Fan Hir, which leads up to Bannau Sir Gaer. The summit is covered by peat, on which hare's tail grass mire grows. Common cotton-grass can be found, together with wavy hair-grass and heath rush.

Continue west of the trig point for a **view** over the Swansea Valley. Down to the left are the spectacular limestone caves of Dan-yr-Ogof and the high land above is their catchment area. Below the caves you can see, with the aid of binoculars, the house of Madam Adelina Patti, the famous opera soprano. Fan Gyhirych is one of the finest panoramic viewpoints in South Wales.

Retrace your steps from the trig point at the summit and follow the permitted right of way down to the gate where you meet the obvious track again. Retrace your outward route by turning right through a gate indicated by a white path arrow. Head downslope in the direction of **Fan Nedd**,

## WALK 25 – FAN GYHIRYCH AND FAN NEDD

returning to the col, and take the path that winds up the ridge to the **trig point** on the summit.

On the last few stretches of the climb, you come across a number of eroded **peat hags**; the loss of peat here has been slowed down considerably by recolonising plants. Finally, the slope eases as you walk over Nardus grassland gently to the summit. The vegetation here is a mixture of hare's tail grass, mat grass and bilberry, with frequent common cotton-grass, wavy hair-grass and some crowberry growing on peat up to a metre deep.

From the **cairn** on the northern end of the summit of Fan Nedd take a bearing east-south-east, aiming for where the track (Sarn Helen) leaves the road. ▶ Keep an eye out for Maen Llia, down to your left across the road, an impressive standing stone and well worth a visit at the end of the walk.

The eastern slope of Fan Nedd is carpeted in a springy cover of ling in places.

*The impressive Maen Llia standing stone*

*Roman Road Sarn Helen leading towards Bryn Melyn*

**Maen Llia** is a Bronze Age standing stone that has served as a distinctive waymarker for thousands of years. Erected by the Beaker folk about 4000 years ago, it is at least 4m high, 3m across and almost 1m thick and has a mystical aura due, in part, to the mythical story that this huge stone disappears at cockcrow, when it is said to go down to the river to drink.

Cross the stile in the hill fence, over the road and follow the track north-north-east, crossing Rhyd Uchaf. You are now walking in the footsteps of Roman legionnaires on the Roman road of Sarn Helen (see 'Sarn Helen', Walk 23). Leave Sarn Helen just after crossing the next stream gully and head west across **Bryn Melyn**, descending to meet the road and head back to the start at the top of the **Senni Bends**.

# 5 WATERFALL COUNTRY

*Sgwd Clun-gwyn (Walks 27, 29 and 30)*

# WALK 26
*Elidir Trail: Sgwd Gwladus and Sgwd Ddwli waterfalls*

| | |
|---|---|
| **Start/finish** | Pontneddfechan (SN 901 077), postcode SA11 5NR |
| **Distance** | 6.25km (3.9 miles) |
| **Total ascent** | 210m (690ft) |
| **Grade** | 1 |
| **Max elevation** | 175m (574ft) |
| **Map** | OL12 Western area |

This low-level walk takes in the beautiful riverside scenery of the Afon Pyrddin and the Afon Nedd. The route is easy to follow and includes a number of impressive waterfalls, which are usually at their best after heavy rainfall, when the rivers are in full spate. Paths are well marked and no great effort is required to complete the route, even in bad weather. The river geology is interesting and there is also evidence of old industrial and mining activity in the valley along the route. You will find a warm welcome at the Old White Horse Inn, where there is good food, real ale and a warm winter fire to enjoy while you read about the stories encountered on your walk.

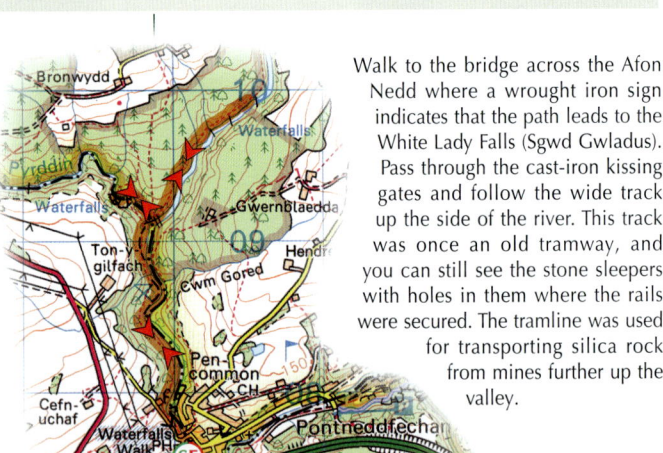

Walk to the bridge across the Afon Nedd where a wrought iron sign indicates that the path leads to the White Lady Falls (Sgwd Gwladus). Pass through the cast-iron kissing gates and follow the wide track up the side of the river. This track was once an old tramway, and you can still see the stone sleepers with holes in them where the rails were secured. The tramline was used for transporting silica rock from mines further up the valley.

There are good exposures of the **rock strata** in a large sandstone cliff to the left of the path. This is the Farewell Rock, so called by miners as it marked the end of the Coal Measures. If you look up at the under surface of the bedding planes, numerous plant fossil fragments can be seen, indicating that these rocks were formed on land some 316 million years ago when Wales was in the tropics. The dip of the Millstone Grit beds to the south is clearly evident, especially in the strata exposed in the river gorge (see 'Geology of Waterfall Country', Walk 30).

### THE TRAVELS OF GIRALDUS CAMBRENSIS – THE ELIDIR TRAIL

Giraldus Cambrensis, also known as Gerald of Wales/Gerallt Gymro, the son of a Norman Baron and a Welsh Princess, wrote *Itinerarium Cambriae* (The Journey through Wales) in the late 12th century. He travelled around Wales spreading propaganda supporting the Crusades, and recorded many interesting stories. One of these concerned Elidyr, who lived in the upper Neath Valley in the fourth century. Elidyr, who was 12 years old, was learning to read but was frequently beaten by his disciplinarian teacher, so to escape his wrath he ran away and hid in a hollow under the banks of the Afon Nedd.

After two days he was hungry and miserable but then two tiny men appeared and offered to take him to a land where all was playtime and pleasure. They led him through an underground tunnel to a beautiful country that was rather dark as the sun did not shine there. The people of this world never lied and lived on a vegetarian diet. Elidyr became friends with the king's son but frequently returned to the upper world where he told only his mother of his adventures. His mother asked him to bring her back a present of gold, a common metal in the land. Elidyr returned with a golden ball, which he stole while playing with the king's son. When he tripped on the doorstep of his house, the little people caught up with him, snatching the ball and running off with it, scorning Elidyr and making derisory remarks. Realising his foolish act, Elidyr ran back to the river but the entrance to the underground tunnel had gone.

The track continues through hazel and sycamore past a number of old mill workings (one on the left has five granite mill stones) and drops back down to the river. The path is wide and suitable for wheelchairs. It passes through a gate or stile where, on the left, there is an old flooded mine working with three adits branching from the entrance.

*Sgwd Gwladus*

On a hot summer's day the air in the **tunnels** is surprisingly cool, but it feels warm and muggy in the winter months, the reason being that air in underground passages remains at a constant temperature of 4°C, regardless of the season. Beyond, on the left, is a bricked entrance to another working, and there are others on the far side of the river where a small side valley, Cwm Gored, branches off.

After a picnic area the path narrows and climbs slightly up some wooden steps, clearly now not suitable for wheelchairs. After a short distance you reach the confluence of the rivers at a deep pool just below a footbridge.

The main route crosses the bridge and turns left following the **Afon Pyrddin** to Sgwd Gwladus. If you are feeling adventurous and fancy walking behind a waterfall

### INDUSTRY ALONG THE NEDD FECHAN

The flooded adits that lead underground on the west side of the Nedd Fechan were once worked for silica, almost 100% SiO2, by about 30 miners. These are just part of a more extensive system of mine workings on both sides of the river. The abutments of three bridges, which once took tramways to the eastern bank, can be seen by the observant walker on the opposite side of the river; one in particular is in good condition on the far side but totally absent from the western bank. Silica mining in the valley began in 1822 and carried on for nearly a hundred years.

William Weston Young discovered how to make firebricks from Dinas Silica. They were used all over Europe and America to line iron- and steel-making furnaces, limekilns and domestic fireplaces. The rock was crushed in the valley and then transported by horse-drawn tram to the firebrick factory at Pont Walby, which closed in 1920.

The hard sandstone was also used for making millstones. You will pass the remains of a double-race mill on the left bank. It was once used to grind corn grown by local farmers. Dinas rock was quarried for limestone, which was transported to Pont Walby where it was crushed and either heated to produce lime for agricultural use or used for road metalling.

do not cross the bridge and continue north-west on the left bank of the Afon Pyrddin to a viewing platform before the fall. Passage behind the fall is only possible if the water levels are low. From the viewing platform, scramble down to the stream bed and pass carefully behind the fall, using the boulders as stepping stones to gain the bank on the other side. These stones are submerged if the river is in spate, and you will have to return to the bridge, cross it and visit Sgwd Gwladus via the northern bank. ▶

After passing behind the fall, you will see an interesting collection of wet-loving plants, such as ferns, up above on the damp rock.

## SGWD GWLADUS

*Sgwd* is Welsh for waterfall and comes from the verb *ysgwd*, which means to toss or fling. This fall has been popular with tourists for many years and is known to English visitors as Lady Falls. The Welsh name comes from Gwladys, a daughter of the fifth-century King Brychan of Brycheiniog, who had 24 daughters and 12 sons! Brychan was, unusually for his time, of Gaelic or Irish descent.

Sgwd Gwladus occurs where the Afon Pyrddin encounters a resistant band of Millstone Grit sandstone. The middle part of the geological formation, known as the Millstone Grit, consists mostly of crumbling black shales but there are also layers of hard sandstone, the most important of which is the Twelve Foot Sandstone, which occurs 13m above the base of the shale division. The general level of the Pyrddin is above the surface of this massive band of grit. Upstream of Sgwd Gwladus, the Pyrddin rapidly cut a steep gorge through the weak upper shales; for some distance the floor of the gorge is the upper surface of the Twelve Foot Sandstone itself. The black shales exposed in the face of the fall are easily eroded by water and, from time to time, blocks of the massive overhanging sandstone bed become undermined to the extent that they collapse. As a result the waterfall is slowly migrating upstream as well as laterally to the west due to the inclination of the strata in this direction.

*Sgwd-y-Bedol*

This is a popular place in warm weather, with swimmers dropping into the pool below from a rope swing.

Ddwli means gushing and these falls really live up to their name when in spate.

Climb up above the fall to the Rocking Stone, a large boulder in the riverbed, which has unfortunately been vandalised and is now immobile. The right bank can be explored for only a short distance upstream before it becomes impassable without wading through the river. From here follow the eastern bank downstream back to the bridge. ◄

Back at the bridge do not cross it but follow the left bank of the Nedd Fechan upstream. A short detour (400 metres) can be made across the bridge to **Cwm Gored**, to visit the entrance to the largest silica mine in the valley.

The path takes you high above the gorge, which has a number of small waterfalls. The path then drops to the level of the river where there are a number of rapids. On the left side, near these falls, is a lovely small stream cascading over moss-covered rocks. As you follow the bend from the rapids, deep river pools can be seen and above these are the photogenic Sgwd-y-Bedol, aptly named the Horseshoe Falls. A little further upstream the river cascades over Sgwd Ddwli Isaf and Sgwd Ddwli Uchaf. ◄

Approach Sgwd Ddwli Isaf either via the flat rocks in the riverbed (if the water is low) or by a track up to the left if they are covered. The falls are in two sections, the second part being higher than the first and in an enclosed cliff area.

To continue upstream from the falls, retrace your steps along the stream bed for about 20 metres to the end of the crags and scramble up the slope to gain the path above. About 50 metres above Sgwd Ddwli Isaf is a pool of about 6m in depth, which was once cut by the Upper Sgwd Ddwli waterfall. This fall is some 200 metres further upstream around a bend in the river. If you are lucky, a dipper may pose in the foreground.

Retrace your steps to the footbridge and back down the western bank of the Afon Nedd to the start in **Pontneddfechan**.

## WALK 27
*Waterfall walk*

| | |
|---|---|
| **Start/finish** | Pontneddfechan (SN 901 077) |
| **Distance** | 15.5km (9.6 miles) |
| **Total ascent** | 510m (1670ft) |
| **Grade** | 2 |
| **Max elevation** | 260m (853ft) |
| **Map** | OL12 Western area |

This classic waterfall walk takes you around the beautiful riverside scenery of the Afon Pyrddin, Afon Nedd, Afon Mellte and Afon Hepste. The route is well defined and includes all the readily accessible impressive cascades in the Waterfall Country. Autumn is the best season to visit, as the route is mostly through deciduous forestry. However, exceptionally hard winters can cause the waterfalls to freeze, providing some spectacular scenes. Although not strenuous in terms of ascents or descents, the distance covered is considerable and the ground may be rough and slippery, so progress can be slow. This is a highly recommended route with some of the finest river scenery in South Wales, but sections can be extremely busy in the summer and at weekends.

Walk to the bridge across the Afon Nedd where a wrought iron sign indicates that the path leads to the Lady Falls (Sgwd Gwladus). Pass through the cast-iron kissing gates and follow the wide track up the left side of the river. This track was once an old tramway, and you can still see the stone sleepers with holes in them where the rails were secured. The tramline was used for transporting silica rock from mines further up the valley (see 'Industry along the Nedd Fechan', Walk 26).

There are good exposures of the **rock strata** in a large sandstone cliff to the left of the path. This is the Farewell Rock, so called by miners as it marked the end of the Coal Measures. If you look up at the bottom of the bedding planes, numerous plant fossil fragments can be seen, indicating that these rocks were formed on land some 316 million years

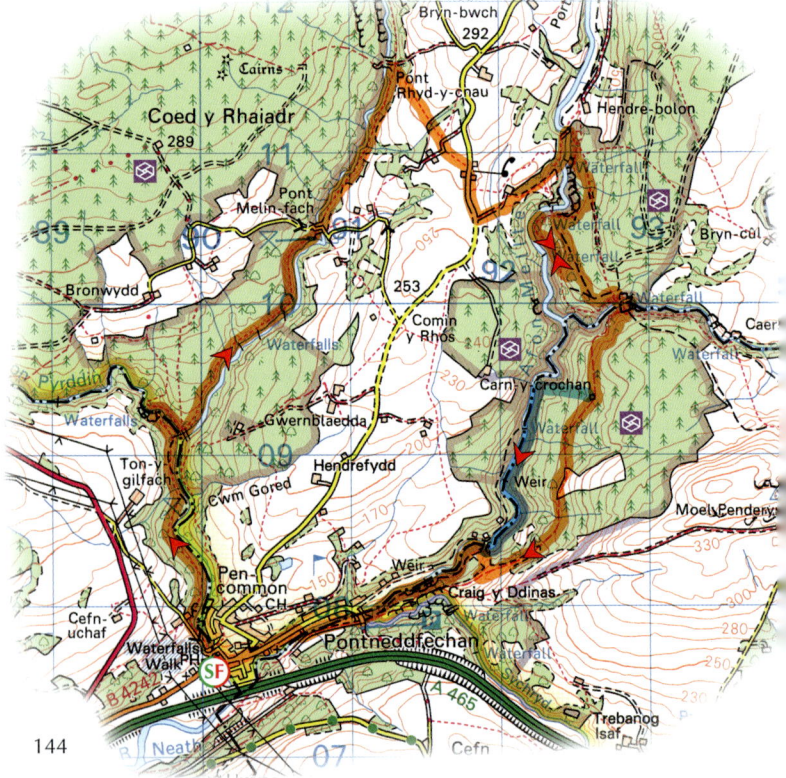

## WALK 27 – WATERFALL WALK

ago when Wales was in the tropics. The dip of the Millstone Grit beds to the south is clearly evident, especially in the strata exposed in the river gorge.

Continue through hazel and sycamore past a number of old mill workings and drop back down to the river. After a picnic area the path narrows and climbs slightly up some wooden steps. A short distance later you reach the confluence of the rivers at a deep pool just below a footbridge. This walk is known as the Elidir Trail (see 'The travels of Giraldus Cambrensis – the Elidir Trail', Walk 26).

The main route crosses the bridge and turns left following the **Afon Pyrddin** to Sgwd Gwladus. If you are feeling adventurous and fancy walking behind a waterfall, do not cross the bridge and continue north-west on the left bank of the Afon Pyrddin to a viewing platform before the fall. Passage behind the fall is only possible if the water levels are low. From the viewing platform, scramble down to the stream bed and pass carefully behind the fall using the boulders as stepping stones to gain the bank on the other side. These stones are submerged if the river is in spate, and you will have to return to the bridge, cross it, and visit Sgwd Gwladus via the northern bank (see 'Sgwd Gwladus', Walk 26). ▶

Climb up above the fall to the Rocking Stone, a large boulder in the riverbed, which has unfortunately been vandalised and is now immobile. From here follow the eastern bank downstream back to the bridge.

Back at the bridge do not cross it but follow the left bank of the Nedd Fechan upstream. As you follow the bend from the rapids, deep river pools can be seen and above these are the photogenic Sgwd-y-Bedol, aptly named the Horseshoe Falls. A little further upstream the river cascades over Sgwd Ddwli Isaf and Sgwd Ddwli Uchaf. ▶

Approach Sgwd Ddwli Isaf either via the flat rocks in the riverbed (if the water is low) or by a track up to the left if they are covered. Sgwd Ddwli Isaf falls are in two sections, the second part being higher than the first and in an enclosed cliff area. To continue upstream from the falls, retrace your steps along the stream bed to the end of the crags and scramble up the slope to gain the path above. About 50 metres above Sgwd Ddwli Isaf is a pool of about 6m in depth, which was once cut by the Upper Sgwd Ddwli waterfall. This fall is

---

After passing behind the fall, you will see up above on the damp rock an interesting collection of wet-loving plants such as ferns.

Ddwli means gushing and these falls really live up to their name when in spate.

145

Sgwd Ddwli Isaf

some 200 metres further upstream around a bend in the river. If you are lucky, a dipper may pose in the foreground.

The route leaves the gorge after the falls and continues along the bank of the river to a picnic area and car park. Turn right across **Pont Melin-fach** and immediately left over a stile, now following the path along the right-hand bank of the stream signed to Pont Rhyd-y-cnau. The path drops to river level and, in a short distance, passes under a small cliff. This may be difficult when the river is in flood and the stones are slippery. In these conditions this section may be passed at a higher level. ◀

*Look out for dippers and wagtails in the stream bed.*

Eventually, it becomes impossible to follow the path at river level and the route skirts below the next set of crags, climbing up to the top of the bank. Climb up to a high level opposite this – the more adventurous can follow the narrow path behind the holly. There is a pleasant plunging waterfall on the opposite bank. This is a spectacular wooded area with boulders covered in a variety of mosses. The closer you stay to the edge, the more exciting – or dangerous – the walk becomes. The river takes a contorted route through steep gorge walls with the odd small waterfall and deep pool. The banks of the river are covered mainly with hazel, ash, holly, rowan and sycamore.

*Other tree species include silver birch and oak.*

The right of way marked on the map runs across the top of the cliff but the walk is more interesting if you follow the bank as far as conditions will allow. ◀ The gorge walls are formed from erosion-resistant Millstone Grit and along this stretch you can see good examples of stratification.

Follow your preferred route here, staying close to the river with some scrambling across boulders, and then strike up right to a stile. Drop again to the river and continue north if water levels allow. This area is well populated with small woodland birds, and herons are commonly seen along the river. Late April is a good time of year to visit, when all the woodland flowers are in bloom.

Just before **Pont Rhyd-y-cnau**, a footpath leaves on your right. Take this south-east across the fields to join a road on a bend. Carry straight on to the next right-angled bend and take the footpath signposted to Capel Hermon. Take the farm track to a stile on the left and a second stile. Cross this and aim straight across the field to a stile opposite a church.

Turn right down the road, cross a cattle grid and just after this, on the left, is a car park. Take the track on the left to a gate and information board about Waterfall Country.

After about 60 metres follow the fingerpost, which directs you right at a fork in the track. Soon you will hear the roar of the Afon Mellte as it plunges over the waterfall of Sgwd Clun-gwyn. Drop through the woods to a junction of paths with the waterfall straight ahead. Ignore the turning back to the right and continue left along the western bank, descending the steep slope to the top of the fall. ▶

From the top of Sgwd Clun-gwyn the adventurous can leap across the river just above the fall where the water runs in a narrow channel. Otherwise, and if the river is in spate, walk upstream a few hundred metres to a bridge. Cross this, turn right and follow the green waymarked path that climbs diagonally up the slope through woodland to meet the red waymarked path at fingerpost 12. Turn right (signed 'Sgwd yr Eira') and at fingerpost 13 make a short two-minute detour to a viewing area of Sgwd Clun-gwyn (White Meadow Fall).

*The deep pools above the fall are ideal for a refreshing dip on warm summer days.*

### SGWD CLUN-GWYN

Sgwd Clun-gwyn is found on the Afon Mellte where it tumbles over a massive band of resistant Millstone Grit sandstone. The lower parts of the fall can be explored by scrambling down its side, using tree roots and good rock handholds, to a middle terrace and then down to the stream bed. When only a little water is flowing, it is possible to walk along the middle terrace for a closer look at the mosses and ferns that thrive in this very damp environment. A deep trough has been carved at the bottom of the fall by the tremendous scouring power of the falling water.

The fall was formed by earth movements bringing shales of the middle Millstone Grit into contact with the pebbly grit that constitutes the lowest stratigraphical member of the same formation. The weak shales are downstream of this geological fault, which now forms the near-vertical face of the waterfall. This same fault crosses the Hepste around 1km to the south-south-east, but the amount of earth movement dies out in this direction and an obvious feature has not formed in the Hepste. The shales were rapidly eroded by tumbling water and have, in fact, been removed completely downstream of the fall, as the river now runs across the same sandstone surface below the fall as it does above. This massive band of sandstone, known as the Twelve Foot Sandstone, is the same as the overhanging bed over which Sgwd Gwladus plunges. The fall has been working its way to the east as the tilt of the sandstone bedding forces the water in this direction.

A cross-section of the fault can be found clearly exposed on the eastern bank in line with the top of the waterfall. The fact that the fault plane which forms the face of the waterfall is still in line with the trace of the fault in the bank means that Sgwd Clun-gwyn has, unusually, not migrated upstream since its inception, in stark contrast with Sgwd yr Eira.

*Sgwd y Pannwr, the Fall of the Fuller or the Fall of the Wool Washer*

# WALK 27 – WATERFALL WALK

Return to the main path and continue above the gorge, signposted 'Sgwd yr Eira'.

Continue on the main route, which runs along the top of the gorge on even ground, to fingerpost 25 where you turn right on a green link path to Sgwd y Pannwr (Fall of the Fuller). From the picturesque fall proceed upstream, close to the riverbank, on an even and well-made path past waymarker 32 to the next falls. From this point, the lower section of Sgwd Isaf Clun-gwyn can be explored with a fine view of the Mellte as it tumbles through the gorge.

## SGWD ISAF CLUN-GWYN

*Sgwd Isaf Clun-gwyn*

This complex of cascades was formed by two parallel faults, fractures in the earth's crust, which brought a long narrow band of pebbly sandstones to the surface. The Mellte generally flows north–south along the outcrop of the Middle Shales of the Millstone Grit, but the band of pebbly sandstone deflects its course to the west, crossing the sandstone by the shortest route and then turning south again once on a narrow tract of shale between the Farewell Rock (the Upper Millstone Grit sandstone) to the west and pebbly sandstone to the east. This present course is anomalous, as the river would not change direction to the west in order to cross a resistant band of rock when by continuing due south it would remain on weaker shales. The likely explanation for this strange course is that it was predetermined by a fault in the shale that overlay the faulted wedge of grit. This shale was then removed by erosion but the stream continued to flow in the same direction, a phenomenon known as superimposed drainage.

Retrace your steps to Sgwd y Pannwr and climb out of the gorge on the route you used earlier. Turn right where the green link path joins the red path at fingerpost 25 and your route then swings east along the top of the Hepste gorge to fingerpost 35. Turn right here and descend the steps to Sgwd yr Eira.

If there is a lot of water flowing, the wall on the left is quite wet and waterproofs are recommended (see 'Sgwd yr Eira', Walk 28).

After passing behind Sgwd yr Eira, the path leads up the steep slope to the left and out of the gorge. Take the path signposted to Craig y Ddinas to the right.

The path, which ascends out of the gorge, crosses a steep gully that has a geological fault running through it. This was responsible for the original formation of the waterfall, which has since retreated upstream.

## ANCIENT WOODLAND

Woodland clinging to the gorge walls of the Afon Mellte, Hepste, Sychryd, Nedd and Pyrddin forms one of the richest and most extensive areas of ancient semi-natural woodland in Wales. A wide variety of botanical types have been identified, ten in all, ranging from ash-maple woods on limestone to sessile oak-downy birch-wood sorrel types on Millstone Grit. Downy birch-purple moor grass and alder-ash woods are found on wet ground conditions. Wet flushes in this type of woodland provide a home for marsh hawk's-beard, its most southerly locality in Britain.

The sheer steepness and inaccessibility of the gorge walls have prevented timber exploitation in the past, leaving an ancient woodland almost untouched by man in places. Only small pockets of truly ancient woodland survive today in Britain. Small-leaved lime thrives on cliff edges and steep slopes and is found together with wood fescue grass. The undisturbed nature of the woodland means that it still has its rich complement of woodland-associated species, including a number of rare ferns: Wilson's filmy fern, Tunbridge filmy fern, hay-scented fern and rare liverworts, mosses and lichens. These are found in a variety of habitats, such as boulder scree, cliff faces, springs, decaying wood, ancient trees and numerous niches associated with streams and rivers.

The path leaves the top of the gorge and heads south. The hill ahead in the distance is the Rhigos Mountain, which has a number of glacial corries. Beyond it is the South Wales Coalfield, and the valley to the south-west is the Neath.

## WALK 27 – WATERFALL WALK

The route swings right and down towards the gorge around the ruins of Cilhepste-fach. ▶

A more adventurous option leaves from here.

Take the next footpath on the right marked with a finger post that you encounter, where the path that you are on starts to descend a spur of land, to a wooden bridge. This part of the Mellte valley was once a hive of industrial activity and was home to Glynneath Gunpowder Works (see 'Glynneath Gunpowder Works', Walk 29). Evidence of this industrial heritage can be found further upstream on both sides of the river and is worth exploring.

Do not cross the wooden bridge but take the path that stays close to the river, past the end of a recently built metal bridge over the Afon Mellte, and follow this to the car park and the impressive cliff of **Craig y Ddinas** (see 'Craig y Ddinas', Walk 28). An old tram route once ran past the cliff, connecting the silica mine with the Vale of Neath Canal. ▶

The extended walk to the Sychryd Valley leaves from here.

*Waterfall on the Afon Mellte*

## RIVERS OF WATERFALL COUNTRY

The rivers that comprise Waterfall Country are the Mellte, Hepste, Sychryd, Pyrddin and the upper parts of the Neath, which all originally flowed into the Cynon Valley to the south-west. Earth movements during late Tertiary times uplifted this area, accelerating the rate at which the rivers of South Wales were carving valleys. The River Neath was particularly rejuvenated and greatly extended its course north-east, using a line of weakness along a narrow belt of greatly folded and faulted rocks, the Neath Disturbance. The River Neath managed to capture the rivers of Waterfall Country so that they flowed faster into the lower levels of the Neath. The revitalised rivers cut steep-sided gorges as the many waterfalls receded upstream.

To continue on the main route follow the road out of the car park and turn left before the bridge and then bear right onto a bridleway that runs parallel to the river. Take the next right, cross the footbridge to the road and turn left back to the start in **Pontneddfechan**.

*Sgwd Ddwli Uchaf from the West*

### Alternative route

Leave the waymarked footpath at the right-angled bend in the path at Cilhepste-fach, following the ride which runs west. Pick up the line of a collapsed stone wall and look out for a conspicuous oak tree near the edge of the gorge at the end of a spur of land. This marks the beginning of the steep descent of an ill-defined zigzag path that leads to an easy path along the eastern bank of the river below. On reaching this path, turn left and walk downstream to the last waterfall on the Hepste, which is in two tiers. Continue past a small brick structure and on to the **weir**. ◄

From the weir continue along the side of the river to join a path. Turn right and descend down to the wooden bridge. You rejoin the main route here.

The extensive collection of ruined buildings, weirs and leats in the lower reaches of the valley were once a gunpowder works.

### Extension

From Craig y Ddinas, there is an option to visit the Sychryd Valley with its waterfalls and silica mines. Take the footpath leading to the right of the crags and enter the narrow gorge with the stream below on the right. Rounding the corner, pass below an impressive cliff. Further up, this gorge becomes very narrow and the river tumbles down over a series of rocks at Sgydau Sychryd. The spectacular rock exposure at the entrance to the gorge on the right is called Bwa Maen. This impressive fold can only be clearly seen during winter months when it is not obscured by foliage.

> **Bwa Maen** means 'bow rock' and well describes the spectacularly exposed arch-like fold with a sharp crest. If you look closely at the large boulders that have fallen from the roof of a cave, you will see that the rounded, convex surfaces have small grooves. These were formed by the beds of rock rubbing together when they folded. The Carboniferous limestone was squeezed into this contorted feature by the Armorican earth movements associated with the Neath Disturbance. A fault occurs immediately to the left of Bwa Maen, along which the Sychryd now flows.

Retrace your steps back to Craig y Ddinas and continue on the main route back to the start of the walk.

# WALK 28
## Sgwd yr Eira

| | |
|---|---|
| **Start/finish** | Penderyn (SN 945 089) |
| **Distance** | 10km (6.2 miles) |
| **Total ascent** | 410m (1340ft) |
| **Grade** | 2 |
| **Max elevation** | 371m (1217ft) |
| **Map** | OL12 Western area |

This excellent walk, packed full of interest, culminates in an unforgettable experience of walking behind a waterfall. An initial easy ascent of Moel Penderyn is followed by an exploration of the Sychryd and Hepste valleys, where you will see evidence of a busy industrial past. Old ruins are left behind as you wind your way through the picturesque Hepste gorge with its tumbling river and steep slopes covered in ancient woodland. The best is left to last, when you climb out of the Hepste Valley and drop into the Mellte gorge and walk behind Sgwd yr Eira (Fall of Snow). The paths are reasonably easy to follow and there are good views in the early parts of the walk, followed by spectacular river scenery. The Red Lion, a few hundred metres south of the end of this walk, is full of character and has fine ales and open fires.

From Penderyn take the track (W) towards the old quarries through a gate with the national park arrow marking the route. Continue straight ahead to another gate and cross the stile. Turn immediately left following the hill fence, leaving some quarry spoils on your right. Work your way up to the col ahead and then leave the fence and cross west to the summit of **Moel Penderyn**, marked by a trig point.

North and slightly west from here you can see Fan Nedd with the Carmarthen Fans further to the west. North-east lie the Brecon Beacons.

There are many clues on the map as to the rock type of this area, such as numerous 'Areas of Shake Holes' and 'Swallow Holes'. These are typical of **limestone country** and, in fact, this area is a

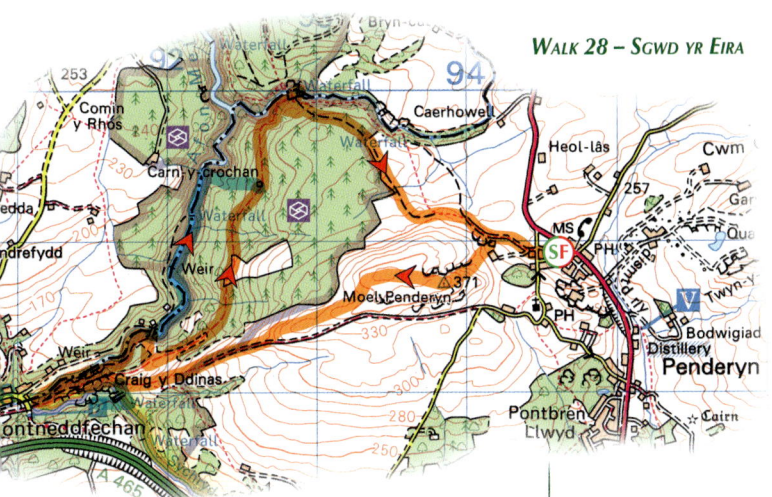

honeycomb of underground passages. The limestone is mostly capped by a layer of Millstone Grit. Swallow holes literally swallow streams when they disappear underground, whereas shake holes are formed when the roof of an underground chamber or passage caves in. The Millstone Grit has often collapsed when the limestone beneath has been dissolved away. The Afon Hepste has changed its underground course many times, moving further south and west, leaving behind an extensive system of caves with spectacular stalagmites and stalactites. Limestone is mainly composed of calcium carbonate, which is slightly soluble in water. Limestone is more vigorously dissolved if weak acids are present in the water. In fact, the groundwater that formed the remarkable cave systems in South Wales is slightly acidic – a result of acid rain, humic acids produced in soil and the breakdown of coniferous pine needles.

To the east is the massive limestone quarry (Cwar Llwynon), overlooking the village. To the south-east is the Cynon Valley and over to the south-west is the Rhigos Mountain with open-cast coal mines on its flanks. Beyond and due west is the Swansea Valley.

Walk due west along the crest of the ridge. A close look at the rock outcrops here reveals that the limestone pavement has been polished by water, indicating that this area once suffered the powerful scouring action of a stream. Beyond the ridge is a bilberry and cotton-grass heath.

**Moel Penderyn** is also geologically interesting for a different reason. Compressive forces in the earth's crust have pushed the rock strata into the form of an elongated dome called a pericline. The axis of this fold, known as the Penderyn Anticline, runs for many kilometres north-eastwards into the Old Red Sandstone and south-westwards into the Coal Measures. This fold was formed during the Caledonian mountain-building period as a result of north-westward compression.

Drop left before you reach a forestry fence to a track known as 'the Ridgeway', an old drovers' road that connected Penderyn with Pontneddfechan. Follow this through a gate, heading in the direction of the head of the Neath Valley, dropping over the brow of the hill. Pass the ruins of Clwyd-rhyd-fan to reach mixed woodland. The track winds between spoil heaps from old silica mines to a wooden sign with a marker pointing back to Penderyn. ◄ At this point you can either take the rising track ahead to **Craig y Ddinas** or, for the first alternative route, take the path off to the left, signposted to the silica mines.

> Looking back, you can see the entrance to some of the mines.

### CRAIG Y DDINAS

Craig y Ddinas is a 50m high limestone cliff of great geological significance, as the continuation of the Vale of Neath Disturbance runs through it. Its name comes from the Iron Age earthworks on its summit, and it is reputed to be one of the last places where fairies lived in Britain.

The contorted limestone strata here are the surface evidence of enormous crustal earth movements, which took place along lines of weakness known as geological faults. The tilted limestone beds of the near-vertical face provide challenging rock-climbing routes, whereas the easy cliffs to its right are popular with beginners learning to climb and abseil. Legend claims that a nearby cave is the final resting place of King Arthur and the Knights of the Round Table, who lie in wait to be called to defend Britain.

## WALK 28 – SGWD YR EIRA

On the left of the crag is an advised path sign, but just opposite the last bay of the car park take a small path down to the left to the riverbed, where there is a sign for the gunpowder works.

Down to the left of the **Afon Mellte** and just beyond is a steep bank that divides the river from a large lagoon. Follow the path which drops to river level. The path passes through mainly hazel, birch and ash woodland (see 'Ancient woodland', Walk 27). It then climbs again, leaving a steep drop to the water below. Further evidence of this area's industrial past can be seen on the opposite side of the river where there is a man-made sluice.

*Windblown trees above Afon Mellte*

About a kilometre from Craig y Ddinas there is a **weir** with a steel cable crossing from a stilling well on the opposite bank. This is used to measure the rise and fall of the river. The path climbs to the right, leaving the river and passing through beech woodland and beds of wild garlic. Look out for a disused mine adit on the right-hand side.

As you leave the wood the track divides. Take the left branch level with the riverbed. ◄ The path follows a bend in the river, arriving at some old workings represented by a stone wall and river race that were once connected with the Glynneath Gunpowder Works (see 'Glynneath Gunpowder Works', Walk 29). Beyond is a wooden bridge built by Norwegians, and it is worth exploring this area where you will find more remains of the works on both sides of the river upstream from the bridge.

*The conifers ahead were planted just after World War 2.*

The main route turns right at the bridge, on the path that climbs up the hillside, but the second alternative option can be taken here should you wish. The path brings you to the bridleway that climbs up from Craig y Ddinas. Turn left here and follow the signs to Sgwd yr Eira.

The track bears slightly right when it meets the Hepste Valley. ◄ Descend into the Hepste gorge at the fingerpost and interpretation board.

*Look carefully here for orchids flowering in spring.*

**Geological cross-section through Sgwd yr Eira**

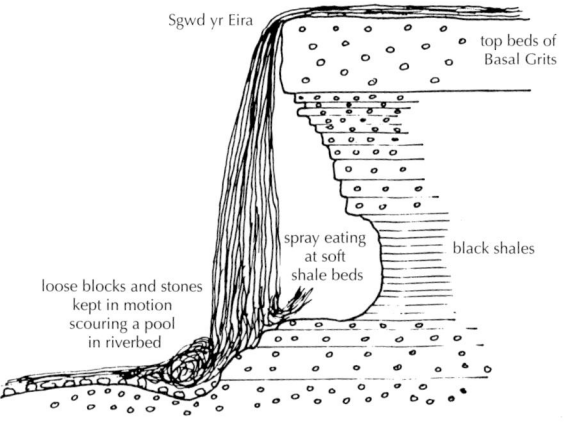

The path crosses a steep gully that formed due to a **geological fault** running through it, weakening the rock. This fault was also responsible for the original formation of the waterfall, which has since retreated upstream.

## SGWD YR EIRA

Of all the falls in the Brecon Beacons National Park, this is the most exciting to visit. It provides the unforgettable experience of walking behind a moving curtain of thundering water. The character of the fall is the result of the local geology. Notice when you stand behind the fall that your feet are on hard sandstone but that the rocks in a 1.5m recessed band at the base of the cliff are relatively weak, thinly bedded shales that crumble away easily. This band is very conspicuous as it is covered in wet-loving vegetation. The rocks above are of a more resistant sandstone but are weakened by numerous bedding planes. The final massive band of sandstone, which forms the protruding shelf over which the water tumbles, is the strongest and so is the most resistant to collapse, resulting in the fall being thrown out spectacularly into space.

*Visitors behind Sgwd yr Eira falls*

The fall developed where a geological fault caused the river to flow from hard sandstone onto soft shales. Removal of the shales undermines the sandstone beds above, causing the waterfall to migrate upstream, now over 70 metres from where the fault crosses the gorge. This point is marked by a gully in the southern side of the gorge, which formed in response to a weakening of the rocks by movement along the fault. This fall shares many characteristics in its formation with the famous Niagara Falls. Amazingly, the fall has frozen in severe winters. Adventurous canoeists have actually shot this fall and, for a short time, the record for the highest drop by canoe in Britain was held here.

After exploring behind the waterfall, return up the steps, turn left and follow the signpost to Penderyn.

> Just around the next bend are a group of four or five large **boulders**. These are a geological oddity as their rock type is not found in the national park. They were, in fact, transported by glaciers from much further afield during the Ice Age and are known as glacial erratics.

This waymarked path brings you back to the start in Penderyn.

**First alternative route**
Take the left turn, signposted to the Dinas Rock Silica Mines, and head down steps to the river. Cross the river bridge by the silica mines, turn right and then climb up left onto the ridge through oak, beech and hawthorn woodland to a large concrete block on the right with metal stanchions let into it.

> These concrete stanchions are all that remains of an unusual aerial ropeway used to transport stone from the **mine** to level ground near Craig y Ddinas. The silica was mined underground and an extensive labyrinth of hallways and passageways remain today, many of which are now flooded with crystal-clear water. They produced large quantities of very pure silica sandstone that was crushed and then used to make refractory bricks for furnace linings.

After exploring the area, retrace your steps back to rejoin the main route.

**Second alternative route**
At the Norwegian bridge, turn right on the path that ascends the slope and look carefully for a small path that leaves on the on the left. The best time to visit this area is early morning when no one else is around. This is when the woods are full of birdsong and you have the best chance of seeing dippers, herons and other birds along the stream course.

The river is forced into a much narrower channel with a number of small waterfalls. Make a short detour here, dropping down to the left to explore the falls and also a fine exposure of Millstone Grit in the opposite bank. ▶ Above are numerous disused workings. The path now climbs and then drops again to the river.

Old iron panels can be seen in the riverbed, and across on the opposite bank there are numerous ruined stone buildings among conifers. Continue to some old stone piers at a former bridging point. Here you can explore an assortment of sluices and weirs that once provided the power for the gunpowder works (see 'Glynneath Gunpowder Works', Walk 29).

From the weir continue upstream, past a small stone structure on the right, to the first **waterfall**. At the entrance to the pond below the fall the river has breached a band of Millstone Grit, and the water actually runs down the dip slope of the bedding plane. The waterfall just beyond has been formed by a resistant band of sandstone. Pass this fall up to the right, crossing a wide boulder-filled gully. There are good exposures in the right-hand wall of well-cleaved Millstone Grit. Leaving the gully, take the path that goes up to the right.

The gorge continues to narrow as you progress upstream, with a steep drop from the path to the river. Both sides of the valley are wooded (see 'Ancient woodland', Walk 27). Rounding the bend, the river straightens into a narrow channel with a number of small falls. The river then swings to the right around a spur of land. Eventually, the path reaches a high point but do not descend where the path drops to river level. This is just before the river swings into a left-hand bend and the gorge further on soon becomes impassable. If you miss this point, retrace your steps to where the path reaches the crest of a small rise.

At the high point on the path is a steep, grassy, wooded slope leading up to the horizon. Make your way up this past an oak tree, passing a small rock outcrop on the right-hand side. There is no clear path at first but keep on the arête of the hill, meeting a path that zigzags up to a large oak tree on the left. From here continue due east to coniferous forestry on the right. Follow a low stone wall on the left which meets the track from Craig y Ddinas at the ruins of Cilhepste-fach where you join the main route.

> The dip of the rocks to the south is clearly evident here.

# WALK 29
## Ystradfellte Falls

| | |
|---|---|
| Start/finish | Car park (SN 919 106), postcode SA11 5US |
| Distance | 10km (6.2 miles) |
| Total ascent | 410m (1350ft) |
| Grade | 2 |
| Max elevation | 254m (833ft) |
| Map | OL12 Western area |

Ystradfellte Waterfall Country has been famous for its natural beauty for many years. This varied route visits the spectacular waterfalls and steep wooded gorges of this area, taking in true ancient woodland, a rich industrial past and excellent geological and geomorphological features. It is quite a long walk along muddy and sometimes slippery river paths, but there should be no difficulty in route finding if the directions are followed carefully.

From the car park walk south on the road and take the footpath on the left, signposted 'Comin y Rhos', which cuts south-south-west across the field to the corner of the coniferous forestry. If this is too wet to cross, walk down the road, leaving it where a road leaves to the right, and take the path to the left across the common to pick up the route at the far corner of the conifer plantation where there is a gate in a fence. Turn right at this gate.

Cross over a stile marked with a yellow national park arrow and continue following the ditch on the left across a field with gorse, silver birch and alder to your left. On the right you can see the farm buildings of Pentred'rysgoed. Cross this field and go over a stile, keeping the ditch on the left, where you pick up the farm track. After about 60 metres the track reaches a gate with another yellow arrow.

Immediately through the gate turn left to the bank of the stream and regain the right of way with the old wall on the right. Shortly, join the farm track and continue down it to a large gate. Beyond this, keep on the track which crosses poor grazing land and runs through a gap in a wall at two solid fence posts.

## WALK 29 – YSTRADFELLTE FALLS

Bear right, south-west, along the south side of the wall by field maple, mountain ash and hawthorn to the junction of several walls. ▶ Head across the bracken-covered field ahead in a south-westerly direction to a junction of several collapsed stone walls. Continue in the same direction, following the wall which leads down the crest of the ridge in the direction of the Neath Valley. The wall more or less disappears but from here you will be able to see the boundary of the golf course. From this point, cut right to a stile in this wall at the apex of the course, marked by a small viewing tower.

You may be lucky enough to see curlews here.

Cross over the stile and proceed along the right of way with a stone wall to the right. From the most southerly tip of this path, before it bends to the right and into the valley, make for the spur of land between a golf tee and green where there are wooden electricity poles. Continue to a stile with a yellow waymarker and drop down the wooded spur, bearing sharply right to a stream on the right and so to some houses.

Turn left round the front of the houses and cross the river by the bridge, below which is the confluence of the Mellte and the Sychryd rivers. Turn left with **Craig y Ddinas** straight ahead. On the left of the crag is an advised path sign, but just before the crag take a small path down to the left to the riverbed, where there is a sign for the gunpowder works.

Down to the left of the **Afon Mellte** and just beyond is a steep bank that divides the river from a large lagoon.

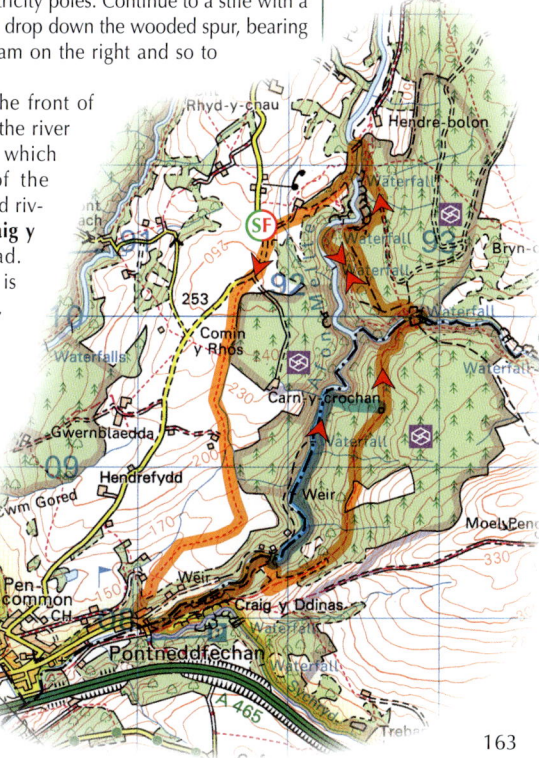

163

*Further evidence of this area's industrial past can be seen on the opposite side of the river where there is a man-made sluice.*

Follow the path which drops to river level. The path passes through mainly hazel, birch and ash woodland. It then climbs again, leaving a steep drop to the water below. ◄

About a kilometre from Craig y Ddinas there is a **weir** with a steel cable crossing from a stilling well on the opposite bank. This is used to measure the rise and fall of the river. The path climbs steeply to the right, leaving the river and passing through beech woodland and beds of wild garlic. Look out for a disused mine adit on the right-hand side.

*The conifers ahead were planted just after World War 2.*

As you leave the wood the track divides. Take the left branch level with the riverbed. ◄ The path follows a bend in the river, arriving at some old workings represented by a stone wall and river race. Beyond is a wooden bridge built by Norwegians. This area was once a hive of industrial activity and it is worth exploring the remains of the Glynneath Gunpowder Works, more of which can be found further upstream on both sides of the river.

### GLYNNEATH GUNPOWDER WORKS

Alongside the Mellte was a gunpowder works, which was unique in Wales at the time. The first owners were the Vale of Neath Powder Company, who started manufacturing in 1857, but in 1862 Curtis and Harvey took over the works and eventually renamed it Nobel's Explosives Company. In 1926 it became part of Imperial Chemical Industries Limited. The site was understandably chosen for its isolation, while the river supplied power and the woodland was used for making charcoal. The site covered about 180 acres, stretching for nearly two miles, which meant that any explosion could be contained.

*The old gunpowder works*

## WALK 29 – YSTRADFELLTE FALLS

> The works are largely in ruins today but stonework and remnants of buildings can still be seen, many of which have only three remaining walls, as the fourth wall and roof were made of timber, which would be blown off if an explosion occurred. The buildings were separated by banks of earth and many were whitewashed, so that an accumulation of gunpowder could be spotted easily. Workers wore special safety slippers made of leather, and women were banned from wearing metal hairpins. Work commenced at 7.30 am and nothing likely to cause a spark could be taken into the buildings. The gunpowder produced here was principally used in coal mines and quarries, including the slate quarries of North Wales. The head of water that fed the waterwheels, which powered the machinery, was supplied via two weirs and a series of leats. Raw materials were hauled on a tramway by horses shod with copper shoes to prevent sparks.

The main route turns right at the bridge on the path that climbs up the hillside but an alternative can be taken here that continues through the gorge with the path coming close to some steep drops.

The main route turns left when it joins the path that comes up from Craig y Ddinas. Follow this to a fingerpost indicating the descent down to Sgwd yr Eira.

The sides of the Hepste gorge are very steep, which, in fact, has prevented the woodland here from being felled. This is an area of genuine ancient woodland, which means that this is a completely natural habitat that has not been interfered with by man (see 'Ancient woodland', Walk 27). Drop steeply down wooden steps towards the river and walk behind Sgwd yr Eira. ▶ Passing behind the falls is one of the most memorable experiences in the national park (see 'Sgwd y Eira', Walk 28). A short excursion can be made by staying alongside the riverbank and descending the gorge. Soon you come across a series of cascades called the Lower Cilhepste Falls. This is an exciting place to explore and discover how these falls were formed. Retrace your steps to join the main route again at the base of the climb out of the gorge.

*The gully you have just crossed on your descent is where the geological fault originally responsible for the creation of the fall lies.*

## LOWER CILHEPSTE FALLS

This part of the gorge is where the Afon Hepste plunges over 70m down a number of steps to reach the confluence with the Afon Mellte. The Hepste gorge has been left as a hanging valley above the Mellte, and these multiple cascades have formed where the steepest gradient is found and where a geological fault crosses the gorge. This same fault is responsible for Sgwd Isaf Clun-gwyn, where it crosses the Mellte. The Mellte was able to capture the Hepste, as its valley is much lower than the Hepste. This triggered a period of rapid erosion in the Hepste, which is at its most active at these falls. The gorge is known as Devil's Glen and is supposed to be inhabited by all manner of otherworldly folk, including ghosts and fairies.

Climb the hillside by the steps, turn left at the top at fingerpost 35 and follow the path to where there is a sign for Sgwd y Pannwr at fingerpost 25. Descend to the gorge, now formed by the Afon Mellte, to Sgwd y Pannwr 'Fall of the Fuller'. Continue upstream along the riverbank to the base of the Sgwd Isaf Clun-Gwyn.

Retrace your steps to Sgwd y Pannwr and climb out of the gorge on the route you used earlier. Turn left where the green-waymarked link path joins the red path at fingerpost 25 and continue following the path above the gorge to fingerpost 12, where you can make a short detour to a viewing area for Sgwd Clun-gwyn. Continue along the main route and then bear left on the path that drops down the valley side to a bridge. Cross this and turn left, following the path running downstream to the top of the falls.

The deep pools above the fall are ideal for a refreshing dip on warm summer days, and the falls' ledge is a good place to learn more about its history (see 'Sgwd Clun-gwyn', Walk 27).

From the top of the fall ascend the path up to the left through oak and hawthorn woodland. The track climbs more steeply to an open area and a gate by the farmhouse of Clungwyn. Cross the stile and turn left (S) and back to the start.

### Alternative route

For a slightly more adventurous option, at the bridge take the path that climbs to the right and then take a small path that leaves on the left that runs along the side of the gorge with the river down below. Continue along the path, now with an alder wood growing in a boggy area to your right. The

*Falls on Afon Mellte*

best time to visit this area is early morning when no one else is around. This is when the woods are full of birdsong and you have the best chance of seeing dippers, herons and other birds along the stream course.

The river is forced into a much narrower channel with a number of small falls. Make a short detour here, dropping down left to explore the falls as well as a fine exposure of Millstone Grit in the opposite bank. ◄ Above are numerous disused workings. The path now climbs and then drops again to the river.

The dip of the rocks to the south is clearly evident here.

Old iron panels can be seen in the riverbed, and across on the opposite bank there are numerous ruined stone buildings among conifers. Continue to some old stone piers at a former bridging point. Here you can explore an assortment of sluices and weirs that once provided the power for the gunpowder works.

From the weir, continue upstream past a small stone structure on the right to the first **waterfall**. At the entrance to the pond below the fall the river has breached a band of Millstone Grit, and the water actually runs down the dip slope of the bedding plane. The waterfall just beyond has been formed by a resistant band of sandstone. Pass this fall up to the right, crossing a wide boulder-filled gully. There are good exposures of well-cleaved Millstone Grit in the right-hand wall. Leaving the gully, take the path that goes up to the right.

The gorge narrows as you progress upstream, with a steep drop from the path to the river. Both sides of the valley are wooded (see 'Ancient woodland', Walk 27). Rounding the bend, the river straightens into a narrow channel with a number of small falls. The river then swings to the right around a spur of land. Eventually, the path reaches a high point but do not descend where the path drops to river level. This is just before the river swings into a left-hand bend and the gorge further on soon becomes impassable. If you miss this point, retrace your steps to where the path reaches the crest of a small rise.

At the high point on the path there is a steep, grassy, wooded slope leading up to the horizon. Make your way up this past an oak tree, keeping a small rock outcrop on the right-hand side. There is no clear path at first but keep on the arête of the hill, meeting a path that zigzags upwards. ◄

*From here there are excellent views north of the interlocking spurs of this valley.*

Continue east along a flattish section to a large oak tree on the left. East from here, a path leads along the side of a ditch on the left to a broken-down wall. The path swings to the right (with the wall on the left) and joins the path that comes up from Craig y Ddinas at Cilhepste-fach. Rejoin the main route here by turning left and on to the path to Sgwd yr Eira.

# WALK 30
*Afon Nedd and Afon Mellte*

| | |
|---|---|
| **Start/finish** | Pont Melin-fach car park (SN 908 105) |
| **Distance** | 11.5km (7.1 miles) |
| **Total ascent** | 305m (1000ft) |
| **Grade** | 1 |
| **Max elevation** | 368m (1207ft) |
| **Map** | OL12 Western area |

Travelling northwards along the banks of the Afon Nedd, this route takes in one of the most interesting and impressive natural features in the area – Pwll-y-rhyd cave. It then crosses a limestone plateau into the Ystradfellte Valley and descends the Afon Mellte past impressive waterfalls. The route is not well frequented, at least in its early stages, and can be quite difficult to follow in places. There can be some problems in route finding as the path often leaves the river, and the passage over the limestone plateau in the north requires good map-reading skills. Also, in wet weather the rocks can be quite slippery under foot. The geology of the valleys, moving from grit to limestone, is interesting and there is an Iron Age fort to the north.

Leave the car park to the north and cross over the bridge. Turn immediately left, cross over a stile and follow the path along the right-hand bank of the stream, signed to Pont Rhyd-y-cnau. The path drops to river level and, in a short distance, passes under a small cliff. This may be difficult when the river is in flood and the stones are slippery. In these conditions this section can be passed at a higher level. ▶

> Look out for dippers and wagtails in the stream bed.

Eventually, it becomes impossible to follow the path at river level and it skirts below the next set of crags, climbing up to the top of the bank. Climb up to a high level opposite this, or the more adventurous can follow the narrow path behind the holly. There is a pleasant plunging waterfall on the opposite bank. This is a spectacular wooded area with boulders covered in a variety of mosses. The closer you stay to the edge, the more exciting – or dangerous – the walk becomes. The river takes a contorted route through steep gorge walls with the odd small waterfall and deep pool. The banks of the river are covered mainly with hazel, ash, holly, rowan and sycamore (see 'Ancient woodland', Walk 27).

The right of way marked on the map runs across the top of the cliff but the walk is more interesting if you follow the bank as far as conditions will allow. ◄ The gorge walls are formed from erosion-resistant Millstone Grit and along this stretch you can see good examples of stratification.

> Other tree species include silver birch and oak.

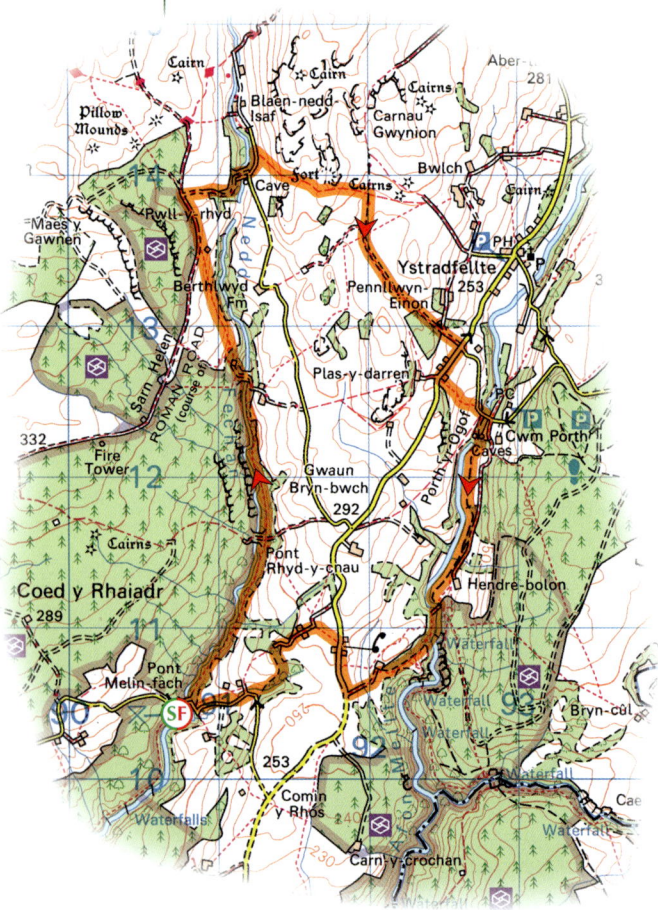

## GEOLOGY OF WATERFALL COUNTRY

The Devonian Period ended when the southern flanks of St George's Land (see 'Geology of the Brecon Beacons', Introduction) subsided, resulting in the sea, which was confined to an area south of the present Bristol Channel, advancing northwards. This marked the beginning of Carboniferous times, when up to 4000ft of grey calcareous shales and massive limestones were deposited. Carboniferous limestone was formed in warm, often clear, shallow seas where corals, shellfish, brachiopods and crinoids (sea-lilies) were abundant. In fact, the skeletal remains of creatures such as these can make up much of the rock. These rocks are divisible into three groups, Lower Limestone Shales, Main Limestone and Upper Limestone Shales, which reflect the establishment, hiatus and waning of a major marine cycle. These stable conditions were interrupted by earth movements caused by approaching continents from the west and the south during the Middle Carboniferous Period, which lifted the southern flanks of St George's Land, resulting in a southward retreat of the sea. The rocks once laid down on the seabed were now exposed to erosion.

Overlying the limestone is Millstone Grit, which, in the Beacons, comprises in its lower layers massive white quartz conglomerates and sandstones, the Basal Grit. This group has very pure bands of over 99% quartz, which were worked for firebrick (silica brick). The Millstone Grit represents a marked change in the depositional conditions of the estuaries of large rivers in which fast currents carried coarse material eroded from mountains to the north. Many of the beds show rapid lateral changes from fine silty muds to coarse sandstones, grits and conglomerates. These resistant layers are overlain by softer grey or blue shales and mudstones, the Middle Shales, which sometimes contain thin bands of coal. These shales are followed by massive beds of sandstone, known commonly by South Wales miners as the Farewell Rock, as they knew that the workable coal bands were left behind once they struck this distinctive geological marker.

Follow your preferred route here, staying close to the river with a bit of scrambling across boulders, and then strike up right to a stile. Drop again to the river and continue north if water levels allow. This area is well populated with small woodland birds and herons are commonly seen along the river. Late April is a good time of year to visit when all the woodland flowers are in bloom.

Now and again you will cross fences using stiles before coming to a sign to Pont Rhyd-y-cnau. Follow this to arrive at a bridge (**Pont Rhyd-y-cnau**) with a gate barring the route. Just below the bridge is a waterfall and a sloping block of Millstone Grit in the riverbed, which gives the true dip direction of the area. Skirt past the bridge without crossing and continue through deciduous forestry along the riverbank. Ignore the wide track down from the right to the bridge. ◄ Continue to the rapids through oak woodland and cross a stile and a stream gully. Fifty metres further on there is an impressive stepped waterfall on the far bank, which is spectacular when frozen.

*Dippers are quite common in the stream bed.*

Parts of the banks are composed of grit and parts are of limestone. The trees on the riverbank are covered in moss on the lower parts with a number of ferns growing from the trunks; these are called epiphytes. In the spring there is an abundance of woodland flowers, including lesser celandine, a yellow flower.

Immediately past these waterfalls, the path enters a narrow gorge with a river pool, Pwll Du, and a limestone cliff beyond it. The water here is extremely clear and flows out through the exit of a cave. This indicates that this pool is the resurgence of an underground cave system. Just after the pool, the path climbs up out of the right-hand side. Follow the path as it drops down below the crag. A short distance up from Pwll Du, the river swings to the right around a tall cliff. In the dry season you can traverse across the front of this, otherwise climb to the top. Above this point the resurgence of the river occurs. Water seeps out of the gravel bed, having travelled underground leaving a dry riverbed upstream. This phenomenon is obscured when the river is in spate after heavy rain.

At the point where the dry riverbed passes through a narrow gorge, cut up right just before the crags on the path. Climb a grassy boulder incline up rock steps to large Millstone Grit boulders and up to the fence on the top of the hillside. Follow the path along the fence on the right. The path comes to a corner of the wire fence, above which a stony track descends to the river. Follow this upstream to the bridge.

Cross the bridge to the left bank and climb the farm track through coppiced hazel, passing a ruined building on the right of the path. The path bends to the left into a gully. This is worth a quick visit because it is headed by a sink hole, over the lip of which fall several small streams that pass underground and eventually find their way down to the river. Below the sink hole turn north through an ungated gap in the fence and into a field. Walk up this, leaving a fence between you and the river far below in a deep gorge.

## WALK 30 – AFON NEDD AND AFON MELLTE

When ruined buildings come into view, head for these and follow the hawthorn hedge and the old wall to a stile. Cross this to the old farm buildings and walk up the track to join the Roman road, **Sarn Helen** (see 'Sarn Helen', Walk 23), at a sign that points back along this road and also back to Dyffryn Nedd.

Follow Sarn Helen along the edge of the coniferous forestry until just before two gates. ▶ A track leaves on the right. Follow this stony road down to a gate where it bends to the left. On the bend, turn right off the track and cut down the riverbank southwards to **Pwll-y-rhyd**, which is about 100 metres downstream. This is an incredible limestone sink hole, where the river pours over its lip and disappears for about 200m underground. You can cross the river with care in dry conditions and explore the opposite bank.

If you have crossed the river, continue northwards up the eastern bank above Pwll-y-rhyd. Otherwise, proceed upstream along the western bank to the bridge. There is a choice of paths along the eastern bank, the lowest one passing below a cliff on rock steps in the river. It might be better to avoid this when the river is in spate. The track now becomes sandy and arrives at a stile and bridge on the track you left before visiting Pwll-y-rhyd. There is a car park here.

The hills ahead are Fan Nedd and the low bulk of Fan Gyhirych.

*The River Nedd disappearing into the Pwll-y-rhyd sinkhole*

Turn right up the tarmac track to a wider road and turn left. After about 150 metres take the footpath on the right, signposted to Ystradfellte. Strike south-east diagonally across the field to a stile and then continue to hawthorn trees on the horizon. From these, aim for the southern edge of the limestone **hill fort**, meeting and following a stone wall. The fort is situated on a limestone pavement.

To the north is **Carnau Gwynion**, a circular ceremonial site probably dating back to the Bronze Age (c.2300–800BC). This was a cemetery containing at least four burial cairns, which are still well defined.

*The dry gorge below Pwll-y-rhyd only floods when the river is in full spate*

## WALK 30 – AFON NEDD AND AFON MELLTE

### LIMESTONE PAVEMENT

*Limestone pavement, Carnau Gwynion*

This route crosses one of the most southerly limestone pavements in Britain. The characteristic appearance results from the limestone, calcium carbonate, being dissolved along joints by slightly acidic rainwater. The raised blocks are known as clints and the clefts as grikes. In the past, this area would have been wooded, as the plants found in the grikes are typical woodland species. The deep grikes have a stable microclimate of low light levels and constant temperatures, characteristics of a woodland floor. Typical grike plant species include lily of the valley, wall lettuce, hard shield fern, hairy rock-cress, brittle bladder-fern, limestone fern, globe flower and unusual limestone pavement species such as common cow-wheat, cowslip and zigzag clover. Rarities include yellow archangel, found only in Wales, narrow-leaved bitter cress and local drifts of mossy saxifrage. Dense hazel scrub is found in places with hawthorn, blackthorn, guelder-rose, dog rose, stone bramble, ivy, elder and honeysuckle.

Cross over the stile, turn right and head down the valley, where you will shortly meet a drovers' road. Follow this through an area of shake holes to the prominent Scots pines and then continue down the gully to meet the main road. These pines mark the route of this old drovers' road. Turn right, ignoring the road that drops down straight ahead. Continue along the road and take the next footpath on the left. Take this across the fields to meet the road where you turn right to the road bridge across the Afon Mellte. The valley on your left, north of the road bridge, can be explored by dropping down a steep path from the car park. The river goes underground through Porth yr Ogof – but don't be tempted to follow it as the cave has extremely deep and fast watercourses.

From the car park exit, go straight across the road and follow the footpath down the eastern bank of the **Afon Mellte**. Here you can wander between limestone boulders and between two fenced-off sink holes, in the depths of which you can hear the rushing river. The route descends to the river here but an easier option stays above. This is Blue Pool, the resurgence of the Afon Mellte.

The path becomes easier and crosses above an open grassy area where the river is wider and more peaceful, and then runs close to the river through woodland. Cross over a rivulet and follow the path as it meanders and climbs above the river, which has narrowed with rapids. Continue on to a wooden bridge. Cross over and follow the clear path south to just above Sgwd Clun-gwyn waterfall. You can detour down to the fall and explore it by climbing down the right-hand edge to a rocky ledge halfway down the fall (see 'Sgwd Clun-gwyn', Walk 27). Rejoin the path and ascend south-west, following the track through bracken and oak and hawthorn woodland. The track climbs steeply at first to an open area and a gate by the renovated farmhouse of Clun-gwyn. Cross the stile and walk up the track to the road.

Turn right (N) over a cattle grid and after 200 metres there is a shop and garage. Beyond is a small church (Capel Hermon). Opposite the church cross a stile, signed to Heol-fawr. Strike across the field towards the farm hidden in the trees, and cross a waymarked stile, turning right to a gate. Turn left on the road to Heol-fawr Farm.

Follow the waymark arrows along a permitted footpath through woodland and then along a stream to the road. Turn right and then just after the entrance to Glyn Mercher Isaf Farm take the footpath on the right, across some fields and back to the road. Turn right down to the bridge and walk back to the start.

# 6 THE BLACK MOUNTAIN (MYNYDD DU)

*The impressive northern scarp of Picws Du (Walk 31)*

# WALK 31
*Carmarthen Fans and glacial cwms*

| | |
|---|---|
| **Start/finish** | Car park, head of the Sawdde Valley (SN 788 243) |
| **Distance** | 15km (9.3 miles) |
| **Total ascent** | 805m (2640ft) |
| **Grade** | 3 |
| **Max elevation** | 802m (2631ft) |
| **Map** | OL12 Western area |

Situated in the Fforest Fawr Geopark, this walk is the shortest route up the highest summits in Mynydd Du, and it is packed full of interest ranging from the mythical stories associated with Llyn y Fan Fach to spectacular glacial features. A long and steady ascent brings you to the high peaks of Picws Du and Fan Foel with their spectacular views and steep cliffs on their northern slopes. There is a steep descent from the ridge down to the lake.

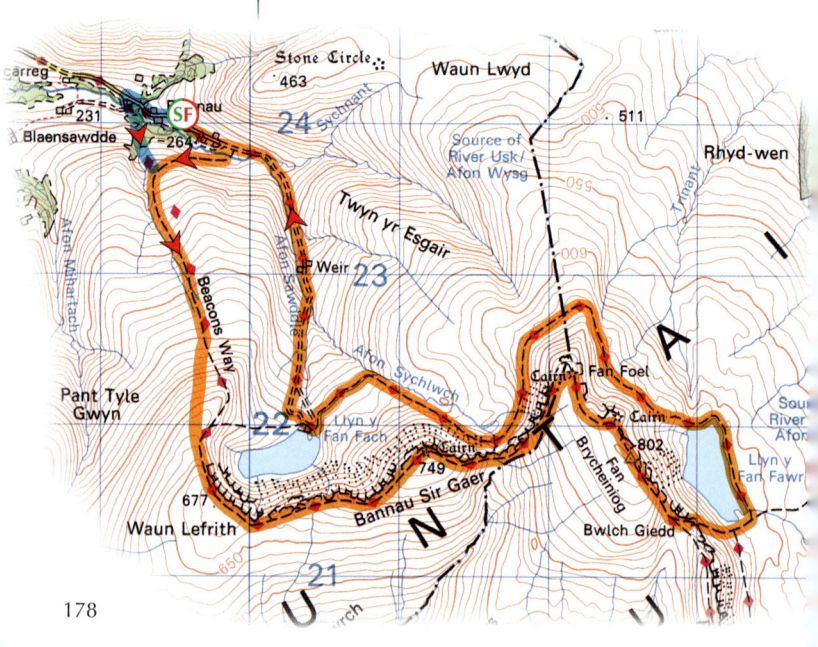

The obvious choice is to take the track with the Afon Sawdde down on your right, but this involves a monotonous slog up to Llyn y Fan Fach. A more interesting and far less busy option is to cross the stream, if water levels are low, near the crossing point used by farm quad bikes. Take the track that leads right diagonally across the slope of Brest y Fedw and then swings left onto the **Beacons Way** above the stream course of Garwnant.

If it is not possible to ford the stream, walk back down the track and take the next road on the left and descend to the stream bridge. Cross over and turn left through the first gate on the path alongside the stream, now on the Beacons Way. Climb through the woodland and cross the hill fence where you join the main route.

Climb steadily along Cefn Nant Lygos and on to the majestic ridge of **Bannau Sir Gaer**, with awe-inspiring views below of the glacial lake and north to the Usk Reservoir.

> Take time to watch the **trout** jumping in the holding pools. In 1994 the Llyn-y-Fan Trout and Salmon Hatchery was opened to rear Towy and Cleddau Salmon in mitigation for the Llyn Brianne and Llys-y-fran reservoirs. Brown trout from the upper Teifi are also reared for restocking rivers and still waters.

### MYTHICAL LAKE

Llyn y Fan Fach is the setting for the legend of the Lady of the Lake. A young man used to take his cattle to graze on the local hills. One day he came across a lady sitting on the water combing her hair. He admired her beauty and offered her bread and cheese but she refused, saying, 'Unbaked is thy bread I will not have thee.' She refused him on a second occasion but on his third visit she accepted his gift and agreed to marry him. Her dowry was sheep, cattle, goats and horses but she warned him, 'Strike me without cause three times and you shall lose me.' They lived together and had a family but sadly he did strike her three times, though not with malice, and she returned to the lake with all her animals. She later appeared to her sons and taught them about herbs with medicinal uses. They went on to become the famous physicians of Myddfai, and a study of their 13th-century recipes shows that Welsh medicine was far more advanced than that in most of Europe. Directions were given as to the quantities and methods of preparation of the ingredients, which was most unusual at that time.

*Standing on Cwar-du-mawr looking east along the ridge to Picws Du*

The highest summits are capped by the resistant Plateau Beds. Continue round the ridge of Bannau Sir Gaer and up to the cairn at Picws Du, which was probably a prehistoric funerary monument.

From here the path drops steeply to the col at Bwlch Blaen Twrch where the **Afon Sychlwch** tumbles down to the north. Take the path east to the summit of **Fan Foel** and follow the ridge to the trig point on **Fan Brycheiniog**. ◀ There are spectacular views down to another glacial lake, Llyn y Fan Fawr, and of the Brecon Beacons to the east.

*This is the highest point of the range at 802m.*

### FAN FOEL

The summit is the site of an early Bronze Age (2000BC) round barrow that was excavated in June 2004. A stone kerb defined the edge of the barrow, which had a central cist comprising a stone box made from stone slabs. A cremation deposit was found inside and an examination of the bone identified the presence of an adult, a young child and an infant, as well as two pigs and possibly a dog. A second cremation deposit contained the remains of an adult and a juvenile. A crushed pottery vessel, which probably contained food, was found in the central cist as well as a triangular-shaped flint knife. There would have been a mound formed by peat and turf covering the cist.

Continue along the ridge to **Bwlch Giedd**, where you turn left and drop down to **Llyn y Fan Fawr**.

*The Sawdde Valley leading up to Bannau Sir Gaer, from the north-west*

Follow the eastern edge of the lake and traverse at the base of the cliffs across Gwal y Cadno to where the path drops down from Fan Foel. Continue in a westerly direction and then swing southwards, keeping to the base of the escarpment, to where you meet the path descending from the ridge above at Pant y Bwlch. The sinuous linear mound you can see is a glacial moraine at the bottom of the cliff.

Keep following the base of the northern cliffs of Bannau Sir Gaer towards Llyn y Fan Fach. When the track divides, take the left-hand path until it reaches a stone-lined channel that diverts part of the Afon Sychlwch into Llyn y Fan Fach. Cross this and follow the path to **Llyn y Fan Fach**. ▶ It is bounded by moraines, which are most obvious on the left-hand side. There is an emergency stone refuge which has an open-hearth fire where the stream exits.

The lake was dammed in the early part of the 20th century and was used as a reservoir for Llanelli from 1918 until 1993.

From here, descend the track back to the start passing Llyn-y-Fan Trout and Salmon Hatchery on the way. Take time to watch the trout jumping in the holding pools.

In 1994 the **Llyn-y-Fan Trout and Salmon Hatchery** was opened to rear Towy and Cleddau Salmon in mitigation for the Llyn Brianne and Llys-y-fran reservoirs. The valley floor, just before the car park, is a great place to spot wheatear, as they come here to breed in late spring and then spend the winter in Central Africa.

# WALK 32
## Tair Carn Isaf via Cwm Pedol

| | |
|---|---|
| Start/finish | Llandeilo road bridge across Nant Pedol (SN 691 140) |
| Distance | 7km (4.3 miles) |
| Total ascent | 330m (1080ft) |
| Grade | 2 |
| Max elevation | 460m (1509ft) |
| Map | OL12 Western area |

This short walk in one of the remotest areas of the national park follows a section of gorge in Cwm Pedol, which has ancient woodland and a beautiful stream. A pleasant walk through upland pasture leads to an easy ascent of Drysgol from where there are fine views. Car parking is limited at the bridge but there are spaces on the right of the track up to Cwm Pedol.

Start at the bridge over the stream, Nant Pedol, on the Llandeilo Road. Facing upstream, take the track on the left through a gate signposted to Cwm Pedol. Walk up the track to the Welsh waterworks, where you cross a stile and continue into mixed deciduous woodland.

◄ The route leaves the track at Cwm Pedol Isaf bungalow and follows a footpath that leads off to the left. Cross over a stile and into a field with a small stream running down the hill, making this area rather wet. Turn left up the slope to the hill fence, cross the stile and turn right.

The path winds its way diagonally up the slope to the right where it meets another path. There is a nice patch of heather here. Turn right and descend a little past a single oak tree on the right. The route passes through substantial areas of bilberry and heather. Continue past three oak trees on the right to a junction. Take the path to the left that runs across the slope in the direction of a farm barn on the opposite side of the valley. Do not take the path that descends to the stream and wooden bridge below.

The path enters pretty oak woodland, where the valley side drops steeply down to the stream below and the understorey is carpeted in flowers in the spring (see 'Ancient

*Keep an eye out for birds of prey during the walk. Buzzards, red kite and kestrels are a common sight here.*

## WALK 32 – TAIR CARN ISAF VIA CWM PEDOL

woodland', Walk 27). Nant Pedol has cut this gorge through the Lower Coal Measures, which comprise mudstones with coal seams. Drysgol, the hill above on your left, is formed from the Farewell Rock and the higher mountains from the Basal Grit.

Follow the waymarked path along the western side of **Nant Pedol**. The route takes a track just to the right of a ruined **stone cottage** and soon afterwards crosses the hill fence. Turn right and follow an indistinct path that brings you to where the hill fence drops to the stream below. Continue diagonally upwards following the edge of the wet boggy area on your right. Eventually, you reach a stream gully. Do not cross this but follow the bank to the ridge above. ▶

There are fine views to the south-west down the Amman Valley and to Gower on the horizon.

Continue on a north-westerly bearing to the summit of **Tair Carn Isaf**, crossing moorland covered with heather, ling, bilberry, purple moor grass and bog cotton.

The National Park Authority is actively managing this **habitat**, as the heather is infested with heather beetle and has become too old and degenerate to benefit wildlife or livestock. Patches are burnt to create a mosaic habitat of different ages of heather stands. The air is full of the sound of singing skylarks in the spring. In late April and early May look out for the dotterel, a wader slightly smaller than a golden plover, around the boulders and rocky outcrops; they favour this habitat when they stop off on their migration from their wintering grounds in North Africa to their breeding grounds in Scandinavia.

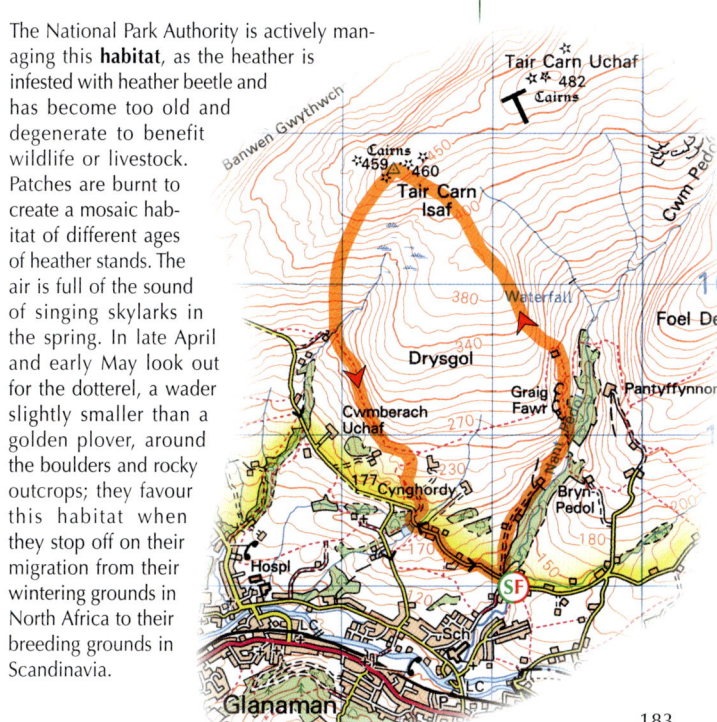

183

*Aerial view of Tair Carn Isaf*

Descend (SSW) from the summit across Pen Bryn Mawr to where a stream meets the hill fence. Cross over the stream and follow the hill fence on your right to a kissing gate. Follow the path down to where it meets a gravel road. Turn left and walk back to the start.

# WALK 33
## Sinc Giedd and Carmarthen Fans

| | |
|---|---|
| **Start/finish** | Gwyn Arms, Pen-y-cae (SN 846 167), postcode SA9 1GP |
| **Distance** | 20.25km (12.6 miles) |
| **Total ascent** | 880m (2890ft) |
| **Grade** | 4 |
| **Max elevation** | 802m (2631ft) |
| **Map** | OL12 Western area |

This classic walk explores the heart of Mynydd Du, providing a real sense of the mountain wilderness and a true taste of the nature of this remote upland massif. The long route meanders through a moonscape of shake holes and takes in Sinc Giedd, a swallow hole where a stream disappears underground. This contrasts with the return route, which follows the spectacular ridge of Bannau Sir Gaer. This walk should only be attempted in good visibility as the path is ill-defined in one featureless moorland section.

## WALK 33 – SINC GIEDD AND CARMARTHEN FANS

From the Gwyn Arms, go back to the main road, turn left and take the gate on the right, signposted 'Danger crossing river in flood', and continue along the road to Carreg Haffes Farm. Cross over the stile and follow the track around to the right to another stile on the left. Continue straight ahead over another stile and across a field, keeping the fence on your left. Follow the blue bridleway arrows and cross over a stile at the end of the fence along a path on the edge of some woodland where you may see some llamas. The path brings you into **Cwm Haffes**.

Cross over the stile and follow the stream for a short distance on the right-hand side. Traverse the small first stream and walk diagonally over an island covered in gorse to where there are some reasonable stepping stones that can be used to cross the main stream when it is not in spate. There is a lovely view up to the right of the boulder-strewn Haffes river valley. The base of the Carboniferous limestone runs along the high right-hand wall of this steep valley.

If this is not safe to cross, retrace your steps to the road, cross over the road bridge and walk south-westwards down the valley. Turn right after the **Shire Horse Centre** and then right again. Follow the footpath signs to bring you into the Haffes Valley where you rejoin the route. Straight ahead is an old quarry track which leads diagonally up the hillside to the left.

There are excellent views down the Swansea Valley to Craig-y-Nos Castle, which once belonged to the celebrated opera diva Adelina Patti. On the right is the entrance to Dan-yr-Ogof, an extensive underground cave system that is open to the public. Beyond is the extensively quarried profile of the Cribarth.

Ignore the track that leaves on the right to some old quarry workings and continue with the hill fence on your left to where this bends down to the left near the highest point of the quarry track. At this point, take the path, not marked with a fingerpost, which heads in the direction of a rocky outcrop on the summit of the hill to the west. ▶

> There is a solitary tree sticking out of a rock outcrop on the right.

The path swings around to the right (N) and runs parallel with the rock outcrop and then gradually swings back to the west, leaving the outcrop to the left (S). It then becomes quite distinct and runs parallel with the Haffes Valley.

The route meanders between shake holes and outcrops of Carboniferous limestone that form a classic karstic landscape and a great habitat for plants. Off to the right in the distance there are good views of the summits and ridges of Fan Hir and Fan Foel, which are formed from the resistant grits and conglomerates of Old Red Sandstone. These form the route for the return part of the walk.

Along this path you will come across a pool on your left and then afterwards, on the right, there is a large upland peat bog, Waun Fignen Felen, below which is an extensive limestone cave system.

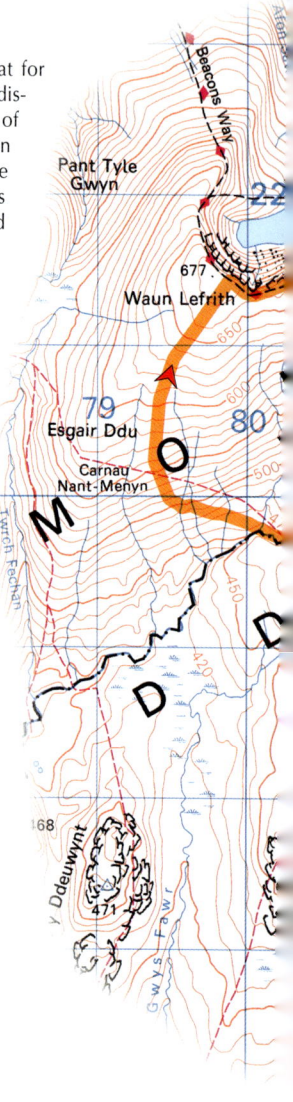

### SHAKE HOLES

The numerous shake holes characteristic of Mynydd Du are depressions caused by the overlying Millstone Grit being undermined by the collapse of cavern roofs in the underlying Carboniferous limestone. Also known as sinkholes or doline, they are bowl-, cone- or well-shaped depressions in limestone-dominated areas. Karst topography is characterised by sinkholes, cave systems and a lack of surface streams. Sinkholes usually form where there is the underground movement of water through caves or rock joints. Rainwater, being naturally mildly acidic, dissolves the limestone, causing voids to form below the land surface. Sinkholes are formed when these voids or caves collapse. They frequently provide access to cave systems or sub-surface streams and rivers. The Brecon Beacons has the greatest density of sinkholes than anywhere else in Britain.

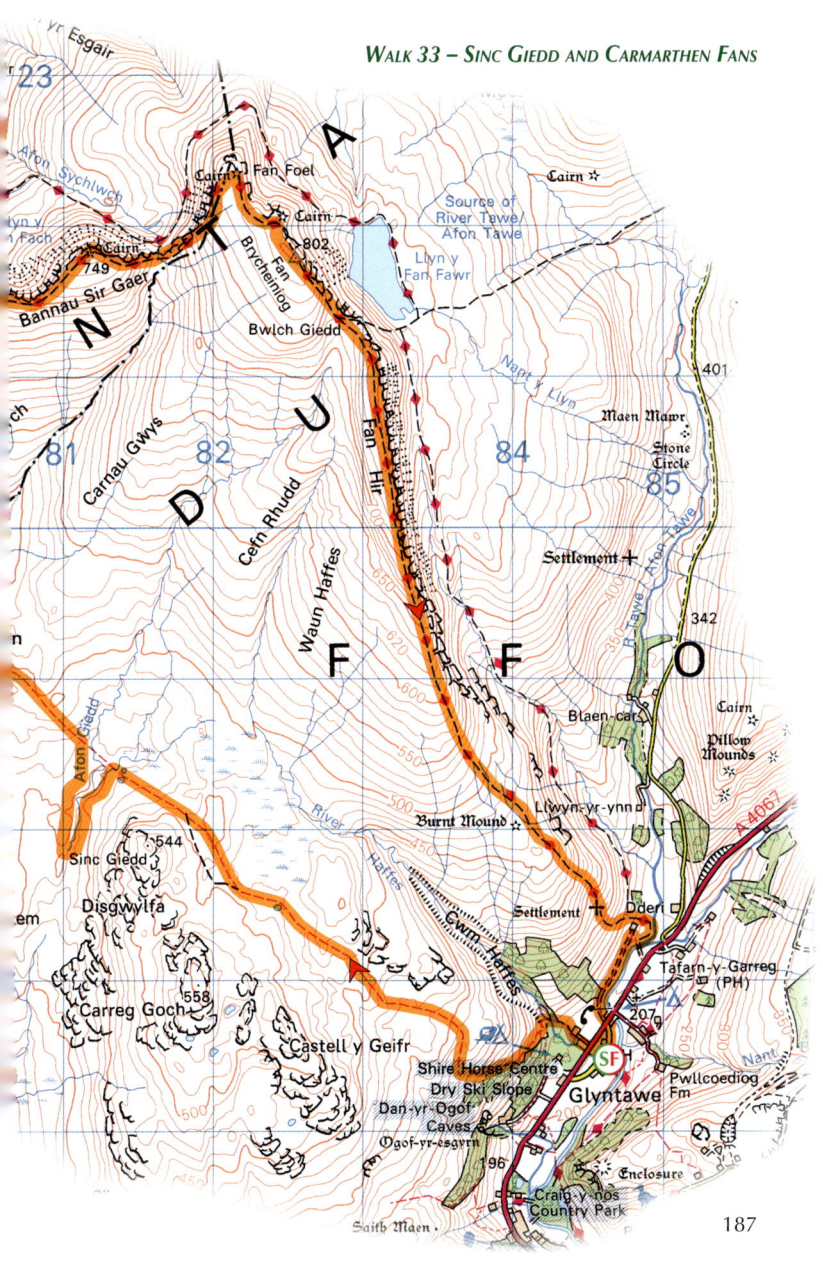

## WALK 33 – SINC GIEDD AND CARMARTHEN FANS

## WAUN FIGNEN FELEN

Waun Fignen Felen was once a basin, formed by glacial action, surrounded by alder woodland, with hazel playing an important role. Mesolithic man made a small clearing by burning the trees around 6000BC, allowing heath vegetation to develop. This was also maintained by burning, perhaps as a strategy to concentrate game animals, which were attracted by the good grazing. The basin's outlet was blocked by peat around 6500BC, forming an open lake surrounded by woodland and a watering place for wild animals. Stone Age hunter-gatherers built a lakeside settlement on the northern shore.

It became clear around 2000 that the rate of erosion of the peat bog was accelerating, with much of the surface comprising exposed black peat. An innovative project, 'Black to Green', was implemented to restore the bog by placing round straw bales to block gullies, thereby slowing down run-off and raising the water table. The aim was to conserve and revegetate 15 hectares using mainly locally generated gorse mulch containing a seedbank of acid grassland species.

*The bridleway marked on the map that joins on the left at Twyn Tal y Ddraenen is an old coffin route.*

The bridleway descends down to Pwll y Cig. Make a short detour at this point to visit Sinc y Giedd. Cross over a small stream, turn left, leaving the track, and follow the stream valley (S). Lying on the surface are many boulders of Millstone Grit containing numerous large pebbles of white quartz. Keep to the left bank on the higher ground until you reach the point where the stream disappears underground at **Sinc Giedd**.

Cross over the valley below the cliff and make your way back to the bridleway. The path becomes very indistinct after Pwll y Cig so care has to be taken in route finding. ◄ Continue north-west, crossing another small stream, and head up the hillside onto a grassy area. On the right is the high ground and the path splits just before this. Take the right-hand fork which heads just to the left of the hillock ahead. You come to the crest of the slope, with the summit on the right, and the track becomes clear again and drops down to the main stream gully below, with a large expanse of bog down to the left.

Head up the slope and cross another stream, Nant Lluestau, and then up to the rocky crags above. Cross **Waun Lefrith** and finally gain the ridge and summit of **Bannau Sir Gaer**. Turn right (E) and follow the ridge to the cairn at Picws Du, which was probably a prehistoric funerary monument.

*The swallow hole of Sinc Giedd where the Afon Giedd disappears underground*

### GLACIAL CIRQUES

The glacial cirques of Llyn y Fan Fawr and Llyn y Fan Fach are among the finest in South Wales, with a further two cwms located to the east at Pwll yr Henllyn and Pant y Bwlch. Their associated Loch Lomond Stadial moraines can be seen clearly from the ridge above.

Descend to the col Bwlch Blaen Twrch, climb the ridge to the summit of **Fan Foel** and continue to the trig point on **Fan Brycheiniog**.

To the east there are excellent **views** of the highest summits in the Brecon Beacons, Pen y Fan and Corn Du, and of the Black Mountains to the left of these. Down below is Llyn y Fan Fawr. To the north lie the Usk Reservoir and Mynydd Epynt. The cairn on Fan Foel is a round barrow.

A fine collection of unusual **plants** can be found in the lime-rich sandstone in the crags above Llyn y Fan Fawr; these include mossy and burnet saxifrage, great burnet and roseroot, as well as green spleenwort.

*Glacial moraines below Fan Foel*

Descend to Bwlch Giedd and climb again to **Fan Hir**.

The origin of the linear ridge, **Fan Fechan**, at the base of the cliff is something of an enigma. It is over 20m high in places and comprises recycled fragments of Old Red Sandstone, possibly on a subdued bedrock ridge base in part. Two different modes of formation have been proposed: first that it is a glacial moraine and second that it is a protalus or nivation ridge (see Walk 22).

Continue along the ridge to the hill fence and cross the stile on the left of some sheep pens at Ty Henry. Follow the path which swings to the right below the pens and turn left through a gate. The path runs between two fields and then comes to the river. Turn right and follow the path along the river and turn right through a gate just before the bridge. Head across the field towards the house at Ty Henry and turn left onto the bridleway. Follow this with the river on your left back to the road. Turn right, cross over and then turn left back to the start.

# WALK 34
*Afon Twrch*

| | |
|---|---|
| **Start/finish** | New Tredegar Arms, Cwmtwrch (SN 757 113), postcode SA9 2XG |
| **Distance** | 17.75km (11 miles) |
| **Total ascent** | 415m (1360ft) |
| **Grade** | 3 |
| **Max elevation** | 468m (1535ft) |
| **Map** | OL12 Western area |

This route explores the finest valley in Mynydd Du. A tranquil river walk is followed by spectacular gorge scenery and a challenging wilderness section in the heart of the upland massif. A wide range of interests are catered for and highlights include its interesting archaeological and geological features. Route finding can be challenging in poor weather and this route is recommended only in good conditions.

With the pub behind you, cross the road and turn left in front of a row of terraced houses, following the fingerpost arrow. The road becomes a track and the right of way makes a short detour left before turning right through a kissing gate and back onto the flat track. This is a disused tramway which used to bring limestone down from quarries in the hills. ▶

Continue on the east side of the river, taking the right-hand track at a fork. Cross a wooden stile and a second stile as you approach the riverbank. There are some cast-iron sleeper shoes to be found. The track briefly meets a road at Bryn-Henllys Bridge on the left. Cross the road to continue along the eastern bank. At a small **weir** there is a picnic stop and a stone shelter.

> Keep a watch for grey heron in the Afon Twrch below.

### CWM TWRCH

Cwm Twrch translates as Valley of the Wild Boar and derives from the Twrch Trwyth, a mythical monster boar. It appears in the story of Culhwch and Olwen recorded in the White Book of Rydderch as part of the Middle Welsh tales now collectively known as the Mabinogion.

Culhwch is the son of a king, Cilydd Wledig, but he is born in a pig pen when his mother gives birth after being frightened by some pigs. After she dies in childbirth, he is raised in secret by the swineherd. Cilydd searches for another wife, which leads to him killing King Doged and taking his widow, daughter and land as his own. His new queen hatches a plan for her daughter to marry Culhwch, but he refuses. Enraged, she places a curse on him so that he can marry only Olwen, the daughter of Ysbaddaden Pencawr, the evil king of the giants.

Culhwch has not yet met Olwen, and his father advises him that he will never find her without the help of his cousin Arthur, who he seeks out at his court in Celliwig in Cornwall. Culhwch finally finds Olwen but is set a series of herculean challenges to complete by Ysbaddaden, who knows he will die if his daughter marries.

One of Culhwch and King Arthur's tasks is to rid the western Brecon Beacons of the pack of wild boars that are terrorising the people. He chases the boars eastward from Dyfed towards Powys. On the Black Mountain he picks up a large stone and hurls it at the pack, killing its leader on the edge of the valley near Craig-y-Fran Gorge. The big boar's body rolls down the valley and into the river, now known as the Afon Twrch.

Cross the river on the wooden bridge and just ahead you will see an impressive brick chimney and on the right an extensive rock exposure. Turn right and follow the path between the fence and the river, ignoring the two metal gates in the fence, and then cross where indicated by the waymark arrow. Shortly afterwards there is an interesting rock outcrop of resistant sandstone beds and weaker shales. A little further on is the well-preserved brick **chimney** and below it three large limestone kilns.

This area is known as the **Llosgi carreg**, or Burning Rock, and was the site of a kiln that was used to produce lime for Ynyscedwyn Ironworks up until the 1880s and later for the nearby brickworks. A rail incline ran due north from here, up to the limestone quarries on Cefn Carn Fadog. It is thought that there were once two chimneys on this site, with a further one on the hill above. Their original function is unclear, but they were an essential part of the engine houses that either powered the incline, hauled coal from the mine or provided ventilation for underground mine workings.

Continue along the path in front of the kilns and then up a small incline in the direction of a rock outcrop on the hillside ahead. Go through a kissing gate and take the path that climbs diagonally up the slope. In the riverbed below, you can see the dip or slope of the sedimentary rocks, these being the same as the hillside you are walking on.

Turn left and follow the boundary wall around Cyllie Farm, ignoring an obvious track on the left, and enter the open hillside beyond the farm buildings in a boggy area. Cross this, bearing right, and follow the path parallel with the river valley. There is a very narrow path below you, which runs just along the top of the cliffs in places, but this is very precarious.

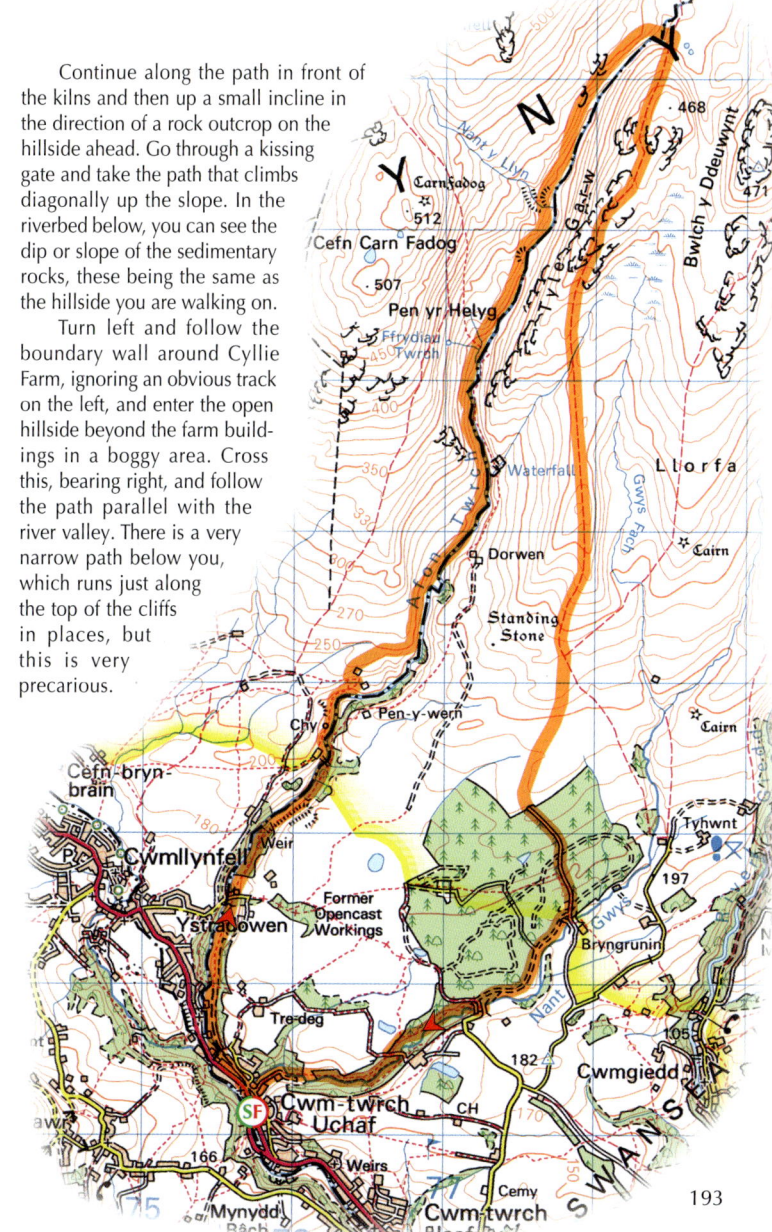

*Disused workings in Cwm Twrch*

The gorge here is one of the finest in Wales, with superb views of the woodland clinging to the steep valley sides and of the deeply incised watercourse (see 'Ancient woodland', Walk 27).

Continue following the river valley northwards, passing a derelict ruin on your right. Just after this, you come across a deep drainage ditch that leads to a stream gully. Cross this and drop down to the stream and follow the bank to a narrow gorge and waterfalls. A tributary coming down on the opposite hillside has a fine **waterfall**. ◄ You will encounter numerous upland and stream birds.

Continue following the stream where the terrain allows as some areas can be boggy. The Basal Grit boulder field on the valley sides has excellent areas of inaccessible bilberry and shows what the rest of the upland areas would be like without grazing animals. The valley side steepens on the eastern side and culminates in the resistant crags of Tyle Garw. Look out for the large spring called **Ffrydiau Twrch**,

This is one of the remotest and wildest areas of Wales.

## WALK 34 – AFON TWRCH

which emerges from the western valley side and another at Ffrwd Las. The route can be cut short by fording the Afon Twrch at any suitable point and climbing up to Tyle Garw. Otherwise, continue upstream until the northern slope of **Tyle Garw** drops down to the stream at a meander.

Cross the stream and ascend the ridge in a southerly direction on a bridleway marked on the map. This is one of the coffin routes that run north–south across Mynydd Du (see 'Coffin routes', Walk 38). ▶ From the summit ridge of Tyle Garw, head south to the rounded summit of the ridge of land that separates the Twrch Valley from the Gwys Fach.

The col down to the left is Bwlch Ddeuwynt, Gap of the Two Winds.

> There are fine panoramic **views** to the north of the desolate heart of Mynydd Du and beyond to the high ridges of Bannau Sir Gaer, Fan Foel and Fan Hir. The distinctive crinkled profile of Cribarth is to the east.

Descend (SW) and cross over a collapsed stone wall and follow this downslope on your right. Cross another wall and shortly afterwards the path finishes near a **standing stone**. From the stone, continue in the same direction to a track, turn left and continue SSW.

Ffrwd Las near the Afon Twrch

Leave the track after you cross a second boggy area and cut across the moorland to a gate in the hill fence. Go through this, keeping to the main track, and turn right just before the river bridge. This track follows **Nant Gwys** down to Tir-y-gof Bridge. Take the bridleway just before the bridge and continue along the wide track. Turn left at a crossroads of paths and then right to follow the bank of the river. The main track is joined again and this leads to a bridge. Cross this and follow the track down to the main road. Turn right and walk back to the start.

# WALK 35
## Henrhyd Falls and River Tawe

| | |
|---|---|
| **Start/finish** | Layby, Ynyswen A4067 (SN 830 128) |
| **Distance** | 7.25km (4.5 miles) |
| **Total ascent** | 180m (590ft) |
| **Grade** | 1 |
| **Max elevation** | 274m (899ft) |
| **Map** | OL12 Western area |

This easy, low-level walk takes you along a spectacular wooded gorge with the highest waterfall in South Wales at its head. Owned and managed by the National Trust, the woodland is of special note and the humid habitat supports a wide variety of damp-loving species. A cross-country traverse then brings you to an impressive section of the River Tawe.

Start at the layby on the bend on the A4067 and walk a short distance along the road to a point opposite the graveyard at **St David's Church**. Turn right and follow the waymarked track that descends to the left to a house. A path continues to the right to the **River Tawe** where there is a metal bridge. Cross this and ascend the steps up to the left, ignoring the wooden bridge across Nant Llech on the right. Go through the kissing gate and follow the path through the woodland along the bank of the stream to the road.

## WALK 35 – HENRHYD FALLS AND RIVER TAWE

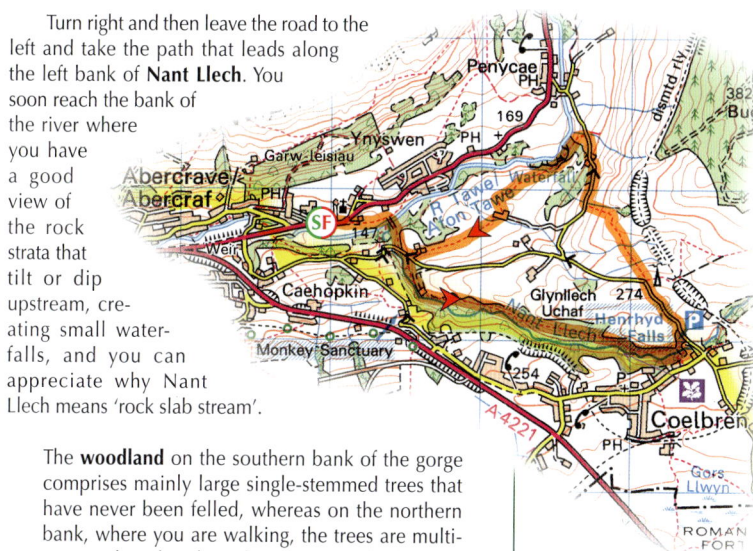

Turn right and then leave the road to the left and take the path that leads along the left bank of **Nant Llech**. You soon reach the bank of the river where you have a good view of the rock strata that tilt or dip upstream, creating small waterfalls, and you can appreciate why Nant Llech means 'rock slab stream'.

The **woodland** on the southern bank of the gorge comprises mainly large single-stemmed trees that have never been felled, whereas on the northern bank, where you are walking, the trees are multi-stemmed as they have been coppiced. This harvesting technique involves felling the tree near its base and allowing it to grow back again. Sessile oaks, which can thrive in poor acidic soils, grow on the drier upper slopes. But as you move closer to the stream, the soils become wetter and more nutrient-rich and ash and alder are found. Wych elm and small-leaved limes also thrive here, indicating that this is ancient woodland (see 'Ancient woodland', Walk 27). Look out for damp-loving vegetation growing on the rocks, boulders and tree branches, as Graig Llech is a Site of Special Scientific Interest for its wide range of rare mosses, ferns, lichens and liverworts.

The path meets a track coming down from the left. Turn right, continuing along the gorge to a wooden bridge. Do not cross but continue along the left-hand side of the valley to a ruined stone building, Melin Llech, which was once a woollen mill. ▶ You may hear the unusual sound of the whoops of howler monkeys in the nearby primate sanctuary, which gives the gorge a rather surreal atmosphere of a tropical jungle.

The gorge is home to a variety of woodland and stream birds, such as pied flycatchers, dippers and kingfishers.

After a while, you come to a National Trust sign for Sgwd Henrhyd and a wooden bridge. Continue to a kissing gate and the path then drops to the river where there is a 3m high waterfall, again formed by a bedding plane in the rock. Take care traversing this as the rock can be slippery, then scramble back to the path again further up on the left.

The path meets a track coming down the valley side from the left, which comes from the car park. Bear right here and continue to a wooden bridge across the main river from where, in the winter, you get a glimpse of the fall further up the gorge. Ascend the wooden steps on the other side to reach the waterfall (Sgwd Henrhyd) on the right bank.

**Sgwd Henrhyd** has a vertical drop of 28m, making it the highest in South Wales. Earth movements along a geological fault 300 million years ago brought the hard sandstone of the Farewell Rock adjacent to the softer, easily eroded Coal Measure shales that normally lie above. The water has worn away the soft shales at a faster rate than the sandstone, resulting in a step in the riverbed. Over the past few thousand years, the size of the step increased as the shale at the base of the waterfall was worn away, and the overhanging Farewell Rock collapsed to produce a spectacular gorge and high waterfall.

These soft shales make Nant Llech a famous location for their rich Westphalian fossil fauna and the rarely found Astel Coal, a thin coal (30cm) that marks the start of the productive Coal Measures.

Retrace your steps to the bridge and follow the track that sweeps back on itself out of the gorge and to the **car park**. Turn left along the tarmac road to a **communications tower** on a bend. Two footpath signs are marked here. Take the one on the left that heads in the direction of Cribarth mountain on the opposite side of the Tawe Valley. Cross the field, heading for the stile in the fence just to the left of an electricity post. Just before this, cross over a boggy area via a boardwalk. Now head upslope to the right of a row of trees.

Do not go through the gate but keep the fence on your left and follow this to a wooded stream gully and down to the road. Turn right and follow the road to an old church on the right. Take the waymarked path on the left before the

*The Tawe Valley looking towards Moel Feity*

bridge. The track divides after 25 metres. Take the right-hand fork where you will see a yellow footpath arrow on a post. This brings you to the edge of a steep cliff with the **River Tawe** below. ▶

Follow the path along the top of the cliff, taking great care, to where a small stream runs down from the left. Just after you cross this, a yellow arrow shows the footpath turning left away from the edge of the cliff. Shortly afterwards you come to a barbed-wire fence. Turn right and then cross over a stile and right again between two fences. Walk along a small streamway and through a gate where there is a stony track. This becomes a wide grassy area between two stone walls and brings you to a stile. Once you cross this, do not take the track to Glyn Llech Isaf Farm, but keep the fence on your left to a gap in the trees where a bridge crosses a stream.

Turn left along a track and then right along a line of trees and a fallen-down stone wall that mark an old field boundary, which you keep on your left. At the fence ahead there is a yellow waymark arrow and a farm building just to the right. Cross the stile and follow the path with the moss-covered wall now on your right. Cross over a further two stiles and a gate and follow the track that leads to the road. Turn right down the hill and retrace your route to the start.

There are excellent views from here of the valley and an impressive stretch of river rapids.

# WALK 36
## Garreg Las via Cwm Sawdde

| | |
|---|---|
| Start/finish | Capel Gwynfe (SN 722 220), postcode SA19 9RE |
| Distance | 19.25km (12 miles) |
| Total ascent | 665m (2180ft) |
| Grade | 3 |
| Max elevation | 635m (2083ft) |
| Map | OL12 Western area |

This is a demanding route in terms of length and route finding in the upland section. The route follows the western side of Cwm Sawdde Fechan and height is gradually gained to reach the summit of Garreg Las. The walk then returns along the other tributary of the Afon Sawdde. This is one of least-visited areas of the park, and you are likely to encounter very few other walkers on the valley paths and mountain summits. Route finding in the upland parts of this route can be difficult in low visibility, but a low-level alternative is available if the weather conditions are poor.

With the chapel at your back, turn left along the road and right on the footpath just before a house. Take this along the trees to meet a track descending to a road with a **church** on the corner. Go straight across onto the footpath through the wood, with a lake on your right, and cross over the **Afon Clydach** to meet the A4069. Turn left and then right up the tarmac lane. Turn left along a farm track to Neuadd Fach when the metalled road ends. The ridge on the horizon is the upland part of the walk. Go through the gate into the farmyard and continue on the bridleway to the Sawdde stream running in the narrow gorge below. This is a pretty area with oak woodland covering the valley sides.

Cross the ford and take the track sweeping up to the right and then left. The bridleway is quite indistinct but cross the boggy field to a gate in the hill fence. The path is difficult to follow but head along the valley side and soon a distinguishable route appears where there is a slight break in the slope. This is one of the coffin routes that crossed from

Llanddeusant in the north to the industrial towns in the Twrch Valley (see 'Coffin routes', Walk 38).

Continue contouring along the valley side until you meet the **Sawdde Fechan** stream. Do not cross but continue following the watercourse where there are some small

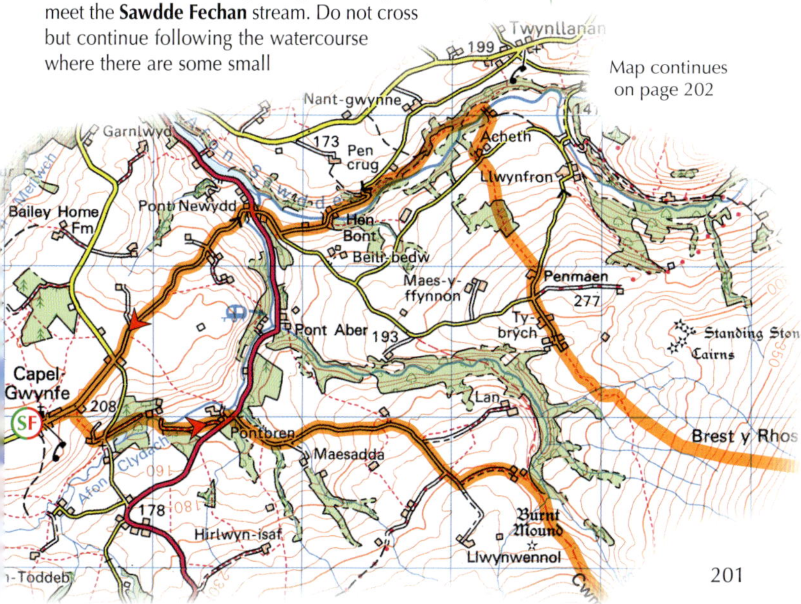

*The Afon Sawdde*

Map continues on page 202

*You might be lucky to see a dipper here.*

waterfalls. ◂ The stone enclosures here are *hafodydd* or sheep pens. Retrace your steps to the start from here if you wish to just explore the valley or if the weather conditions have worsened.

The main route ascends the headwall of the valley and continues (S) across flat open moorland to meet a small path, which forms part of the Beacons Way.

Turn left (E) and ascend the stony ridge ahead and then (N) to **Garreg Las**. To the south is the Amman Valley. The rocks here are very hard, well-bedded quartz sandstones, which are the Basal Grits of the Millstone Grit formation that was formed in the Carboniferous Period. There isn't an obvious path to follow but make sure you keep to the highest ground to avoid crossing the boulder fields that are found closer to the crags. ◂

*There are good views to the east of Fan Hir and Bannau Brycheiniog.*

Towards the end of the ridge there are two distinct large Bronze Age circular burial cairns, **Carnau'r Gareg Las**. Continue north, descending the ridge to **Carreg Yr Ogof**. The route swings west at the end of the crags and descends across **Brest y Rhos**, with Nant Ffynnon-wen on your right, to a quad-bike track and the hill fence. Ford the stream and follow the track down to the road. Continue straight on at the next junction and turn left off the road just past **Penmaen**. The footpath crosses fields and passes through a wood to **Acheth**. Cross over the road and onto a footpath that brings you to a bridge over the river at Ynyswen. Cross over and turn left on the footpath which climbs

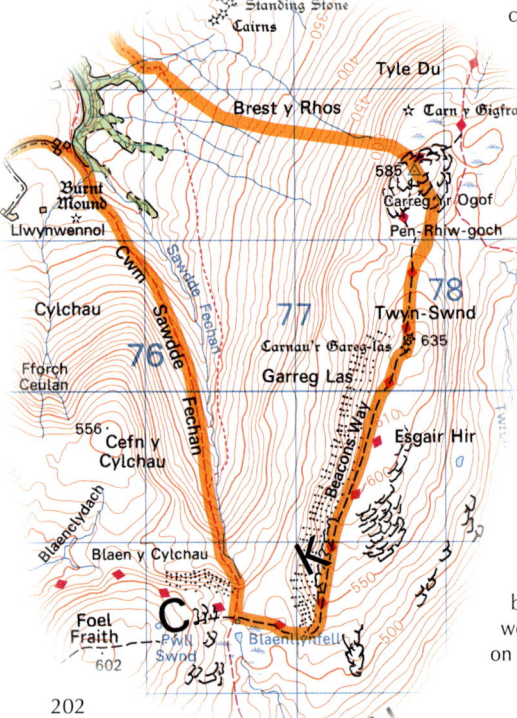

high above a steep-sided gorge with beautiful cascades and pools below.

Turn left at the road, walk down the hill and bear right at the next junction down to **Pont Newydd**. Cross over the A4069 and continue over crossroads at Bryn-Clydach back to the start.

# WALK 37
*Cribarth*

| | |
|---|---|
| **Start/finish** | Abercrave Inn, Abercrave (SN 825 129), postcode SA9 1XS |
| **Distance** | 11km (6.8 miles) |
| **Total ascent** | 420m (1380ft) |
| **Grade** | 2 |
| **Max elevation** | 428m (1404ft) |
| **Map** | OL12 Western area |

Man's endeavours in the past have created the character of this route, as the whole summit of this mountain has been sculpted by quarrying. Along the way there are impressive views of the upper Swansea Valley and some sections along the Afon Tawe. A steep descent from the ridge takes you to Craig-y-nos Country Park, where there is a café. The return route crosses farmland before gaining the open hillside beneath the impressive cliffs of the 'Sleeping Giant' above.

Take the road behind the Abercrave Inn and turn left just before the road ends, along a track to Abercrave Farm. Look out for large boulders of Old Red Sandstone next to the path in the field. These are glacial erratics that were transported by the Tawe Valley glacier from the mountains further north at the end of the last Ice Age. Carry on through the woodland to the open hillside where you turn left, leaving the main track, on the footpath that runs above the wood and then bears right up the hillside to a waymarked stile. Cross over, follow the stone wall to another stile and turn right after this to a waymark post. Climb the path (NW) to where it becomes wider as it was once a tramway for a silica quarry.

## WALKING IN THE BRECON BEACONS

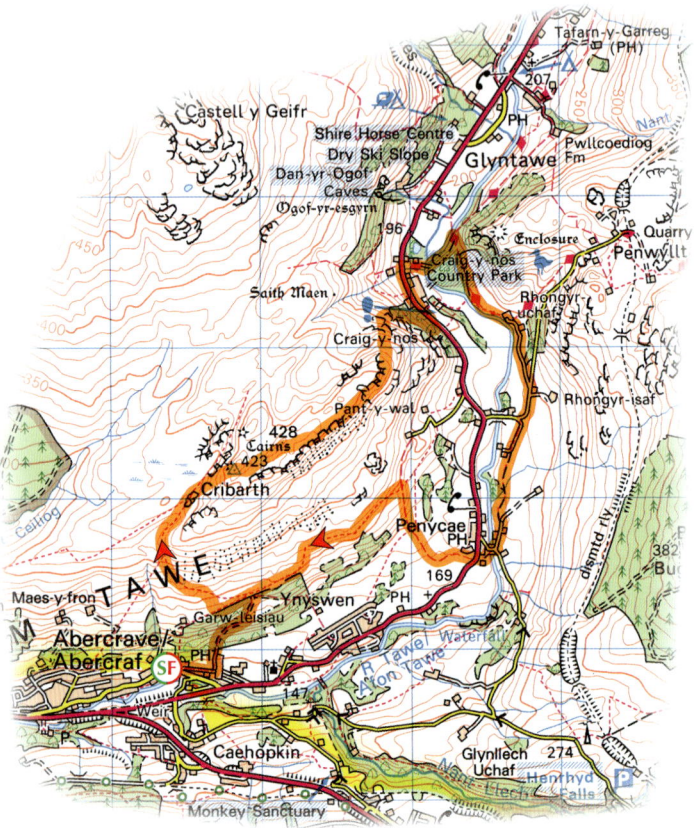

There are a number of silica rock workings on either side of the path. The rock was used to make refractory bricks for the lining of furnaces.

Bear right at a fork and then right again onto the old tramway at Pen Cribarth. This is part of the main tramway that ran in a straight line back down to Abercrave and then west to the former Swansea Canal wharf at Rheolau. Built in 1798, it transported thousands of tons of quarried limestone. Fork left soon afterwards and follow the path around the hillside and cross over the stone wall. ◄ Follow this on your right and then cross over to the left to the steeply inclined 19th-century limestone quarry tramway and use this to ascend the mountain to where it bends to the right.

## CRIBARTH

This mountain, known locally as the 'Sleeping Giant', owing to its profile when seen from down-valley, was extensively quarried in the 19th century. The ridge runs along the Cribarth Disturbance, an ancient fault line in the earth's crust that manifests itself here as a couple of tight anticlinal folds in the rock. The limestone exposed along the ridge was extensively cracked when these rocks were folded by movements in the earth's crust nearly 300 million years ago, making it and the gritstone easily quarried using the hand tools of the time. It is flanked by steeply dipping beds of gritstone and an area of rottenstone to the north. The latter is a unit of sandy limestone found at the contact between the limestone and Millstone Grit, and it was quarried and used as an abrasive and polish in the copper and tinplate industries of South Wales.

*An aerial view of Cribarth*

Look out for a hollow at the top of the tramway, which was the site of the drum around which ran the cable attached to the trams. These were loaded with stone at the top of the incline, and they would then pull up the trams that had been emptied at the bottom, which were linked to the other end of the cable.

Continue to the Bronze Age funerary cairn on the summit of **Cribarth** from where there are panoramic views of the upper part of the Swansea Valley and the Beacons to the east. Cross (NE) to the stone wall and follow this until you encounter a raised tramway on your left. Follow this along the edge of the ridge, passing a number of quarries, and descend to a ladder stile over the wall. Cross over with the wire fence on your left and take this path down to the main road.

Cross over, turn left and walk up the road. Turn right into the car park at **Craig-y-nos Country Park**. The castle was once the home of Adelina Patti, the famous opera singer, who lived here between 1878 and 1919. ◄

> There is a café here.

Carry straight on through the car park and over the bridge that spans the **Afon Tawe**. Walk upstream and then turn right onto the Beacons Way, just before another bridge, and continue through the **nature reserve** of Craig y Rhiwarth and Allt Rhongyr. The ground vegetation of the ash woodland contains lily of the valley, and the limestone grassland is one of the finest in Brecknock.

The path joins a road at Grithrig Cottage, just after which you bear right on a narrow lane and right again when this meets another road. Continue straight on at the right-hand bend in the road and straight again when this finishes on a footpath. This meets the end of a road where you bear right to **Pen-y-cae**. Turn right at the T-junction, cross over the bridge and take the footpath on the left to the apex of the field. Pass between the houses to the main road. Cross straight over and follow the bridleway to the hill fence, ignoring a footpath that crosses it. Go through the gate, turn left and follow the wall. The path is indistinct at first but bear right up a well-worn path to a plateau. Turn left and follow a grassy track to cross a stile in the stone wall. Continue on the path and turn left just before a gate in the fence. Cross a ruined stone wall, turn right and take the path around the edge of the field. Climb the next stile and walk across the field to cross the stile and continue on a grassy track that meets the hill fence you crossed earlier. Retrace your steps to the start.

# WALK 38
## Carmarthen Fans via Cwm Giedd

| | |
|---|---|
| Start/finish | Cwm Giedd Forest car park (SN 792 127) |
| Distance | 24km (14.9 miles) |
| Total ascent | 690m (2260ft) |
| Grade | 4 |
| Max elevation | 749m (2457ft) |
| Map | OL12 Western area |

This is the most demanding walk in the book in terms of sustained altitude and remoteness and should only be attempted by fit and experienced hillwalkers. The vast majority of the route is in the desolate heart of Mynydd Du, where there are no footpaths to be found on the ground today. These ways were, however, known and used centuries ago. Good visibility is essential for this route as there are sections that are featureless. Navigation is aided by the Giedd stream valley and the ridges running south–north to the Carmarthen Fans. This is probably the remotest upland massif in Wales, and there is no sign of any human habitation in any direction for most of the day.

From the car park and picnic area head north on the bridleway up Cwm Giedd, crossing over **Nant Cyw** and **River Giedd**, to the hill fence.

### COFFIN ROUTES

This walk uses the coffin routes, whose origins go back hundreds of years to hard times when the men from the farms around Llanddeusant were forced to seek work south of Mynydd Du in quarries and coal mines in the Amman, Twrch and Swansea valleys. This was the time of the Rebecca Riots, when wool had reached rock-bottom prices. Fatalities in these industries were commonplace, and the bodies of workers would be carried back over the mountain by the men of Brynamman. They were met halfway by the villagers of Llanddeusant, so that the body could be buried in the graveyard of St Simon and St Jude. The bodies were wrapped symbolically in fleece, as centuries earlier, in 1666, an Act of Parliament made it law that all corpses were to be interred in a woollen blanket in an attempt to protect the domestic wool industry from foreign imports.

*An aerial view of the Gwys Fawr and Afon Twrch valleys*

Ascend the spur of land ahead to **Cefn Mawr**, with the Afon Giedd down to your right and the Gwys Fawr on your left. These are left behind as the route enters an area that resembles a cratered moonscape, with numerous shake holes marked on the OS 1:25,000 map. Leave the bridleway marked on the map at grid reference SN 8040 1791 and strike east to find **Sinc Giedd**.

### SINC GIEDD

During wet periods the stream flows beneath this cliff of the Llandyfan Limestone. The Giedd Valley is eroded along a north–south geological fault, but the water that disappears here does not continue underground to feed the Afon Giedd; instead it joins the Mazeways series in the Dan-yr-Ogof cave system 3km away as the crow flies. Cavers have made many attempts to connect the sink holes in this area with Dan-yr-Ogof cave, but these have so far been unsuccessful.

Head north from Sinc Giedd along the left-hand side of the stream gully to the bridleway. Turn left along the path and then strike right, passing a derelict stone sheep enclosure. Continue climbing across **Carnau Gŵys** to the col between Fan Foel and Picws Du. Turn left and follow the ridge to the summit of Picws Du. Down below is the glacial cirque of Llyn y Fan Fach.

## WALK 38 – CARMARTHEN FANS VIA CWM GIEDD

On a clear day there are fine panoramic views from **Picws Du** of Plinlimon to the north, the Preseli Hills to the west, the Devon coast and Gower to the south and the Black Mountains to the east. A circular cairn, 19.5m in diameter by 1m high, crowns the summit; this is probably a prehistoric funerary monument. Down below is Llyn y Fan Fach, the setting of the local legend of the Lady of the Lake.

Continue (SW) along the ridge of **Bannau Sir Gaer** and leave it by striking south across Cefn Twrch and **Brest Twrch** to the ford where the Afon Twrch starts to flow in an westerly direction. Cross the stream at a convenient point and traverse a featureless area with the stream gully of the Afon Twrch on your right (see 'Cwm Twrch', Walk 34). Head for the high ground ahead to join the bridleway, another coffin route, marked on the map. Descend (SW) and cross over a collapsed stone wall and follow this downslope on your right. Cross another wall and shortly afterwards the path finishes near a **standing stone**. From the stone, continue walking in the same direction to a track, turn left and continue SSW.

Map continues on page 210

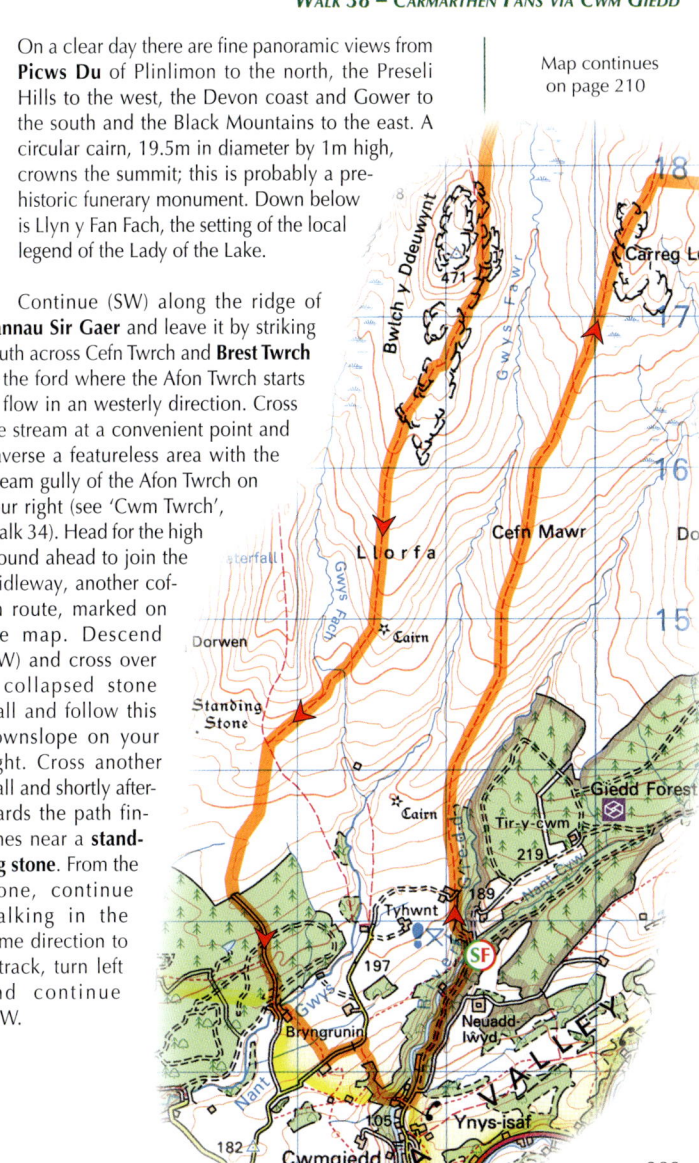

Leave the track after you cross a second boggy area and cut across the moorland to a gate in the hill fence. Go through this keeping to the main track. Carry straight on at a junction and cross the river bridge to Beudy Bach. Pass between the buildings and follow the footpath through fields to the road at Hen-Glyn-Isaf. Turn left and then right at the next fingerpost onto the bridleway to Nant-gwinau Bridge. Turn left and take the track back to the start.

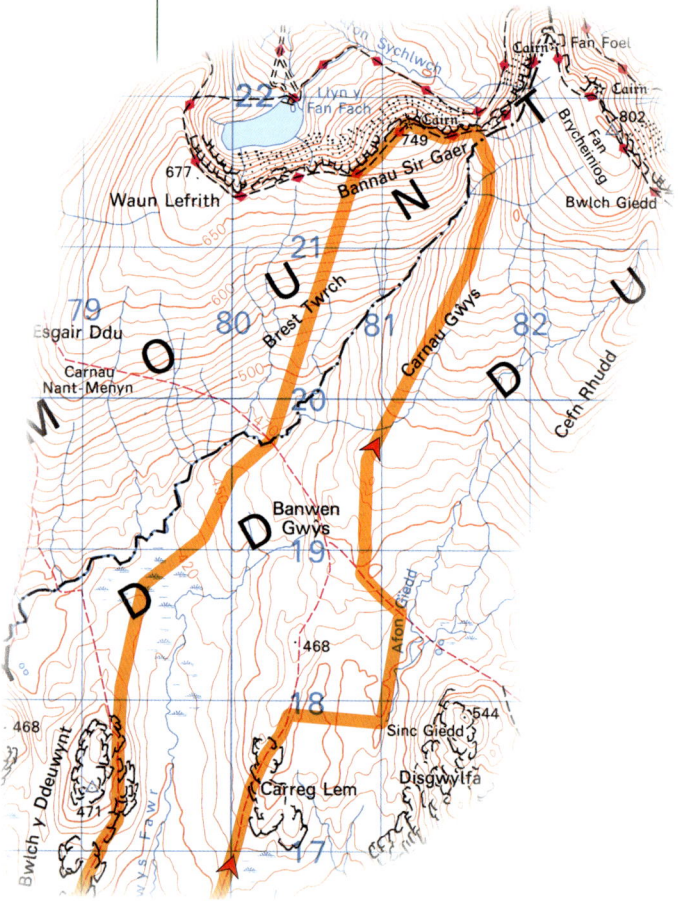

# WALK 39
## *Carreg Cennen*

| | |
|---|---|
| **Start/finish** | Carreg Cennen Castle car park (SN 666 193), postcode SA19 6UA |
| **Distance** | 5.5km (3.4 miles) |
| **Total ascent** | 215m (710ft) |
| **Grade** | 1 |
| **Max elevation** | 262m (859ft) |
| **Map** | OL12 Western area |

This short walk, which has spectacular views of Carreg Cennen Castle, encompasses plenty of valley and mountain wildlife as well as interesting limestone features. An exploration of the castle and its cave is a real adventure but remember to bring a torch, so you can venture into the bowels of the subterranean world on offer here.

There are two waymarked routes and this one follows the 'red castle' path. Go through the gate in the middle of the bottom of the car park and cross the fields on the waymarked path to the road. Turn left and descend the hill, ignoring the footpath that leaves on the right. Turn right at the next fingerpost and follow the 'red castle' sign down to the stream.

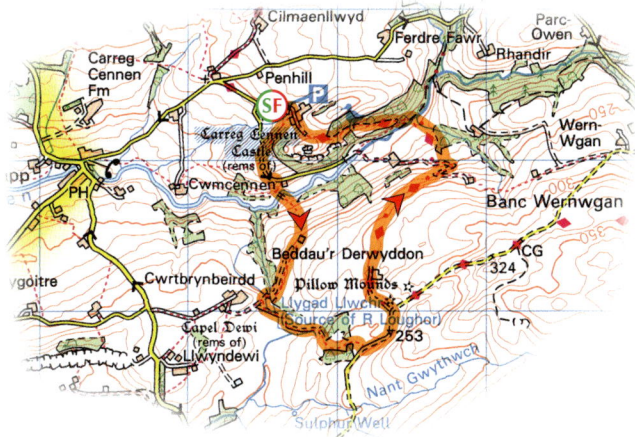

*Aerial view of Carreg Cennen on its limestone cliff*

Cross over the Afon Cennen and head up to Llwyn-bedw. The route continues across fields to the mountain road passing **Llygad Llwchr**, the source of the River Loughor.

The water coming out of the **cave** entrance emanates from an underground lake beneath Mynydd Du and has travelled for over four miles underground and from over 300m higher up. The limestone cave system was first explored in 1841 and nearly 1km of passages has been discovered to date.

### CARREG CENNEN CASTLE

This impressive strategic location was probably the site of an Iron Age hill fort before Rhys ap Gruffudd, Lord Rhys, most likely constructed a masonry castle here. It was captured by the English during the First War of Welsh Independence in 1277, and the castle was granted to John Giffard, Lord Giffard of Brimpsfield, who, with his son, built the current stone structure. Owain Glyndŵr attacked the castle in 1403 with the initial attempt being repulsed. However, John Scudamore, the garrison's commander, was forced to surrender when the castle was besieged. A supply of clean water would not have been a problem, as fresh water rises up at the end of a cave that lies deep within the castle walls. The castle came back into English ownership when a Yorkist army seized it and partially demolished the walls to prevent its further use.

Turn left on the road and carry straight on at the right-hand bend onto a farm track, which forms part of the Beacons Way. Keep following the 'red castle' waymarkers across the fields and down to the bridge over the Afon Cennen. On this part of the walk there are wonderful views of the castle perched atop the limestone crag.

> The cliffs are the only known location in South Wales of a collection of limestone- and sun-loving **lichens**. Look out for the dominant white crustose lichen, *Aspicilia calcarea*, particularly on the tops of the castle walls. There are also rare **plants** here, such as the spiked speedwell, which has beautiful deep-violet-blue flowers; they can be seen growing on the vertical rock face below the castle. Wild chives can also be found; the name 'Cennen' comes from the Welsh word for the leek family. Autumn is the time to see a spectacular display of wild **fungi** of exceptional variety growing on the tightly grazed grassland around the castle. Species include golden spindles, crazed cap, lilac pinkgill and toasted, crimson and persistent waxcaps.

*There is a café here and a quaint pub in the village of Trapp nearby.*

Climb through the woodland and up to the **castle**. There is an entry fee but this is well worth it, even for just exploring the cave deep within the limestone. ◄

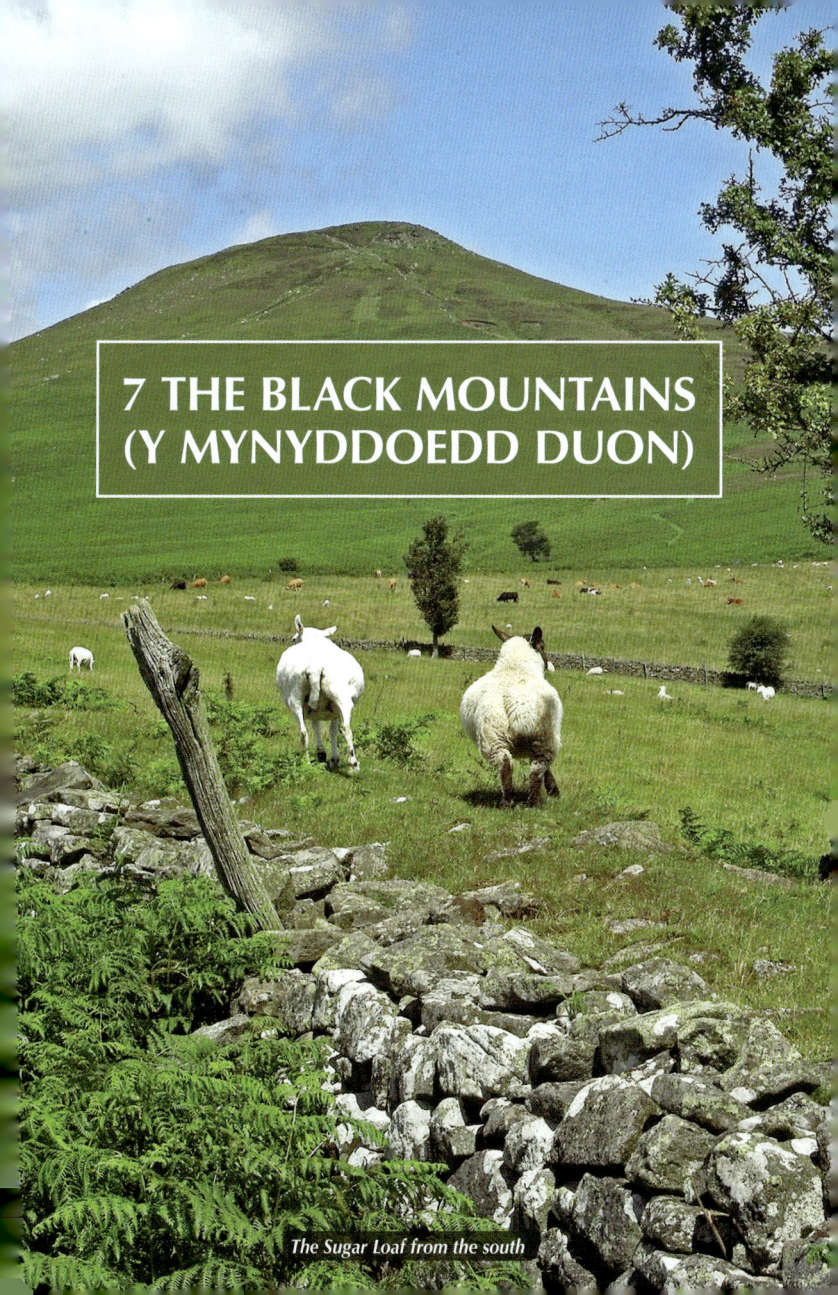

# 7 THE BLACK MOUNTAINS (Y MYNYDDOEDD DUON)

*The Sugar Loaf from the south*

# WALK 40

*Pen Cerrig-calch and Table Mountain*

| | |
|---|---|
| **Start/finish** | Crickhowell, car park (SO 216 190) |
| **Distance** | 9.5km (5.9 miles); with extension 18.25km (11.3 miles) |
| **Total ascent** | 635m (2080ft); with extension 925m (3030ft) |
| **Grade** | 3; with extension 3 |
| **Max elevation** | 701m (2300ft); with extension 719m (2359ft) |
| **Map** | OL13 Eastern area |

This is one of the best of the high walks in the Black Mountains. The summit of Pen Cerrig-calch is reached via Darren and this avoids the well-used ascent route via Table Mountain. The descent includes the added bonus of following 1.5km of Cwm Cumbeth, a wooded valley that is full of wildlife interest. The extension to Pen Allt-mawr and around the valley of Cwm Banw is well worthwhile.

This route follows the Beacons Way to the hill fence. Walk back up the road from the car park and turn left after the second house, just past the apex of the bend. Cross over the next road on the path between the houses, straight over again and turn left by the metal gate. Turn right at the road and walk up to the farm. Go through the gate, bear left and then right on the track around **Gwern-vale Farm**. Continue on the waymarked path through the fields to **Twyn**. Cross over a path here and climb up to the hill fence, still on the Beacons Way.

If the weather conditions are poor, a low-level alternative route can be taken here by turning right on the path above the hill fence, rejoining the main route just before Table Mountain.

*The extended route to Pen Allt-mawr and Pen Twyn Glas leaves from here.*

Continue on the path up the slope and look out for a path on the right that climbs upslope after the end of the woodland on the left. Take this and then strike up to the summit of **Pen Cerrig-calch**. ◂

## WALK 40 – PEN CERRIG-CALCH AND TABLE MOUNTAIN

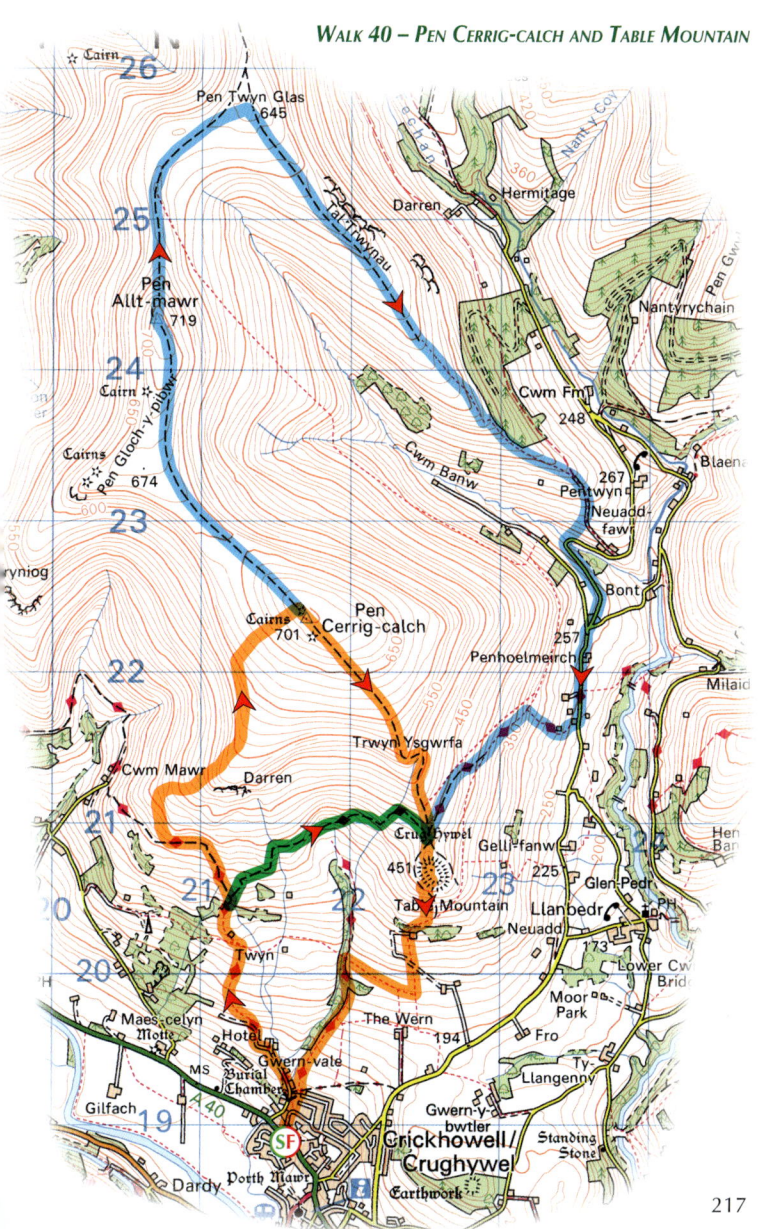

217

*The Grwyne Fechan Valley and Cerrig-calch*

The **summit** itself comprises Millstone Grit, but just below this is a band of Carboniferous limestone that was once part of the Llangattock escarpment before the Usk Valley was formed; this is the only occurrence of limestone in the Black Mountains. Quartz conglomerates of the Plateau Beds are found below and then Brownstones and Senni Beds on lower ground. A variety of upland birds live here, including skylarks, meadow pipits, stonechats and ravens.

To continue on the main route descend the path southeast from the summit, clamber down the steep section at **Trwyn Ysgwrfa** and climb the steps through the earth and stone ditches and ramparts onto **Table Mountain**.

Formed by the dip slope of the resistant Plateau Beds, Table Mountain is the impressive setting for **Crug Hywel**, an Iron Age hill fort that is thought to have been owned by Hywel Dda, a well-respected prince of South Wales, in the 10th century. He was the grandson of Rhodri the Great, famous for killing the leader of the Viking invaders at Anglesey. Hywel introduced the Law of Wales, a set of social rules to free the common man from oppression by the upper classes.

## WALK 40 – PEN CERRIG-CALCH AND TABLE MOUNTAIN

Continue southwards down the sloping flat summit, keeping to the right-hand edge above the crags, and descend the steps at the end. Drop down to the path below on the right and to the hill fence where the two drystone walls meet. Cross the stile and follow the path, which then turns to the left and drops down the slope through the fields. Turn right on a footpath that leaves the path in the field just below the farm of Ysgubor Newydd and contour along the slope to join a path that descends along Cumberth Brook.

*Robin*

> This is a good location for **wildlife and plant** spotting. The route is bordered by lesser celandine (a yellow flower) and the woodland on the right has a rich tapestry of bluebells, dog violets, wood sorrel and wood anemones in the spring; the latter are often an indication of ancient woodland. A mixture of beech, oak, ash, hazel and holly can also be seen. A variety of woodland birds, including the tit, pied flycatcher, nuthatch, redstart, tawny owl, woodpecker and treecreeper, frequent the woodland as well as butterflies.

This will bring you back to the metal gate you went through at the beginning of the walk. Retrace your steps back to the start.

### Extension

Continue north along the ridge and drop down slightly to a col. The path becomes stony and exposed to high winds and leads to the summit of **Pen Allt-Mawr**, where there is a trig point. Descend north from the summit to **Pen Twyn Glas** around the head of Cwm Banw. Keep below the crest of the ridge on your right and merge with a path descending **Tal Trwynau** ridge on your right.

> The summit of **Pen Twyn Glas** (645m) is marked by two upright stones, 19th-century boundary markers, which are inscribed with the names of local

landowners, 'Mrs Macnamara 1811 and Sir J Bailey Bart 1847', whose estates met at this point.

Follow the ridge downhill, passing a tall cairn, and cross the stile in the hill fence. Continue down the prow of the hill and keep right at a fork, ignoring the more obvious farm track on the left. Leave this track when it turns to the left and carry straight on ahead alongside a hedge to the corner of the road. Turn right and walk up the road ahead to where the next footpath leaves on the right at Green Cottage, where you join the Beacons Way. The path just after the cottage bears right along a wall to the ruins of Graig-lwyd. Continue up the hill past some holly bushes and meet the path contouring around the lower slopes of Pen Cerrig-calch. Turn right and shortly after left, to meet a junction of paths. Take the left path climbing gently upwards, taking the higher path, when it divides, to the col, with **Table Mountain** on the left, where you rejoin the main route.

# WALK 41
## *Craig y Cilau*

| | |
|---|---|
| **Start/finish** | Llangattock Quarry car park (SO 209 154) |
| **Distance** | 8km (5 miles) |
| **Total ascent** | 350m (1150ft) |
| **Grade** | 2 |
| **Max elevation** | 490m (1607ft) |
| **Map** | OL13 Eastern area |

This short walk visits Craig y Cilau National Nature Reserve, which is designated for its rich limestone plant life and is one of the national park's treasures. Unusual trees are found here, including a species of whitebeam that is found nowhere else. Once a quarry, the area is now a caver's paradise with an entrance to the famous Ogof Agen Allwedd system.

## WALK 41 – CRAIG Y CILAU

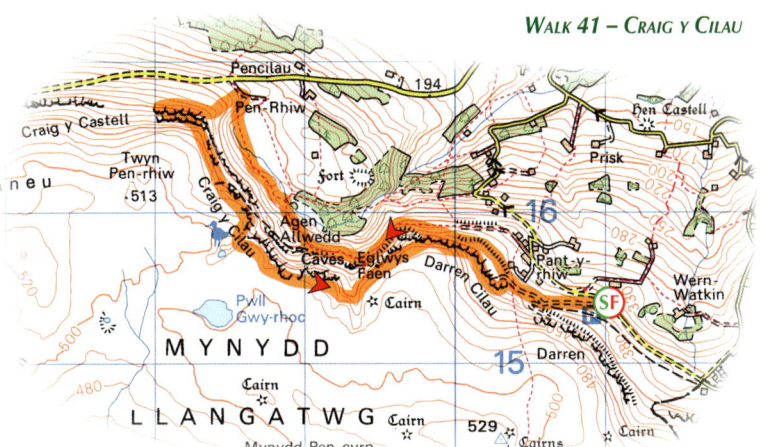

Leave the car park on a track with the escarpment up on your left. Continue past an old lime kiln and bear right onto a disused tramway that winds between spoil heaps and beneath the worked face of the old quarry at **Darren Cilau**. ▶ Continue along the terrace to the National Nature Reserve information board.

The Sugar Loaf Mountain is over to the east.

### CRAIG Y CILAU

Craig y Cilau, which was designated a National Nature Reserve in 1959, contains several caves, rich plant life and a number of uncommon trees, including several species of whitebeam. The short limestone cliffs were once quarried but now contain some of the finest limestone vegetation in the national park.

*Craig y Cilau*

The varied habitat, from the scrub woodland on the lower slopes up through the short limestone grassland and sparsely wooded cliffs to the open moorland of the summit, makes this an excellent reserve for many different insects and birds. Around 40 bird species have been recorded here, including ring ouzels: a migrant thrush that resembles a blackbird with a white bib. Clinging to the ledges of the cliffs, out of reach of grazing sheep, are five notable species of whitebeam, one of which is unique to this locality. In the shaded woody area on the lower slopes is another rarity in this area: the alpine enchanter's nightshade, thriving at the southern limit of its distribution in Britain. Other rare lime-loving plants, such as Angular Solomon's Seal and rue leaved saxifrage, can be found here.

Above the limestone escarpment is a capping of Millstone Grit and below the limestone are the sandstones, silts and clays of the Old Red Sandstone formation. The reserve, therefore, enjoys a very wide range of soil types, which is reflected in the huge variety of flowering plants.

Continue round the terrace in a long sweeping arc (W and N). On a clear day the views and situation are remarkable. After the hollow of **Eglwys Faen** you reach the extensive limestone cliffs, and a waymarked path descends on the right into the valley. Leave this for the moment and continue to the end of the terrace to view the entrance to the **Agen Allwedd** cave system.

The limestone itself is peppered with **caves**, and Mynydd Llangattock contains extensive cave systems, including Ogof Agen Allwedd (37.5 km), Ogof Daren Cilau and Eglwys Faen. Agen Allwedd is an important winter roost for lesser horseshoe bats. It also has a colony of long-eared bats.

Backtrack to the waymarked path and descend gently to the valley. On the way down there is a fine view north past the high summits of Pen Cerrig-calch and Pen Allt-mawr to Pen Tir and Mynydd Troed. Castell Dinas can be seen in the far distance to the right of Mynydd Troed. Waun Fach, the highest point in the Black Mountains, is just visible to the east.

The path branches at a waymarked post. Follow the yellow arrow down to the right between bracken and hawthorn trees. At the valley base turn left and continue up the valley, climbing slightly alongside a moss-covered wall on the right.

At the sharp right bend in the wall continue straight ahead and into an interesting high bog, Waun Ddu. ▶ Continue onwards and turn left just before a track and climb the slope at the end of the escarpment. Follow the path along the top of ridge and then above the quarries. Descend back to the old tramway track that you used earlier at the end of **Darren Cilau** and retrace your steps back to the start.

Small areas have been fenced off for experimental purposes and these harbour rushes and heathers.

# WALK 42
*Crug Mawr and Sugar Loaf*

| | |
|---|---|
| **Start/finish** | Red Lion, Llanbedr (SO 240 204) |
| **Distance** | 20.5km (12.7 miles) |
| **Total ascent** | 985m (3230ft) |
| **Grade** | 3 |
| **Max elevation** | 596m (1955ft) |
| **Map** | OL13 Eastern area |

With two upland sections linked by tranquil wooded river valleys and two excellent pubs along the way, this all-day walk is full of variety and interest. The highlight is a visit to the extraordinary Partrishow Church, which has a wealth of history spanning a thousand years. The return route climbs the Sugar Loaf and then drops down to Llangenny and a well-earned break at the Dragon's Head pub. A relaxing river walk brings you back to the start.

Start at the Red Lion pub in the village of Llanbedr. With the pub and church in front of you, take the track with a 'No-through road' sign on the right, which then swings around the edge of the graveyard and down to the river, the Grwyne Fechan, in the valley below. Cross Upper Cwm Bridge and take the stile on the left and follow the zigzag path up the valley side. The bridleway on your right is your return route. The path divides halfway up the slope. Take the left-hand fork.

The **woodland** is a mixture of ash, beech, sycamore and hazel and is particularly impressive in April and May when the understorey is carpeted with a mixture of lesser celandine (yellow flower), wood sorrel (delicate white flower), wood anemones (white flower), dog violets and bluebells.

Cross the stile where the woodland finishes and continue into a field and to the road. There are excellent views to your right of the north slope of the Sugar Loaf, which is on the return route. On your left is the Grwyne Fechan Valley with Table Mountain and Pen Cerrig-calch. Cross the road and the stile into a field. There is a break in the line of trees ahead and the route crosses an upright rock slab and a stile in the hedge just before this on your right. Head across the field to the left of the house (Henbant Fach) to the start of a track. Shortly afterwards, take the bridleway on the left with a mossy drystone wall. ◀

> The woodland here has a superb carpet of bluebells in the spring.

Ignore the track that leaves on the right just before the woodland finishes and carry on to the gate where you turn right along the Beacons Way. Ahead are excellent views of the Grwyne Fechan Valley and up to the summits of Waun Fach and Pen y Gadair Fawr. Follow the path which runs alongside the drystone wall and ignore a gate

WALK 42 – CRUG MAWR AND SUGAR LOAF

in this. At a junction take the right-hand fork to the summit of **Blaen-yr-Henbant** where you can follow a sheep track along its left-hand edge along the top of a line of crags. The area here is covered in bilberry and the songs of skylarks can be heard in spring and summer. A closer inspection of the Old Red Sandstone rocks shows they are red in colour and well bedded.

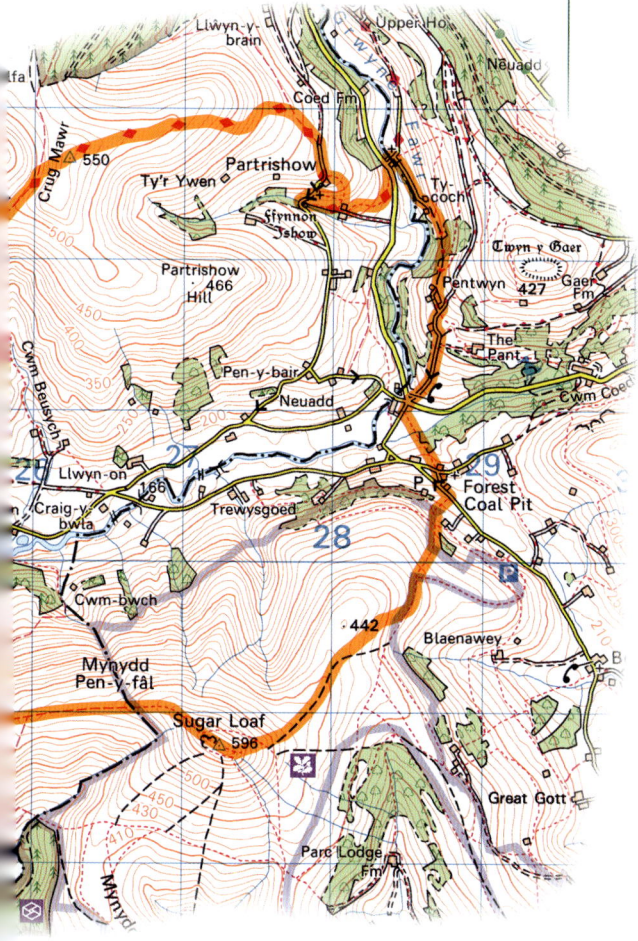

Drop down to a col with Cwm Beusych to your right and Cwm Milaid to your left. The Beacons Way skirts below the summit of **Crug Mawr** but take the small path that leads to the trig point. The area is covered with heather and bilberry and has excellent panoramic views. On a clear day it is possible to see the Cotswolds and the Malvern Hills to the east and the Severn Estuary to the south.

From the trig point descend east along a path, passing a small pond, to where it runs alongside the hill fence to a gate marked 'Beacons Way'. Go through this down to the road and continue straight ahead to where a footpath signposted to Ty'n-y-llwyn leaves on a bend just before a stone barn. Take this and cross the field and then turn right along a break in the slope, before you reach the farm, to **Partrishow Church**.

> **Partrishow Church** was established in the mid 11th century and has a rare surviving medieval rood screen and loft, which date back to about 1500. The church is entered through a 14th-century porch and as well as the splendidly carved oak rood screen, it also houses two stone altars in front and a 16th-century chest hewn out of a single tree trunk. The font at the rear is carved out of one block of stone and bears an inscription from around 1055, making it one of the oldest in Wales. A number of old wall paintings were discovered during the restoration in 1909, one of which is a chillingly eerie 'Doom Figure' that depicts a skeleton carrying a scythe, an hourglass and a spade and which was reputedly painted with human blood in the 17th century. A copy of the Ten Commandments, which also dates back to the 17th century, is the clearest of the many other interesting wall paintings.

Carry on through the graveyard to the road, turn left and follow the road to the bend and **Ffynnon Ishow**.

> **Ffynnon Ishow** is the secluded holy well of St Issui, an early Christian priest who lived near the well and gave hospitality to pilgrims. Legend has it that a continental pilgrim was cured of leprosy here and left much gold to build the church. The approach

## WALK 42 – CRUG MAWR AND SUGAR LOAF

to the well is indicated by a stone marked with a Maltese cross, which is thought to have been a medieval pilgrim's stone. Unfortunately, Issui met his death at the hands of an ungrateful traveller.

Take the footpath on the left just above the well. It crosses the field, with the church up to the left, and leads

*17th-century painting, Partrishow Church; Rood screen, Partrishow Church*

to the impressive house of Tyn-y-llwyn. Cross the stile and take the path on the left, marked 'Beacons Way', and follow this to the road. Cross this and walk down to the bridge over the **Grwyne Fawr** and turn right on the tarmac road before **Tabernacle Church**. This becomes a footpath at **Ty-coch** where you continue straight ahead above a house, following the valley to **Pentwyn** and then to a T-junction with a road.

Turn right here and drop down to a five-way road junction. Continue straight ahead to Pontyspig, in the direction of the Sugar Loaf. After about 100 metres take the footpath on the left and head straight across the field to a stile and cross a small stream. Head for the stile in the opposite fence. Pass through woodland using boardwalks, cross a stile and head for the house across the field.

Turn left at the road and first right to a junction where you bear left. Continue to a large oak tree on the right that marks where the path leaves for the Sugar Loaf 3.2km away. Take this and shortly after cross the stile in the hill fence where there is a National Trust sign. Carry straight on, ignoring the path on the right. The path runs along a fence with trees on the left and then cuts up the hill through bracken that changes to heather and bilberry. It follows a stone wall then leaves this where the wall turns left.

Take the right-hand fork heading for the summit. This meets a path coming up from the left. Bear right at this point and take the path, an old quarry track, which works its way around the northern side of the summit and eventually to the top of the **Sugar Loaf**.

> Your great effort is rewarded with superb **panoramic views**. Due east is the steep slope of Ysgyryd Fawr, north-west is Pen Cerrig-calch and to the west in the distance are Pen y Fan and Corn Du, the highest summits in South Wales. On a clear day it is possible to look south over Abergavenny and to the Severn Estuary and the Devon hills beyond. The Grwyne Fawr Valley, below to the north, formed as a result of a major geological fault in the earth's crust called the Neath Disturbance.

Head (W) down the path across **Mynydd Pen-y-fal**. At the junction take the right-hand fork, with Llanbedr down to the right, and then head left when the path divides again

*The view west from the Sugar Loaf*

and drops to the hill fence in the direction of Llangenny. Turn left and before the path starts to rise again there is a gate. Go through this and follow the valley down to a track and then the road. Carry straight on to the bridge over the Grwyne Fawr in **Llangenny**. ▶

Just before the bridge on the east bank is a stile and a footpath that runs upstream. The woodland has a great show of flowers in the spring. The path comes to a stone bridge and this is where you have to leave the riverbank. A yellow arrow directs you to turn right along a fence to a post with a sign warning 'Danger'. Turn left here along the obvious path to a stile and a narrow path. Cross over at the junction of the paths and cross the stile. Shortly after, ignore the path that drops down to the left and continue to some cottages and the road.

Turn left and then left again when there is a 'Private Road' sign. Descend the track and take the first footpath on the left. The path drops down through the woodland to a bridge across the river and across a field to a road. Cross over the road into a field with the river on your left. A path climbs up to a track where you turn left and keep following the river. Ignore the first bridge and continue to the bridge you crossed at the beginning of the walk. Turn left over the bridge and retrace your steps to the start.

The Dragon's Head pub is just on the other side of the river.

# WALK 43
## Llanthony Priory, Offa's Dyke and Bal Mawr

| | |
|---|---|
| **Start/finish** | Llanthony Priory, Vale of Ewyas (SO 288 278) |
| **Distance** | 17km (10.6 miles) |
| **Total ascent** | 795m (2610ft) |
| **Grade** | 3 |
| **Max elevation** | 616m (2021ft) |
| **Map** | OL13 Eastern area |

This classic route takes in two ridges and the beautiful Vale of Ewyas. Starting at the impressive Llanthony Priory, the walk climbs up to Offa's Dyke, the boundary between England and Wales. Other important religious buildings are discovered at Capel-y-ffin before another ascent to the ridge and on to Bal Mawr. The excellent pub at the priory is a welcome treat at the end of the day.

Start in front of Llanthony Priory where there is a sign marked 'Hill walks' on the left. Take the indicated path to the northern side of the priory, follow the track marked 'Offa's Dyke North' and then take the path marked 'All Routes', on your left, to a gate. The path takes the western flank of Cwm Siarpal to the corner of Loxidge Wood, crosses the hill fence and then climbs **Loxidge Tump** to Offa's Dyke. Look back for a superb view of Llanthony Priory.

**Offa's Dyke** marks the border between Wales and England. The deep ditch and dyke structure was built in the eighth century by the Mercian ruler King Offa in an attempt to keep the Welsh out of his kingdom.

The heather **moorland** here is important for rowan and merlin, with 2700 acres having been acquired by the national park. It is managed as a grouse moor and has the largest breeding population in the national park.

## Walk 43 – Llanthony Priory, Offa's Dyke and Bal Mawr

## LLANTHONY PRIORY

*Llanthony Priory Nave*

Llanthony Priory was one of the earliest houses of Augustinian canons to be founded in Britain. The knight William de Lacy is said to have come across a ruined chapel of St David while out hunting. A church, dedicated to John the Baptist, was built on this site and was reorganised as a priory in about 1118. Giraldus Cambrensis visited in the 12th century and wrote of the priory as being 'fixed amongst a barbarous people'. In 1135 the 40 canons were forced to retreat to Hereford and Gloucester and the building was destroyed. They were brought back by the de Lacy family, and a great rebuilding phase between 1180 and 1230 resulted in the construction of the priory's church, one of the greatest medieval buildings in Wales.

*The Honddu Valley is a classic U-shape and was cut by a glacier during the last Ice Age.*

Turn left (NW) along the ridge to a milepost indicating Red Daren down to the east. Continue along the peaty crest of the ridge where some of the wettest parts have been protected by large flagstones. Pass the **trig point** where there are good views down into the picturesque Olchon Valley. Turn left at another milestone, taking the path south-west down a spur and picking up a stony path to the left towards Nant Vision. Follow the path that zigzags through bracken and then turns west along the hill fence to a stile after around 100 metres. ◀

Cross this and descend steeply through woodland to another stile. Aim for the farm and follow a fingerpost right, above the hedgerow, to a stile and the lane to **Vision Farm**. Turn right up the valley, passing behind Ty'r-onen Farm, onto a wide unmade track to a ford. Cross this and a stile ahead and cross the field to the corner of the trees. Cross a small stream over a stone stile and continue to a second stone stile. Cross the field ahead to a sandy track and a gate behind Blaenau Farm leading to the yew-tree-encircled St Mary's Church at **Capel-y-ffin**. ▶

Walk down to the main road, crossing the river bridge, and take the road on your right to the Grange Trekking Centre. Pass the first footpath on the left and then take the narrow road on the left from where you can see the old monastery.

*Capel-y-ffin*

Measuring 8m by 4m, St Mary's Church is one of the smallest in the country and was built in 1762.

### LLANTHONY TERTIA MONASTERY

The Anglican monastery of Llanthony Tertia was founded in 1870 by the eccentric Joseph Leycester Lyne, who took the religious name of Father Ignatius. Lyne, an Anglican lay reader, was inspired by the monastic revival of the late 19th century and was determined to found an Anglican Benedictine religious order. There was a great deal of opposition to his ideas, and he found it impossible to persuade any of the Anglican bishops to ordain him as a priest or to support him in any way. This was hardly surprising as he practised a daily ritual where the monks would take it in turns to be led into the cloister with a halter, spat on, walked over by the rest of the community and made to beg for their bread.

Walk up to the **Grange Guest House** and turn left up a stony lane through a gate. Follow a zigzag track up the hillside to the crest of the hill to a stone called the Blacksmith's Anvil. Down to the west is the glacially cut, U-shaped Grwyne Fawr Valley. On the left to the north is Lord Hereford's Knob and Hay Bluff is to the right. Below the reservoir is the Mynydd Du conifer plantation, a huge blight on the landscape, and beyond are the high summits of Pen Allt-mawr and Pen Cerrig-calch.

Continue (SE) along **Chwarel y Fan**, **Bwlch Bach** and **Bwlch Isaf** to the summit of **Bâl Mawr**. The Sugar Loaf Mountain is over to the south-west and Ysgwrd Fawr is to the south-east. Descend south-east from the trig point to meet a crossroads on the level ground at **Bâl Bach**. Turn left onto the Beacons Way and descend the path that leads into **Cwm-bwchel** and follows the stream course on its northern side. ◄ Cross the hill fence just above the buildings and follow the waymark signs for the Beacons Way down to the road and back to the start at the priory.

*There are fine views of the priory in the valley below.*

# WALK 44
## Lord Hereford's Knob

| | |
|---|---|
| **Start/finish** | Bridge over the Afon Honddu, Capel-y-ffin (SO 255 315) |
| **Distance** | 10.5km (6.5 miles) |
| **Total ascent** | 405m (1330ft) |
| **Grade** | 3 |
| **Max elevation** | 690m (2264ft) |
| **Map** | OL13 Eastern area |

This excellent walk explores a picturesque and surprisingly remote side valley of the Vale of Ewyas. A steep initial ascent is followed by a ridge walk to Lord Hereford's Knob from where there are fine panoramic views of Mid Wales to the north-west and of the glacial U-shaped valley of the River Honddu. There is plenty of historical interest with two churches and a monastery along the route.

## WALK 44 – LORD HEREFORD'S KNOB

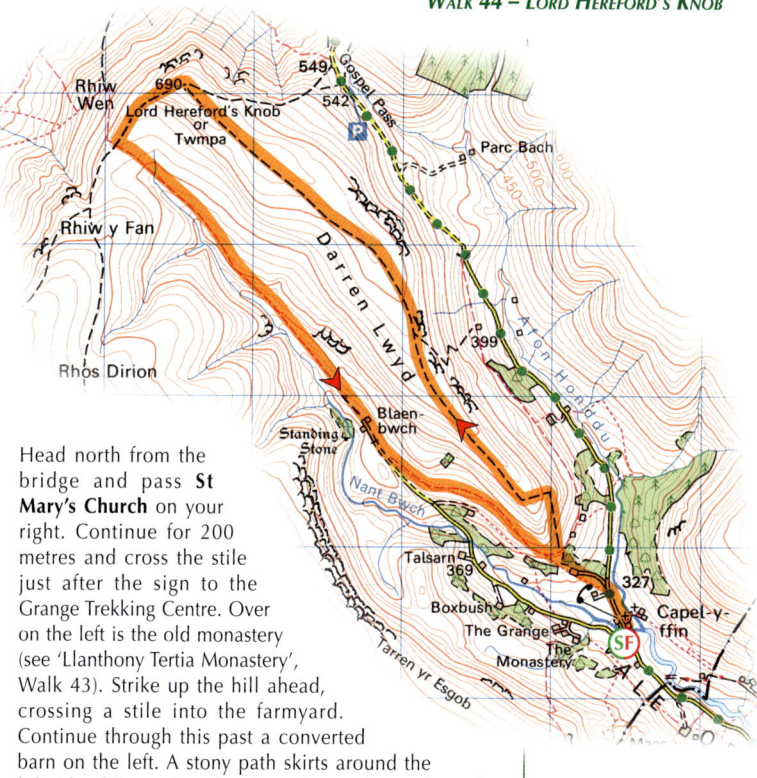

Head north from the bridge and pass **St Mary's Church** on your right. Continue for 200 metres and cross the stile just after the sign to the Grange Trekking Centre. Over on the left is the old monastery (see 'Llanthony Tertia Monastery', Walk 43). Strike up the hill ahead, crossing a stile into the farmyard. Continue through this past a converted barn on the left. A stony path skirts around the left side of Darren Lwyd and at a large ash tree the path divides. Take a sharp right up onto the hillside. Shortly after there is an excellent view south to the Vale of Ewyas and the monastery on the right. The path swings round to the left. ▶

At the divide in the path take the left-hand climbing path which shortly doubles back (SW) and onto the prow of the hill. Turn right (N) and you will soon reach a well-built shelter below the summit of **Darren Lwyd**. Continue north to a true cairn, still below the summit. Continue up the ridge, climbing gently, and the path becomes alternately sandy and muddy between heather. At the fork, take the right path and continue gently to the badly eroded summit area with first a collapsed cairn and then a standing cairn. There is a small

Across to the right is the hill ridge carrying Offa's Dyke, which forms the boundary between Wales and England.

*Nant Bwch from Lord Hereford's Knob*

There are small waterfalls in a side valley joining from the west.

cairn on the summit of **Lord Hereford's Knob**, also known as the Twmpa.

Descend south-west from the summit. On a clear day the Brecon Beacons can be seen straight ahead. At the lowest point on the escarpment a track descends steeply (N) into the valley. At this point take the bridleway (SE), soon picking up a small stream, the start of **Nant Bwch**. Make sure to descend on its left bank into a quickly steepening valley. ◀ The path remains well above the river and follows a man-made ledge, presumably a quarry route.

The path drops down the valley and fords a small stream joining from the east where there is a fine waterfall and stone refuge. Continue to **Blaen-Bwch Farm**. Leave the road on a footpath on the left opposite the first stand of trees on the hillside above. This soon joins the bridleway that contours around the hillside to where you crossed the hill fence earlier. Retrace your steps to the start.

# WALK 45
*Castell Dinas and Waun Fach*

| | |
|---|---|
| **Start/finish** | Castle Inn, Pengenffordd, A479 Talgarth to Tretower (SO 174 296) |
| **Distance** | 11.5km (7.1 miles) |
| **Total ascent** | 640m (2100ft) |
| **Grade** | 3 |
| **Max elevation** | 811m (2661ft) |
| **Map** | OL13 Eastern area |

This superb walk ascends Waun Fach, the highest mountain in the Black Mountains, and has stunning panoramic views. The route descends Y Grib, a narrow spur of land, to Castell Dinas, an impressive Iron Age hill fort with a commanding view of the Rhiangoll Valley.

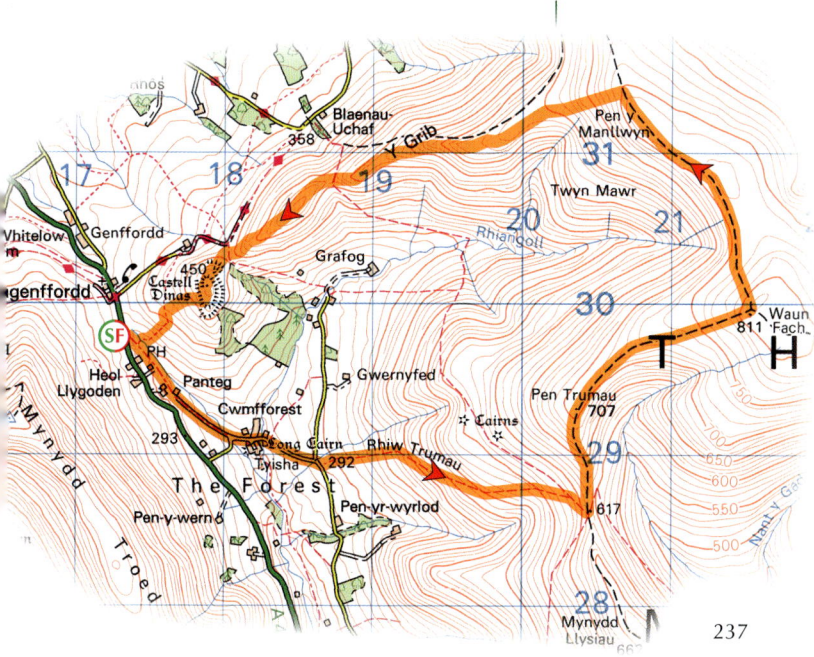

*View south from Y Grib*

At the northern end of the pub car park descend a set of wooden steps, marked with a waymark arrow to Castell Dinas, into the lane below and turn right down the track. After about 50 metres there is a stile on the left. Ignore this – it will be your descent route at the end of the walk. Walk behind and below the Castle Inn and after 200 metres the track divides. Keep to the left past a farm and cross a ford to meet a road on a bend. Turn left and follow the road, passing **Cwmfforest Farm** on the left, to where another road joins from the left.

Shortly afterwards, turn left onto a bridleway to the hill fence. ◄ Cross **Rhiw Trumau** to the cairn at the col. Turn north and follow the ridge along **Pen Trumau** to **Waun Fach**. Far to the east the Shropshire Clee Hills are visible and to the south you may glimpse the Bristol Channel. To the west are the Brecon Beacons and the Carmarthen Fans. Listen out for skylarks singing in the spring and summer.

Take the obvious path that descends a little to the north and then skirts around the eastern ridge of the Rhiangoll Valley. Climb slightly to **Pen y Manllwyn** and about 500 metres from the rather unclear summit drop down the hillside in a westerly direction to **Y Grib**. Keep to the summit of the ridge, avoiding the paths to the right and left which descend below the ridge itself. There are three sections to the ridge with short descents and climbs to the separate summits, and you will pass a substantial cairn on the way down past a few rocky outcrops. On the last summit before the castle hill is a round stone shelter.

Drop down quite steeply from this to a gate ahead. Cross the stile and climb up ahead to the remains of **Castell Dinas**. A more obvious path to the right should be avoided as it bypasses the castle remains.

The lower slopes of the mountains ahead are formed from the Senni Beds, with the summits composed of the more resistant Brownstones.

**Castell Dinas** is an Iron Age hill fort whose ramparts, steep sides and great ditches are still well defined. It is hard to believe that these were probably built as early as 500BC. A Norman motte and bailey style castle was also built on the site, but there is little remaining of this stone stronghold.

Drop to the right, leaving the small coniferous plantation on your left, to a stile. Descend the field, keeping the fence to your right, to reach another stile. Keep descending to the stream, which is easily crossed, to a stile leading into the lane where the walk began. Turn right and walk 50 metres to the steps and back to the start.

*Wild ponies on Pen Trumau*

# APPENDIX A
*Route summary table*

| Walk | Name | Start/finish | Distance | Total ascent | Grade | Page |
|---|---|---|---|---|---|---|
| 1 | Corn Du and Pen y Fan via Cwm Llwch | Cwm Llwch | 10.75km (6.7 miles) | 655m (2150ft) | 3 | 22 |
| 1a | *Alternative via Cwm Llwch ridge* | *Cwm Llwch* | *12.5km (7.7 miles)* | *725m (2380ft)* | *3* | *28* |
| 1b | *Cwm Llwch Valley alternative* | *Cwm Llwch* | *6km (3.7 miles)* | *335m (1100ft)* | *1* | *29* |
| 2 | Pen y Fan via Cwm Sere | Cwm Gwdi | 10.75km (6.7 miles) | 655m (2150ft) | 3 | 30 |
| 2a | *Cwm Sere Valley alternative* | *Cwm Gwdi* | *8.25km (5.1 miles)* | *275m (900ft)* | *1* | *30* |
| 3 | Cribyn via Cwm Sere | Cwm Gwdi | 10.75km (6.6 miles) | 600m (1970ft) | 3 | 35 |
| 3a | *Pen y Fan extension* | *Cwm Gwdi* | *12.5km (7.7 miles)* | *815m (2670ft)* | *3* | *38* |
| 4 | Cwm Sere ridge | Cwm Gwdi | 11.5km (7.1 miles) | 755m (2480ft) | 3 | 39 |
| 5 | Cribyn via Cwm Cynwyn | Cwm Gwdi | 13.5km (8.3 miles) | 660m (2160ft) | 3 | 43 |
| 6 | Fan y Bîg via Cwm Cynwyn | Llanfrynach | 16km (10 miles) | 570m (1870ft) | 3 | 48 |
| 7 | Cwm Cynwyn ridge | Llanfrynach | 17.5km (10.9 miles) | 770m (2530ft) | 3 | 51 |
| 8 | Fan y Bîg via Cwm Oergwm | Llanfrynach | 16km (10 miles) | 600m (1970ft) | 3 | 55 |
| 8a | *Craig Cwareli alternative* | *Llanfrynach* | *17km (10.6 miles)* | *740m (2430ft)* | *3* | *59* |
| 9 | Cwm Oergwm and Gist Wen | Llanfrynach | 17.25km (10.7 miles) | 710m (2330ft) | 3 | 60 |
| 9a | *Cwm Cwareli* | *Llanfrynach* | *13.5km (8.4 miles)* | *640m (2100ft)* | *3* | *63* |
| 10 | Cwm Oergwm ridge | Llanfrynach | 16.75km (10.4 miles) | 695m (2280ft) | 3 | 64 |
| 11 | Cwm Oergwm Valley | Llanfrynach | 11km (6.8 miles) | 285m (930ft) | 1 | 68 |
| 12 | Bryn | St Meugan's Church | 8km (5 miles) | 400m (1310ft) | 1 | 72 |

## Appendix A – Route summary table

| Walk | Name | Start/finish | Distance | Total ascent | Grade | Page |
|---|---|---|---|---|---|---|
| 13 | Cwm Tarthwynni circuit | Talybont Reservoir | 8.5km (5.2 miles) | 595m (1950ft) | 2 | 75 |
| 13a | Rhiw Bwlch y Ddwyallt extension | Talybont Reservoir | 11.5km (7.1 miles) | 720m (2360ft) | 2 | 79 |
| 14 | Blaen-y-glyn and Allt Forgan | Blaen-y-glyn Isaf | 8.75km (5.4 miles) | 530m (1740ft) | 2 | 80 |
| 15 | Blaen-y-glyn and Craig y Fan Ddu | Blaen-y-glyn Isaf | 9.25km (5.7 miles) | 525m (1720ft) | 2 | 86 |
| 15a | Craig Cwareli extension | Blaen-y-glyn Isaf | 12.75km (7.9 miles) | 640m (2100ft) | 2 | 90 |
| 15b | Valley-head alternative | Blaen-y-glyn Isaf | 9.75km (6 miles) | 640m (2100ft) | 2 | 90 |
| 15c | Low-level route | Blaen-y-glyn Isaf | 4km (2.5 miles) | 220m (720ft) | 2 | 90 |
| 16 | Torpantau circuit | Torpantau-Talybont | 13.75km (8.5 miles) | 505m (1660ft) | 3 | 91 |
| 17 | Neuadd Horseshoe | Taf Fechan | 13.25km (8.2 miles) | 640m (2100ft) | 3 | 96 |
| 17a | Craig Cwmoergwm extension | Taf Fechan | 14.5km (8.9 miles) | 835m (2735ft) | 2 | 100 |
| 18 | Cwm Llysiog and Waun Wen | Layby N of Pont Nant Gwinau | 10.5km (6.5 miles) | 345m (1130ft) | 2 | 101 |
| 19 | Corn Du and Pen y Fan via Cwm Crew | Forestry plantation off A470 | 8.5km (5.3 miles) | 495m (1620ft) | 3 | 105 |
| 19a | Corn Du and Pen y Fan extension | Forestry plantation off A470 | 11.5km (7.1 miles) | 505m (1660ft) | 3 | 109 |
| 20 | Corn Du and Pen y Fan from Pont ar Daf | Pont ar Daf | 7.5km (4.7 miles) | 520m (1700ft) | 3 | 112 |
| 21 | Craig Cerrig-gleisiad | Layby off A470 | 4km (2.4 miles) | 330m (1080ft) | 2 | 116 |
| 22 | Fan Fawr | Beacons Reservoir | 6km (3.7 miles) | 340m (1110ft) | 2 | 120 |
| 23 | Craig Cwm-du and Fan Frynych | Brecon Beacons NP Visitor Centre | 13.75km (8.5 miles) | 380m (1250ft) | 2 | 122 |
| 24 | Fan Frynych, Fan Dringarth and Fan Llia | Blaen Llia car park | 18km (11 miles) | 515m (1690ft) | 2 | 126 |
| 25 | Fan Gyhirych and Fan Nedd | Top of the Senni Bends | 13km (8 miles) | 580m (1900ft) | 2 | 130 |
| 26 | Elidir Trail | Pontneddfechan | 6.25km (3.9 miles) | 210m (690ft) | 1 | 138 |

241

## WALKING IN THE BRECON BEACONS

| Walk | Name | Start/finish | Distance | Total ascent | Grade | Page |
|---|---|---|---|---|---|---|
| 27 | Waterfall walk | Pontneddfechan | 15.5km (9.6 miles) | 510m (1670ft) | 2 | 143 |
| 28 | Sgwd yr Eira | Penderyn | 10km (6.2 miles) | 410m (1340ft) | 2 | 154 |
| 29 | Ystradfellte Falls | Car park at SA11 5US | 10km (6.2 miles) | 410m (1350ft) | 2 | 162 |
| 30 | Afon Nedd and Afon Mellte | Pont Melin-fach | 11.5km (7.1 miles) | 305m (1000ft) | 1 | 169 |
| 31 | Carmarthen Fans | Head of the Sawdde Valley | 15km (9.3 miles) | 805m (2640ft) | 3 | 178 |
| 32 | Tair Carn Isaf | Llandeilo road bridge | 7km (4.3 miles) | 330m (1080ft) | 2 | 182 |
| 33 | Sinc Giedd and the Carmarthen Fans | Gwyn Arms, Pen-y-cae | 20.25km (12.6 miles) | 880m (2890ft) | 4 | 184 |
| 34 | Afon Twrch | New Tredegar Arms, Cwmtwrch | 17.75km (11 miles) | 415m (1360ft) | 3 | 191 |
| 35 | Henrhyd Falls | Layby off A4067, Ynyswen | 7.25km (4.5 miles) | 180m (590ft) | 1 | 196 |
| 36 | Garreg Las | Capel Gwynfe | 19.25km (12 miles) | 665m (2180ft) | 3 | 200 |
| 37 | Cribarth | Abercrave Inn, Abercrave | 11km (6.8 miles) | 420m (1380ft) | 2 | 203 |
| 38 | Carmarthen Fans via Cwm Giedd | Cwm Giedd Forest | 24km (14.9 miles) | 690m (2260ft) | 4 | 207 |
| 39 | Carreg Cennen | Carreg Cennen Castle | 5.5km (3.4 miles) | 215m (710ft) | 1 | 211 |
| 40 | Pen Cerrig-calch and Table Mountain | Crickhowell | 9.5km (5.9 miles) | 635m (2080ft) | 3 | 216 |
| 40a | *Pen Cerrig-calch extension* | *Crickhowell* | *18.25km (11.3 miles)* | *925m (3030ft)* | *3* | *219* |
| 41 | Craig y Cilau | Llangattock Quarry | 8km (5 miles) | 350m (1150ft) | 2 | 220 |
| 42 | Crug Mawr and Sugar Loaf | Red Lion, Llanbedr | 20.5km (12.7 miles) | 985m (3230ft) | 3 | 223 |
| 43 | Llanthony Priory, Offa's Dyke and Bal Mawr | Llanthony Priory, Vale of Ewyas | 17km (10.6 miles) | 795m (2610ft) | 3 | 230 |
| 44 | Lord Hereford's Knob | Capel-y-ffin | 10.5km (6.5 miles) | 405m (1330 ft) | 3 | 234 |
| 45 | Castell Dinas and Waun Fach | Castle Inn, Pengenffordd | 11.5km (7.1 miles) | 640m (2100ft) | 3 | 237 |

# APPENDIX B
## Routes by interest

Routes are scored out of five for each interest category.

| Walk | Name | Geomorphology (glacial) | Geology | Birds | Flowers | Waterfalls | Panoramas | Archaeology |
|---|---|---|---|---|---|---|---|---|
| 1 | Corn Du and Pen y Fan via Cwm Llwch | 5 | 3 | 4 | 5 | 2 | 5 | 3 |
| 2 | Pen y Fan via Cwm Sere | 5 | 4 | 3 | 4 | 0 | 5 | 4 |
| 3 | Cribyn via Cwm Sere | 3 | 3 | 4 | 3 | 0 | 4 | 1 |
| 4 | Cwm Sere ridge | 5 | 4 | 2 | 4 | 0 | 5 | 4 |
| 5 | Cribyn via Cwm Cynwyn | 3 | 3 | 3 | 4 | 0 | 4 | 0 |
| 6 | Fan y Big via Cwm Cynwyn | 3 | 2 | 4 | 2 | 0 | 4 | 1 |
| 7 | Cwm Cynwyn ridge | 4 | 3 | 3 | 2 | 0 | 4 | 1 |
| 8 | Fan y Big via Cwm Oergwm | 2 | 2 | 2 | 2 | 0 | 0 | 1 |
| 9 | Cwm Oergwm and Gist Wen | 2 | 2 | 4 | 3 | 1 | 5 | 4 |
| 10 | Cwm Oergwm ridge | 2 | 2 | 3 | 2 | 0 | 5 | 1 |
| 11 | Cwm Oergwm Valley | 2 | 2 | 3 | 3 | 1 | 0 | 1 |
| 12 | Bryn | 2 | 1 | 2 | 2 | 0 | 5 | 0 |
| 13 | Cwm Tarthwynni circuit | 2 | 2 | 2 | 2 | 0 | 4 | 2 |
| 14 | Blaen-y-glyn and Allt Forgan | 3 | 3 | 4 | 3 | 3 | 5 | 0 |
| 15 | Blaen-y-glyn and Craig y Fan Ddu | 3 | 3 | 4 | 3 | 4 | 5 | 0 |

## WALKING IN THE BRECON BEACONS

| Walk | Name | Geomorphology (glacial) | Geology | Birds | Flowers | Waterfalls | Panoramas | Archaeology |
|---|---|---|---|---|---|---|---|---|
| 16 | Torpantau circuit | 3 | 3 | 3 | 2 | 1 | 5 | 1 |
| 17 | Neuadd Horseshoe | 4 | 3 | 3 | 3 | 0 | 5 | 3 |
| 18 | Cwm Llysiog and Waun Wen | 2 | 2 | 2 | 2 | 1 | 2 | 0 |
| 19 | Corn Du and Pen y Fan via Cwm Crew | 3 | 3 | 2 | 2 | 1 | 3 | 0 |
| 20 | Corn Du and Pen y Fan from Pont ar Daf | 4 | 3 | 2 | 2 | 0 | 5 | 3 |
| 21 | Craig Cerrig-gleisiad | 4 | 3 | 5 | 5 | 0 | 2 | 1 |
| 22 | Fan Fawr | 3 | 2 | 2 | 2 | 0 | 4 | 0 |
| 23 | Craig Cwm-du and Fan Frynych | 3 | 3 | 5 | 5 | 0 | 3 | 3 |
| 24 | Fan Frynych, Fan Dringarth and Fan Llia | 4 | 3 | 5 | 5 | 0 | 3 | 3 |
| 25 | Fan Gyhirych and Fan Nedd | 2 | 2 | 1 | 2 | 0 | 5 | 2 |
| 26 | Elidir Trail | 2 | 4 | 4 | 4 | 5 | 0 | 5 |
| 27 | Waterfall walk | 2 | 5 | 5 | 4 | 5 | 0 | 5 |
| 28 | Sgwd yr Eira | 5 | 5 | 5 | 4 | 5 | 2 | 5 |
| 29 | Ystradfellte Falls | 5 | 5 | 5 | 4 | 5 | 0 | 5 |
| 30 | Afon Nedd and Afon Mellte | 5 | 5 | 5 | 5 | 5 | 0 | 2 |
| 31 | Carmarthen Fans | 5 | 3 | 3 | 2 | 0 | 5 | 3 |
| 32 | Tair Carn Isaf | 1 | 2 | 5 | 3 | 0 | 3 | 0 |
| 33 | Sinc Giedd and the Carmarthen Fans | 5 | 4 | 2 | 2 | 0 | 5 | 3 |
| 34 | Afon Twrch | 2 | 5 | 4 | 3 | 3 | 1 | 5 |

## Appendix B – Routes by interest

| Walk | Name | Geomorphology (glacial) | Geology | Birds | Flowers | Waterfalls | Panoramas | Archaeology |
|---|---|---|---|---|---|---|---|---|
| 35 | Henrhyd Falls | 1 | 5 | 5 | 4 | 5 | 2 | 0 |
| 36 | Garreg Las | 2 | 2 | 3 | 1 | 0 | 3 | 2 |
| 37 | Cribarth | 1 | 5 | 3 | 1 | 0 | 4 | 5 |
| 38 | Carmarthen Fans via Cwm Giedd | 5 | 3 | 3 | 2 | 0 | 5 | 1 |
| 39 | Carreg Cennen | 0 | 2 | 2 | 1 | 0 | 2 | 5 |
| 40 | Pen Cerrig-calch and Table Mountain | 3 | 2 | 3 | 4 | 0 | 5 | 3 |
| 41 | Craig y Cilau | 1 | 2 | 5 | 5 | 0 | 3 | 3 |
| 42 | Crug Mawr and Sugar Loaf | 2 | 2 | 4 | 4 | 0 | 5 | 5 |
| 43 | Llanthony Priory, Offa's Dyke and Bal Mawr | 2 | 1 | 2 | 2 | 0 | 4 | 5 |
| 44 | Lord Hereford's Knob | 2 | 2 | 3 | 1 | 1 | 5 | 4 |
| 45 | Castell Dinas and Waun Fach | 2 | 2 | 3 | 2 | 0 | 5 | 4 |

# APPENDIX C
## Brief Welsh–English glossary

| Welsh | English |
|---|---|
| aber | river mouth |
| aderyn | bird |
| afon | river |
| allt | wooded slope |
| aran | high place |
| bach | little or small |
| ban, bannau | peak or crest |
| blaen | end, point, top, head of |
| bod | dwelling |
| bont | bridge |
| bryn | hill |
| bwlch | pass |
| cadair | chair |
| cae | field |
| caer | fort, stronghold |
| canol | middle |
| capel | chapel |
| carn/carnedd | cairn or heap |
| carreg | stone or rock |
| castell | castle |
| cau | hollow |
| cefn | ridge |
| celli | grove, copse |
| cemaes | river bends |
| cerrig | stones |
| cilfach | corner, nook |
| clawdd | hedge or ditch |
| clog | crag, cliff |
| clogwyn | cliff |
| clun | meadow |

| Welsh | English |
|---|---|
| clydach | torrent |
| clyn-gwyn | white meadow |
| coch | red |
| coed | wood |
| comin | common |
| craig | rock/crag |
| crib | combe/sharp ridge |
| cribin | rocky ridge |
| croes | crossroads |
| cwar | quarry |
| cwm | valley |
| cymmer | meeting of rivers |
| ddinas | fort |
| dol | meadow |
| drws | door |
| du, ddu | black |
| duwynt | windy |
| dwfr, dwr | water |
| dyffryn | valley |
| eglwys | church |
| eira | snow |
| esgair | ridge |
| fach | little |
| fan | peak or crest |
| fawr | great or large |
| fechan | smaller |
| felin | mill |
| ffordd | road |
| ffynnon | spring/well |
| foel | rounded bare hill |

## APPENDIX C – BRIEF WELSH–ENGLISH GLOSSARY

| Welsh | English |
|---|---|
| gallt | wooded hill |
| garn/garnedd | cairn/heap |
| garth | hill |
| glas | blue/green |
| gleisiad | young salmon |
| glyn | valley |
| goch | red |
| gwaun | moor |
| gwladus | white lady |
| gwyn/gwen | white |
| gwynt | wind |
| hafodydd | summer dwellings |
| hebog | hawk |
| hen | old |
| heol | road |
| isaf | lower |
| llan | village/church |
| llech | flat stone/slate |
| llithrig | slippery |
| llwch | lake |
| llwyd | grey, brown |
| llyn | lake |
| maen | stone/block |
| maes | field/meadow |
| melin | mill |
| melyn | yellow |
| moel | rounded/bare hill |
| mynydd | mountain |
| nant | stream |

| Welsh | English |
|---|---|
| neuadd | hall |
| ogof | cave |
| pant | hollow, valley |
| pen yr | end of or top of |
| perfedd | middle |
| pistyll | spring, waterfall |
| plas | hall, mansion |
| pont | bridge |
| porth | gateway |
| pwll | pool |
| rhaeadr | waterfall |
| rhiw | hill/slope |
| rhos | moorland |
| rhyd | ford |
| sarn | causeway, old road |
| sgwd | waterfall |
| sticill | stile |
| sych | dry |
| twll | hole |
| twyn | hill |
| uchaf | upper, highest |
| waun | moor |
| wen | white |
| y, yr | the |
| y groes | crossroads |
| y pannwr | the fuller [person who pleats cloth] |
| yr eira | snowy |
| ystrad | valley floor |

# APPENDIX D
*Useful contacts*

The **Brecon Beacons National Park** website (www.breconbeacons.org) is a great resource for things to do and see, transport, outdoor activities and where to stay.

**Traveline Cymru** (www.traveline-cymru.info) is a comprehensive interactive transport information site that will help you plan your best route to the park. Abergavenny in the east is served by trains from Newport and Crewe while Llandeilo and Llandovery in the west are on the magical Heart of Wales line from Swansea. Merthyr Tydfil in the south has a direct connection to Cardiff. Train routes and timetables can be found at www.nationalrail.co.uk.

Coach travellers can reach Brecon via Cardiff and Abergavenny via Birmingham. **National Express** can be found at www.nationalexpress.com and **Stagecoach** at www.stagecoachbus.com. The **TrawsCymru network** (www.trawscymru.info) has a service from Newtown/Llandrindod Wells (704) which connects with X43 in Brecon to Abergavenny or Merthyr Tydfil and Cardiff as well as the 714 to Llandovery.

The park has a number of **information centres:**

**National Park Visitor Centre** (Mountain Centre) at Libanus, six miles south of Brecon. Open all year, tel 01874 623366.

**Craig-y-nos Country Park** in the upper Swansea Valley near Abercraf. Open all year, tel 01639 730395.

**Abergavenny Tourist Information and National Park Centre**, 61 Cross Street, Abergavenny NP7 5EH, www.visitabergavenny.co.uk, tel 01873 853254.

**Llandovery Tourist Information and Heritage Centre**, Town Centre, Llandovery SA20 0AW, tel 01550 720693.

## DOWNLOAD THE ROUTES
## IN GPX FORMAT

All the routes in this guide are available for download from:

**www.cicerone.co.uk/1089/GPX**

as standard format GPX files. You should be able to load them into most online GPX systems and mobile devices, whether GPS or smartphone. You may need to convert the file into your preferred format using a conversion programme such as gpsvisualizer.com or one of the many other such websites and programmes.

When you follow this link, you will be asked for your email address and where you purchased the guidebook, and have the option to subscribe to the Cicerone e-newsletter.

www.cicerone.co.uk

# NOTES

# NOTES

# NOTES

# LISTING OF CICERONE GUIDES

**BRITISH ISLES CHALLENGES, COLLECTIONS AND ACTIVITIES**
Great Walks on the England Coast Path
Map and Compass
The Big Rounds
The Book of the Bivvy
The Book of the Bothy
The Mountains of England and Wales:
　Vol 1 Wales
　Vol 2 England
The National Trails
Walking the End to End Trail

**SHORT WALKS SERIES**
Short Walks Hadrian's Wall
Short Walks in the Lake District: Keswick, Borrowdale and Buttermere
Short Walks in the Lake District: Windermere Ambleside and Grasmere
Short Walks in the Lake District: Coniston and Langdale
Short Walks in Arnside and Silverdale
Short Walks in Nidderdale
Short Walks in Northumberland: Wooler, Rothbury, Alnwick and the coast
Short Walks on the Malvern Hills
Short Walks in Cornwall: Falmouth and the Lizard
Short Walks in Cornwall: Land's End and Penzance
Short Walks in the South Downs: Brighton, Eastbourne and Arundel
Short Walks in the Surrey Hills
Short Walks Winchester
Short Walks in Pembrokeshire: Tenby and the south
Short Walks on the Isle of Mull
Short Walks on the Orkney Islands

**SCOTLAND**
Ben Nevis and Glen Coe
Cycling in the Hebrides
Cycling the North Coast 500
Great Mountain Days in Scotland
Mountain Biking in Southern and Central Scotland
Mountain Biking in West and North West Scotland
Not the West Highland Way
Scotland
Scotland's Best Small Mountains
Scotland's Mountain Ridges
Scottish Wild Country Backpacking
Short Walks in Dumfries and Galloway
Skye's Cuillin Ridge Traverse
The Borders Abbeys Way
The Great Glen Way

The Great Glen Way Map Booklet
The Hebridean Way
The Hebrides
The Isle of Mull
The Isle of Skye
The Skye Trail
The Southern Upland Way
The West Highland Way
West Highland Way Map Booklet
Walking Ben Lawers, Rannoch and Atholl
Walking in the Cairngorms
Walking in the Pentland Hills
Walking in the Scottish Borders
Walking in the Southern Uplands
Walking in Torridon, Fisherfield, Fannichs and An Teallach
Walking Loch Lomond and the Trossachs
Walking on Arran
Walking on Harris and Lewis
Walking on Jura, Islay and Colonsay
Walking on Rum and the Small Isles
Walking on the Orkney and Shetland Isles
Walking on Uist and Barra
Walking the Cape Wrath Trail
Walking the Corbetts
　Vol 1 South of the Great Glen
　Vol 2 North of the Great Glen
Walking the Galloway Hills
Walking the John o' Groats Trail
Walking the Munros
　Vol 1 — Southern, Central and Western Highlands
　Vol 2 — Northern Highlands and the Cairngorms
Winter Climbs in the Cairngorms
Winter Climbs: Ben Nevis and Glen Coe

**NORTHERN ENGLAND ROUTES**
Cycling the Reivers Route
Cycling the Way of the Roses
Hadrian's Cycleway
Hadrian's Wall Path
Hadrian's Wall Path Map Booklet
Pennine Way Map Booklet
The Coast to Coast Cycle Route
The Coast to Coast Walk
The Coast to Coast Map Booklet
The Pennine Way
Walking the Dales Way
The Dales Way Map Booklet

**LAKE DISTRICT**
Bikepacking in the Lake District
Cycling in the Lake District
Great Mountain Days in the Lake District
Joss Naylor's Lakes, Meres and Waters of the Lake District

Lake District Winter Climbs
Lake District: High Level and Fell Walks
Low Level and Lake Walks
Mountain Biking in the Lake District
Outdoor Adventures with Children — Lake District
Scrambles in the Lake District —
　North
　South
Trail and Fell Running in the Lake District
Walking The Cumbria Way
Walking the Lake District Fells —
　Borrowdale
　Buttermere
　Coniston
　Keswick
　Langdale
　Mardale and the Far East
　Patterdale
　Wasdale
Walking the Tour of the Lake District

**NORTH—WEST ENGLAND AND THE ISLE OF MAN**
Cycling the Pennine Bridleway
Isle of Man Coastal Path
The Lancashire Cycleway
The Lune Valley and Howgills
Walking in Cumbria's Eden Valley
Walking in Lancashire
Walking in the Forest of Bowland and Pendle
Walking on the Isle of Man
Walking on the West Pennine Moors
Walking the Ribble Way
Walks in Silverdale and Arnside

**NORTH—EAST ENGLAND, YORKSHIRE DALES AND PENNINES**
Cycling in the Yorkshire Dales
Great Mountain Days in the Pennines
Mountain Biking in the Yorkshire Dales
The Cleveland Way and the Yorkshire Wolds Way
The Cleveland Way Map Booklet
The North York Moors
Trail and Fell Running in the Yorkshire Dales
Walking in County Durham
Walking in Northumberland
Walking in the North Pennines
Walking in the Yorkshire Dales:
　North and East
　South and West
Walking St Cuthbert's Way
Walking St Oswald's Way and Northumberland Coast Path

## DERBYSHIRE, PEAK DISTRICT AND MIDLANDS
Cycling in the Peak District
Dark Peak Walks
Scrambles in the Dark Peak
Walking in Derbyshire
Walking in the Peak District — White Peak East
Walking in the Peak District — White Peak West

## WALES AND WELSH BORDERS
Cycle Touring in Wales
Cycling Lon Las Cymru
Great Mountain Days in Snowdonia
Hillwalking in Shropshire
Mountain Walking in Snowdonia
Offa's Dyke Path
Offa's Dyke Map Booklet
Scrambles in Snowdonia
Snowdonia: 30 Low-level and Easy Walks
 — North
 — South
The Cambrian Way
The Pembrokeshire Coast Path
Pembrokeshire Coast Path Map Booklet
The Snowdonia Way
The Wye Valley Walk
Walking Glyndwr's Way
Walking in Carmarthenshire
Walking in Pembrokeshire
Walking in the Brecon Beacons
Walking in the Forest of Dean
Walking in the Wye Valley
Walking on Gower
Walking the Severn Way
Walking the Shropshire Way
Walking the Wales Coast Path

## SOUTHERN ENGLAND
20 Classic Sportive Rides in South East England
20 Classic Sportive Rides in South West England
Cycling in the Cotswolds
Mountain Biking on the North Downs
Mountain Biking on the South Downs
Suffolk Coast and Heath Walks
The Cotswold Way
The Cotswold Way Map Booklet
The Kennet and Avon Canal
The Lea Valley Walk
The North Downs Way
North Downs Way Map Booklet
The Peddars Way and Norfolk Coast Path
The Pilgrims' Way
The Ridgeway National Trail
The Ridgeway Map Booklet
The South Downs Way
The South Downs Way Map Booklet
The Thames Path
The Thames Path Map Booklet
The Two Moors Way
Two Moors Way Map Booklet
Walking Hampshire's Test Way
Walking in Cornwall
Walking in Essex
Walking in Kent
Walking in London
Walking in Norfolk
Walking in the Chilterns
Walking in the Cotswolds
Walking in the Isles of Scilly
Walking in the New Forest
Walking in the North Wessex Downs
Walking on Dartmoor
Walking on Guernsey
Walking on Jersey
Walking on the Isle of Wight
Walking the Dartmoor Way
Walking the Jurassic Coast
Walking the Sarsen Way
Walking the South West Coast Path
South West Coast Path Map Booklet
 — Vol 1: Minehead to St Ives
 — Vol 2: St Ives to Plymouth
 — Vol 3: Plymouth to Poole
Walks in the South Downs National Park
Cycling Land's End to John o' Groats

## ALPS CROSS—BORDER ROUTES
100 Hut Walks in the Alps
Alpine Ski Mountaineering Vol 1 — Western Alps
The Karnischer Hohenweg
The Tour of the Bernina
Trail Running — Chamonix and the Mont Blanc region
Trekking Chamonix to Zermatt
Trekking in the Alps
Trekking in the Silvretta and Ratikon Alps
Trekking Munich to Venice
Trekking the Tour du Mont Blanc
Tour du Mont Blanc Map Booklet
Walking in the Alps

## FRANCE, BELGIUM, AND LUXEMBOURG
Camino de Santiago — Via Podiensis
Chamonix Mountain Adventures
Cycle Touring in France
Cycling London to Paris
Cycling the Canal de la Garonne
Cycling the Canal du Midi
Mont Blanc Walks
Mountain Adventures in the Maurienne
Short Treks on Corsica
The GR5 Trail
The GR5 Trail — Vosges and Jura Benelux and Lorraine
The Grand Traverse of the Massif Central
The Moselle Cycle Route
Trekking in the Vanoise
Trekking the Cathar Way
Trekking the GR10
Trekking the GR20 Corsica
Trekking the Robert Louis Stevenson Trail
Via Ferratas of the French Alps
Walking in Provence — East
Walking in Provence — West
Walking in the Auvergne
Walking in the Briançonnais
Walking in the Dordogne
Walking in the Haute Savoie: North
Walking in the Haute Savoie: South
Walking on Corsica
Walking the Brittany Coast Path
Walking in the Ardennes

## PYRENEES AND FRANCE/SPAIN CROSS—BORDER ROUTES
Shorter Treks in the Pyrenees
The Pyrenean Haute Route
The Pyrenees
Trekking the Cami dels Bons Homes
Trekking the GR11 Trail
Walks and Climbs in the Pyrenees

## SPAIN AND PORTUGAL
Camino de Santiago: Camino Frances
Costa Blanca Mountain Adventures
Cycling the Camino de Santiago
Mountain Walking in Mallorca
Mountain Walking in Southern Catalunya
Spain's Sendero Historico: The GR1
The Andalucian Coast to Coast Walk
The Camino del Norte and Camino Primitivo
The Camino Ingles and Ruta do Mar
The Mountains Around Nerja
The Sierras of Extremadura
Trekking in Mallorca
Trekking in the Canary Islands
Trekking the GR7 in Andalucia
Walking and Trekking in the Sierra Nevada
Walking in Andalucia
Walking in Catalunya — Barcelona
Girona Pyrenees
Walking in the Picos de Europa
Walking La Via de la Plata and Camino Sanabres
Walking on Gran Canaria
Walking on La Gomera and El Hierro
Walking on La Palma
Walking on Lanzarote and Fuerteventura
Walking on Tenerife
Walking on the Costa Blanca
Walking the Camino dos Faros
Portugal's Rota Vicentina
The Camino Portugues
Walking in Portugal
Walking in the Algarve

Walking on Madeira
Walking on the Azores

## SWITZERLAND
Switzerland's Jura Crest Trail
The Swiss Alps
Tour of the Jungfrau Region
Trekking the Swiss Via Alpina
Walking in Arolla and Zinal
Walking in the Bernese Oberland — Jungfrau region
Walking in the Engadine — Switzerland
Walking in the Valais
Walking in Ticino
Walking in Zermatt and Saas-Fee

## GERMANY
Hiking and Cycling in the Black Forest
The Danube Cycleway Vol 1
The Rhine Cycle Route
The Westweg
Walking in the Bavarian Alps

## POLAND, SLOVAKIA, ROMANIA, HUNGARY AND BULGARIA
The Danube Cycleway Vol 2
The High Tatras
The Mountains of Romania

## SCANDINAVIA, ICELAND AND GREENLAND
Hiking in Norway — South
Trekking the Kungsleden
Trekking in Greenland — The Arctic Circle Trail
Walking and Trekking in Iceland

## SLOVENIA, CROATIA, SERBIA, MONTENEGRO AND ALBANIA
Hiking Slovenia's Juliana Trail
Mountain Biking in Slovenia
The Islands of Croatia
The Julian Alps of Slovenia
The Mountains of Montenegro
The Peaks of the Balkans Trail
The Slovene Mountain Trail
Walking in Slovenia: The Karavanke
Walks and Treks in Croatia

## ITALY
Alta Via 1 — Trekking in the Dolomites
Alta Via 2 — Trekking in the Dolomites
Day Walks in the Dolomites
Italy's Grande Traversata delle Alpi
Italy's Sibillini National Park
Ski Touring and Snowshoeing in the Dolomites
The Way of St Francis
Trekking Gran Paradiso: Alta Via 2
Trekking in the Apennines
Trekking the Giants' Trail: Alta Via 1 through the Italian Pennine Alps
Via Ferratas of the Italian Dolomites Vol 1
Vol 2
Walking in Abruzzo
Walking in Italy's Cinque Terre
Walking in Italy's Stelvio National Park
Walking in Sicily
Walking in the Aosta Valley
Walking in the Dolomites
Walking in Tuscany
Walking in Umbria
Walking Lake Como and Maggiore
Walking Lake Garda and Iseo
Walking on the Amalfi Coast
Walks and Treks in the Maritime Alps

## IRELAND
The Wild Atlantic Way and Western Ireland
Walking the Kerry Way
Walking the Wicklow Way

## EUROPEAN CYCLING
Cycling the Route des Grandes Alpes
Cycling the Ruta Via de la Plata
The Elbe Cycle Route
The River Loire Cycle Route
The River Rhone Cycle Route

## INTERNATIONAL CHALLENGES, COLLECTIONS AND ACTIVITIES
Europe's High Points
Walking the Via Francigena Pilgrim Route —
Part 1
Part 2
Part 3

## AUSTRIA
Innsbruck Mountain Adventures
Trekking Austria's Adlerweg
Trekking in Austria's Hohe Tauern
Trekking in Austria's Zillertal Alps
Trekking in the Stubai Alps
Walking in Austria
Walking in the Salzkammergut: the Austrian Lake District

## MEDITERRANEAN
The High Mountains of Crete
Trekking in Greece
Walking and Trekking in Zagori
Walking and Trekking on Corfu
Walking on the Greek Islands — the Cyclades
Walking in Cyprus
Walking on Malta

## HIMALAYA
8000 metres
Everest: A Trekker's Guide
Trekking in the Karakoram

## NORTH AMERICA
Hiking and Cycling the California Missions Trail
The John Muir Trail
The Pacific Crest Trail

## SOUTH AMERICA
Aconcagua and the Southern Andes
Hiking and Biking Peru's Inca Trails
Trekking in Torres del Paine

## AFRICA
Kilimanjaro
Walking in the Drakensberg
Walks and Scrambles in the Moroccan Anti-Atlas

## NEW ZEALAND AND AUSTRALIA
Hiking the Overland Track

## CHINA, JAPAN, AND ASIA
Annapurna
Hiking and Trekking in the Japan Alps and Mount Fuji
Hiking in Hong Kong
Japan's Kumano Kodo Pilgrimage
Trekking in Bhutan
Trekking in Ladakh
Trekking in Tajikistan
Trekking in the Himalaya

## TECHNIQUES
Fastpacking
The Mountain Hut Book

## MINI GUIDES
Alpine Flowers
Navigation
Pocket First Aid and Wilderness Medicine
Snow

## MOUNTAIN LITERATURE
A Walk in the Clouds
Abode of the Gods
Fifty Years of Adventure
The Pennine Way — the Path, the People, the Journey
Unjustifiable Risk?

For full information on all our guides, books and eBooks, visit our website:
**www.cicerone.co.uk**

# CICERONE

Trust Cicerone to guide your next adventure, wherever it may be around the world...

Discover guides for hiking, mountain walking, backpacking, trekking, trail running, cycling and mountain biking, ski touring, climbing and scrambling in Britain, Europe and worldwide.

Connect with Cicerone online and find inspiration.

- buy books and ebooks
- articles, advice and trip reports
- podcasts and live events
- GPX files and updates
- regular newsletter

**cicerone.co.uk**